Labour of Love

Labour of Love

THE FIGHT TO CREATE
A MORE HUMANE CANADA

Buzz Hargrove

WITH WAYNE SKENE

MACFARLANE WALTER & ROSS
TORONTO

Macfarlane Walter & Ross
37A Hazelton Avenue
Toronto, Canada M5R 2E3

Canadian Cataloguing in Publication Data

Hargrove, Buzz, 1944 –
Labour of love: the fight to create a more humane Canada

Includes index.
ISBN 1-55199-033-4

1. Trade-unions – Canada.
2. Canada – Politics and government – 1993 – .
3. Industrial policy – Canada.
4. Hargrove, Buzz, 1944 – . I. Skene, Wayne, 1941 – . II. Title.

HD6524.H37 1998   331.88'0971   C98-932264-5

Macfarlane Walter & Ross gratefully acknowledges
the financial support for its publishing program from
the Canada Council for the Arts, the Ontario Arts Council,
and the Government of Canada through the
Book Publishing Industry Development Program.

Printed and bound in Canada

For Denise

Power concedes nothing
without a demand.
It never did and it never will.

— *Frederick Douglass,
former American slave, 1849*

CONTENTS

PREFACE

Why would a union leader write a book about the state of Canada's political, economic, and social affairs? Why would he train his gaze beyond his presumed area of expertise – the labour movement? The short answer is that I'm gravely concerned about the direction in which my country is heading and I'd like to spark broad debate about whether it's changing for the better or the worse.

I want to communicate my concerns from my perspective as a trade unionist and a politically active citizen. The labour movement is not an alien, self-interested force, existing outside the mainstream of society, as some in the media like to depict it. Our members are not merely "workers." We send our kids to schools and universities. We line up to vote. We feel, like other Canadians, the impact of our governments' increasingly right-wing political agendas. We see first-hand the hold that corporations have gained over the country's political leadership. I'm writing this book because I fear that corporate interests are eroding the very basis of democracy in this country, and I'm not sure most Canadians understand just how far down this road we have already travelled.

Canada in the late 1990s is a strange place. We pride ourselves on being a society committed to equality and compassion, yet we're living through a period of unparalleled inequality and bitterness. Prime Minister Chrétien addressed the Liberal convention in March 1998 and announced that we had entered "a new golden age comparable to that of the postwar period." Yet 1.5 million Canadians are out of work, and our official rate of unemployment remains stuck above 8 percent, approximately double that of both the United States (another country enjoying an economic "golden age") and Japan (a country going through its worst recession in more than fifty years). When those who have given up looking for work are taken into account, real unemployment in Canada ranges between 11 and 13 percent. Hundreds of thousands of laid-off workers have simply stopped searching for work because their job prospects, in this "golden age," are nonexistent.

These are certainly good times if you're wealthy. But what if you're not? Since 1989, the average income of the bottom fifth of all Canadians has fallen 32 percent, the number of poor children has grown by 46 percent, and the number of Canadians living on social assistance has grown by 68 percent. Yet federal spending on social programs, as a percentage of Gross Domestic Product, is at its lowest level since 1949. Good times if you've been invited to the party, not so good if your nose is pressed against the glass.

Corporate profits are substantial. In 1997, earnings at 165 major publicly traded companies rose 18 percent to $24.6 billion. Executive salaries, bonuses, pensions, and other perks reached unprecedented heights. The typical chief executive officer's take-home pay went up 112 percent. The average Canadian worker's after-tax income, meanwhile, *dropped* 9 percent between 1990 and 1997. In real terms, most Canadian workers now earn less than they would have in 1975.

Membership in Canada's millionaires club tripled between 1989 and 1996, and is expected to triple again by 2005. Many of these millionaires pay modest income taxes, and corporations on average pay less tax than they did ten years ago. The average worker, meanwhile, pays 22 percent *more* income tax than a decade ago.

These "good times" remind me of a statement made by a Brazilian general in the 1950s. Asked how the economy was doing under the military junta, he replied: "The economy is doing great. Unfortunately, the people in it are not."

JEAN CHRÉTIEN'S SO-CALLED GOLDEN AGE was largely achieved through deep cuts to social programs and health care. Those cuts allowed the Liberals to build a budget surplus of roughly $4 billion for the 1997–98 fiscal year. Canada has become a country in which the prime minister basks in the glory of a budget surplus achieved by eviscerating national health care, welfare, and an education system meant to prepare our youth to meet tomorrow's challenges.

The Liberals have purposely made qualification for unemployment insurance benefits more difficult. As recently as 1990–91, the UI fund covered 80 percent of those unemployed; today it covers 36 percent. In fiscal 1997–98, the finance department pocketed $6.8 billion more in revenue than was paid out to unemployed workers. While the unemployed and their families struggle to survive, the federal government sits on a growing pile of cash originally meant to assist them.

At the same moment we're being told what great times these are, corporations insist they must continue to cut costs, increase "efficiency," and become "globally competitive" by laying off tens of thousands more Canadian workers. Our banks "must" merge to compete internationally – further layoffs ahead. Canada, goes the rhetoric, is just too expensive a place to do business. For one thing, wages are too high.

Bunkum. As *The Economist* pointed out in a survey released in December 1997, Canada is one of the cheapest places to do business in the industrialized world. The report's authors found that Canadian businesses enjoy moderate wages, low housing costs, high-quality and inexpensive telecommunications, a good transportation system, and lack of corruption. According to *The Economist*, Canadian businesses are already more competitive than American ones, even when our relatively high unionization is taken into account.

Right-wing lobbyists claim that Canadian unions reduce productivity, profits, investment, and growth. To these people, high wages are bad for the nation's economy. Yet some of the most profitable corporations have strong unions and some of the best paid and most productive workers.

TODAY WE ALSO HAVE any number of provincial governments subscribing to the right-wing, corporate agenda that puts profit above citizenship and insists on reducing social programs. Nowhere is this more evident these days than in Ontario. A December 1997 study showing that

1.5 million Canadian children live in poverty also disclosed that 506,000 of them live in the home of Mike Harris's "Common Sense Revolution." Thanks to the Harris government, the number of poor children in Ontario is almost double the national average.

The Tories cut social services by almost 25 percent. Surprise – the need for welfare increased. Then they slashed welfare funding by 22 percent. Surprise, surprise – there was a 30 percent increase in 1997 in the number of Ontarians seeking emergency food bank assistance. All this from a government that claims to be "doing what the people of Ontario want."

It is working people who elect our governments – federal, provincial, and municipal – based on the promises politicians make during election campaigns. Once in office, however, these politicians govern in the interests not of the people who elected them but of the corporations. What about the social and economic damage their policies inflict on so many Canadians? A small price to pay, apparently, for the implementation of the corporate agenda.

Where will it end? At least one senior member of the federal cabinet wants to see Canada's medicare program privatized and made more like the American model. His right-wing ideology would have him dismantle one of the world's best health care systems to adopt one of the worst.

By catering to corporations and right-wing lobby groups, the Chrétien government has taken over the space on the political spectrum once occupied by the Reform Party and the Conservatives. It's getting so crowded on Canada's right you can hardly tell who's who. Bob Rae, a "lefty," gets elected in Ontario in 1990 and spends five years doing his impression of Ralph Klein. One minute federal Conservative leader Jean Charest is attacking Liberal policies on the floor of the House of Commons in Ottawa; next he's leading the Liberal Party in Quebec. While Charest does his political pirouette, Preston Manning woos Conservatives to join with the Reform Party in a new United Alternative movement to fight the Liberals.

Undaunted by a brief setback in mid-1998, the Chrétien government will undoubtedly continue to push for ratification of the Multilateral Agreement on Investment, a treaty that would effectively place cultural, financial, and public-policy control of this country in the hands of international investors. Systematically our governments remove impediments to the free flow of capital. National borders grow less important; there's little dialogue about what kind of country we want Canada to be; rate of return is all that matters.

Respondents to a 1997, year-end Southam poll painted a much darker picture of their personal economic reality than the one that emerges from government handouts. Increasingly Canadians sense two things about this "golden age." First, it does not apply to them. And second, our political leaders have little idea how bad things really are for many of the people who elected them.

Talking to working Canadians, as I do almost every day, I sense deep misgivings about whose interests our governments – federal and provincial – have come to represent. Many Canadians are living through difficult times. As their anger and frustration build, increasing numbers of them are forming coalitions, demonstrating, and making their voices heard in support of economic and social justice. This is a country we used to be intensely proud of. We felt our politicians understood the need to act in the interests of the average citizen, not just the privileged few. We felt they understood the difference between government as an extension of business and government as a means by which we achieve equality and fairness.

Not so long ago such things mattered in this country. That was the Canada I grew up in, the Canada I love, and the Canada I hope to see restored.

ACKNOWLEDGMENTS

In writing this book I inevitably found myself indebted to any number of friends and co-workers who offered their opinions, their time, and their moral support.

In particular, I wish to express my appreciation to Wayne Skene for his insight and his patience. I want to thank Sam Gindin, the conscience of the CAW, as well as our chief economist, for sharing his knowledge of Canada's labour movement and his perspective on where we might be heading – economically, politically, and socially – as a nation. And I want to thank my secretary, Rita Lori, for her dedication, her loyalty, and her tireless support.

I

SMALL VICTORIES

Workers don't need a union
to walk them backwards.
They can do that on their own.
— *Bob White*

I sat across the huge table in Transport Minister David Anderson's Ottawa office and realized we were getting nowhere. Neither Anderson nor Kevin Benson, Canadian Airlines International's president and chief executive officer, was prepared to make the slightest compromise. We were spinning our wheels. It was December 4, 1996, a little over a month since Benson had announced that Canadian Airlines would go bankrupt unless its 16,400 employees agreed to an across-the-board 10 percent cut in wages and benefits.

According to Benson, the cut was "absolutely essential" to save Canadian from going belly up. More important, he wanted to go over the heads of the six duly certified unions at the airline and put his pitch for wage concessions directly to the employees. Benson's request was highly unorthodox. It also happened to be illegal under Canada's Labour Code. He wanted to sweep the union leadership out of the way so he could spook the employees into accepting his cuts. And the transport minister was backing him all the way.

By the time I arrived at Anderson's office at eleven o'clock that morning, Benson's threats of imminent bankruptcy had succeeded in getting five of the six unions to recommend that their members agree to his wage-cut demand. Only our union, the National Automobile, Aerospace, Transportation and General Workers Union of Canada – CAW, for short – was still holding out on behalf of our 3,700 members working at Canadian.

I knew the majority of our members were behind our bargaining committee. But I, personally, was being depicted in the media as a stubborn and undemocratic union boss for not allowing CAW members to vote on Benson's proposal. True, my office was getting calls, most from employees who belonged to other unions, demanding, "What the hell is Hargrove doing? It's not his position that's at stake. He'll have a job when we're out of work!" But the majority were saying, "Right on, Buzz! It's time somebody told Anderson and Benson to go to hell!"

At the meeting, it was clear to me they were working as a philosophical tag-team – business and government aligned against working people. I have spent much of my life at the bargaining table and I can sense when the other guy thinks he's holding all the aces. Both Anderson and Benson were inflexible. They sat there, stiff as a couple of Latin American dictators, offering no compromises and no options. "Well then, I'm out of here," I announced, packing my papers. "The CAW is not going to be part of your plan."

The problem with their ultimatum was that Benson had been waffling about his airline's potential demise ever since his first public pronouncement. Friday, November 1, 1996, had been the day he announced that Canadian might run out of cash unless a pay cut was agreed to by November 27. His original restructuring plan was aimed at reducing the beleaguered air carrier's costs by $800 million over four years. He claimed the wage rollbacks were not only a requirement but also "non-negotiable." Early on he informed everyone who would listen that there was no Plan B. His Plan A was immutable: $70 million a year out of the employees' pockets for four years, or bankruptcy for the airline. His demand for wage concessions, he said, was not a charade.

What was doubly aggravating for the employees was that they had been danced through this doomsday scenario before. Three times since 1992, management had insisted on wage rollbacks. The message was always the same: x million dollars were urgently needed out of their pockets to save the airline. Months later, management would be back with another threat of demise and a new number that employees "had" to pony up.

Canadian had not seen a profit since 1988. The airline had racked up $1.53 billion in losses between 1989 and 1996. For Benson to come along now and preach to his employees that he knew the absolute number required for corporate salvation was ludicrous. It's good to have firm beliefs. It's okay to dig in when you're negotiating. But to pretend that your way is the only way, particularly at the bargaining table, is sheer stubbornness.

Benson also maintained that he had no intention of approaching the Chrétien government – or any government, for that matter – for financial help. He did say he would approach Canadian Airlines's largest shareholder, AMR Corp. of Fort Worth, Texas, to renegotiate the fees it charged for computer reservation services. He would also search for other cost savings in the airline's operations and talk to creditors about extending their credit conditions. But the major burden of bailing the airline out of its latest financial troubles would rest, as usual, on the collective shoulders of the employees.

As Yogi Berra used to say, "it was déjà vu all over again." The total value of worker concessions made since 1992 already added up to well over $300 million. In the interests of saving the airline from imminent bankruptcy that first year, the employees had agreed to take $210 million in wage and benefit cuts in exchange for shares in the airline. Those shares at the time were valued at $16 each. A day after Benson's latest announcement they were worth $1.25. The employees had been losing ground with every management-induced crisis. Between 1993 and 1996 they had contributed another $100 million in wage cuts and productivity gains. And while Benson was seeking these latest concessions, a freeze on employee wages was already in effect to the end of 1998. If we accepted what Benson was now demanding in rollbacks, most employees would be working in 1997 for 1970s wages. The employees were being used by the airline's board and management as a bank of last resort.

Still, there was one slim windfall from these constant demands: the frequency of this cap-in-hand routine was stiffening the resolve of our members. My position has always been that unions should never give in to wage-cut demands. Any reading of labour history shows that employee concessions do not solve management financial problems. At best they are a short-term, stopgap measure. If management fails to come to grips with the real problems – poor decision-making, flawed planning, inept control of capital – the company inevitably comes back to its employees for more.

In the past, our members had voted to join with the other unions to make concessions. But people got tougher and held out a little longer each time. In many cases they bargained a better deal than the one initially offered by management or accepted by other unions. Knowing you can go to the well only so many times before the members cry "no more!" helped our committee tough out this latest round. But with Anderson and the Liberal government acting like Benson cheerleaders, I knew this would be a tough fight. By the time we met in Anderson's office on December 4, the seemingly fruitless negotiations had been going on for more than a month.

I PICKED UP MY COAT, nodded goodbye, and headed back to the Delta Hotel to get my bags and catch my 3 p.m. flight to Toronto – on Canadian Airlines, of course. Despite the standoff with Anderson and Benson, I felt good about what our bargaining committee had accomplished. Through hard negotiations, the committee, led by Local 1990 president Anne Davidson, staff representative Sue Szczawinska, and my assistant Peggy Nash, had been able to drive Benson's "$70 million or bankruptcy" threat off the table and save wages for all the employees, not just the CAW members.

The issue that ticked me off was Benson's insistence on bypassing the six certified unions and going directly to the employees for a vote on wage concessions. He had first raised the matter at a dinner meeting at Toronto's Sutton Place Hotel in late October. He said to me: "I have this plan. I've tested it on some of the major investors. Initially, I got a good response. I tried it on government and I got a good response. All I need is your cooperation."

"What are you talking about? What plan?"

"A ten percent pay cut over four years."

I was furious. We had just concluded negotiations in April 1996 with Canadian and signed a new collective agreement that gave the airline productivity gains representing a saving of 17 percent. That rollback was worth about $17 million to them. Now, barely six months later,

Benson was back looking for another 10 percent in concessions – a total of 27 percent in less than a year. I could not believe the gall.

Over dinner (which we hardly touched because we argued long and hard), Benson claimed he was the new kid on the block. Sure, he had not been chief executive officer when discussions were taking place over the productivity gains, but he'd been part of the management negotiating team. He knew the company was already ahead by 17 percent in 1996 before he started making noises about more employee wage and benefit cuts. We were even joined at the dinner by one of Benson's senior managers who had received more than $200,000 the previous year in bonuses for having got Canadian employees to agree to a previous cut.

"Kevin," I said, with as much patience as I could muster, "at your salary level or mine, ten percent would not make much difference to our standard of living. But employees who've been hit with wage cuts already – some, two or three times – are working at 1978-level wages. And you want to move them back even further. By the time you guys are finished it will take employees to the year 2010 to get back what they earn today – if your people don't come back again asking for more."

"Look, we're not asking for your union's support or help," he said. "All we're asking is for you to step aside and let us talk to the employees to see how they feel about it."

"You're coming back for the third time to ask for wage concessions. If giving up wages and benefits and conceding on working conditions could have solved your operating problems, we wouldn't be here tonight."

The airline's problems were not caused by the cost of its labour, as Benson well knew. Labour costs represented only about 26 percent of the company's operating costs. Air Canada had labour costs of roughly 33 percent. In the United States, labour costs as a percentage of operating costs run as high as 37 percent. In truth, employee wages were an unbelievable bargain for Canadian. If it could ever get its management problems fixed, its low employee costs would make it tremendously competitive. The problem was bad management – from the board of directors down – coupled with the disastrous decision of the Mulroney and Chrétien governments to deregulate the industry.

The market this country represents is not big enough to support two major air carriers competing on almost all routes. On any given day, there are too many empty seats chasing too few customers. Each time employees agreed to wage concessions, Canadian used that money to increase capacity and throw more empty seats on the market. Costs went up and revenues down. You would think management had a death wish. Overcapacity is the basic insanity of today's domestic airline industry, yet neither Benson nor his predecessors addressed that reality.

Jim Stanford, one of the CAW's economists, prepared an astute analysis of the financial problems at Canada's two major airlines. There was no disputing that flying expensive, half-empty airplanes was a root cause of Canadian's woes. Yet management refused to accept responsibility for this peculiar way of doing business. "Who then is responsible for all those empty seats in the air?" Stanford asked puckishly. "There must be some god out there – some God of Empty Seats – who wants all those unoccupied seats flying in both Canadian Airlines and Air Canada aircraft, heading to the same destinations, at roughly the same time of the night or day."

Canadian has achieved something that few companies in the world have done: it recorded net losses for eight consecutive years. Finally, the airline reported a minuscule profit for the 1996–97 fiscal year. This $5.4 million profit on $3 billion in revenue was achieved in arguably the best year for running an airline since commercial aviation began in North America in 1914. But the airline's health was still so shaky that, in the spring of 1998, its debt issue was given junk-bond status by U.S. debt-rating agencies when it tried to secure US$175 million in new capital.

The 1988 decision by the Mulroney government to deregulate Canada's airline industry ranks as one of the most damaging public policy decisions ever implemented in this country. Canadians were promised that deregulation would give them more airlines competing for their travel business, cheaper fares, greater frequency of flights, better service, more airline jobs, and a stronger airline industry. Under deregulation, Canadians actually got fewer competitive airlines, higher fares on average, reduced service on most major routes, the loss of thousands of jobs, and a domestic airline industry that is in such bad shape that

Canadian Airlines flies in effect courtesy of AMR Corp. and the repeated generosity of its own employees.

"All I need is your cooperation," Benson said. "Just let me go to our people and talk to them."

"We're definitely not buying into your idea of speaking directly to our members," I replied. "It's a clear violation of the Labour Code. You are not the duly elected bargaining agent for our members. We are. And we're going to be out there talking to them, telling them your idea for wage cuts makes no sense."

Now it was Benson's turn to be furious. He has quite a temper. I got up and, with the rest of our committee, left the Sutton Place. That was the last meeting he and I had on any kind of cordial basis until we convened in Anderson's office in Ottawa on December 4.

FROM THE MINUTE I WALKED into Anderson's conference room, I knew that our transport minister was not attending the meeting in an effort to mediate a settlement. He came with the same notepad he had used in a meeting in Vancouver a few days previously. I could read, upside down, the notes he had jotted down for this meeting, and they were the same points he had made earlier: *No* to further financial support for Canadian from the federal government. *No* to discussions on deregulation. And the wage-cut proposals must be put to an open vote of the employees. There were no new options for discussion. Anderson, like Benson, wanted to see our members, who for weeks had been told they were going to lose their jobs, vote for concessions. He began the meeting by lecturing me that the only solution was for Canadian employees to accept wage cuts.

I was dumbfounded by the rigidity of his pro-business stance. Here was a federal cabinet minister saying to working people: "You guys have to give here. Not the employer. Not the creditors. Not the shareholders. You, the employees, have to accept life with lower wages." In all my years in collective bargaining I have never heard an elected official say to a union leader that our members were the *only* ones who had to cough up. I found him rude and insufferably aloof. He had no interest in finding any other solution.

"Look, I haven't heard anything new," I told them. I tried to make an argument that had been crafted by our economic research staff. Canadian Airlines and its employees paid about $500 million a year in taxes, federal as well as provincial. What was wrong with governments forgiving about $100 million a year of that amount over the next four years? It was not a bailout, and it would be more than Benson needed – $30 million more a year for four years. That $30 million might, by providing a small operating surplus, allow management finally to get its financial house in order. The government had created the problem with deregulation. Surely it could be part of the solution.

Not only did Anderson refuse to discuss our alternative, but Benson also turned up his nose at the idea. That made no sense at all, unless he and Anderson had only one goal: to squeeze the employees. Benson had said all along that he did not want any government money. We considered that a strange position for a CEO to take when his company was melting around him. Benson kept referring to Canadian's looming bankruptcy as a "family problem." The family, not government or outsiders, had to solve it.

"Well," I said, "Anderson is evidently not going to bite, but what about you? You know there is nothing scientific about your $70 million a year in wage cuts. Out of consideration for those employees at the low end of the wage scale – earning under $30,000 a year, for instance – why don't you reduce your target number to $62 million a year? If you throw another $8 million in the pot, that would mean those low-paid employees would escape wage cuts. You could come across as a hero."

"Not one penny less than $70 million," Benson replied sternly. I could almost hear his teeth grinding.

Hell, he didn't even know if $70 million was the right number. How could he? Seventy million dollars represents about eight days of operating costs for Canadian. Eight million dollars a year in a gracious, giveback package meant diddly-squat to a major airline that burns that much in fuel in a day. But Benson was saying that even those on the low end of the wage scale would take a hit. It made no sense, and it was no way to treat "family." Still, it would send a message about who was in charge. The more he put the fear into the employees about their jobs, the more pressure he was able to put on the CAW as the holdout union.

This was the same guy who had told the news media in Vancouver after our first meeting that if the CAW did not agree to his terms, it was all over for Canadian the next day. A lot of people had this vision that, as the clock struck 12 midnight, planes would start dropping from the skies. That evening as we watched the late TV news in our hotel room after we broke off talks, reporters climbed all over Benson asking him to explain what was going to happen to customers expecting to fly the next business day. Only then did he seem to comprehend how much public uncertainty his deadline was causing.

"What's going to happen to Canadian Airlines tomorrow?" the reporters asked.

"Nothing is going to happen," he finally admitted. "We'll be operating as usual."

I almost fell off my chair. Benson had been hoisted with his own petard. Every time he tried to spook his holdout employees by threatening that the airline was about to collapse, he had to reverse himself because his tactics scared potential passengers into cancelling their flights. It was not a great business strategy, to say the least, but it helped raise the tension among our members and those of other unions. Every time he mumbled about another looming bankruptcy date, our telephones would light up with calls from pilots and employees from other unions threatening us because we refused to put Benson's demands to a vote of our members.

Our union's position was clear and defendable. The CAW had bargained a legal contract for our members working for Canadian – reservation agents and customer agents. The contract was in force until 1998. Nobody could take that away from us – or so we thought. By now, however, the other five unions had agreed to allow their members to vote on wage cuts. Only the CAW was holding out, for a couple of important reasons beyond the legal collective agreement. First, we knew from experience that employee wage concessions only destroy what union members have worked for years to build up. Every concession opened the door for management to come back and demand more concessions. Second, concessions inevitably trigger a series of knee-jerk demands from other employers. The unions at Canadian Airlines were the same as at Air Canada. Once we gave in to Canadian, we would have to deal with Air Canada, or any other employer associated with the industry. "You gave them concessions," they'd say. "Now, what about us?"

BY THE TIME I'd picked up our bargaining committee members at the hotel after the December 4 meeting and we'd made our way to the Ottawa airport, there was already a delegation of Canadian employees there to confront us. They had received word that the meeting with Anderson and Benson had been a bust. Within minutes of my leaving Anderson's office, I discovered later, Benson and his management group had sent an internal e-mail to all employees and put out a media release claiming I had just dealt the airline the "final death blow" – that it was about to go under because of Buzz Hargrove's refusal to allow Benson to conduct his vote on wage concessions.

Television cameras were eating up the scene at the airport. The anger, the jostling, the in-your-face shouts and swearing were grist for the news mill. We had already talked with many of our members and explained the bargaining committee's position. It was clear that most supported our stand. Many CAW members in the air terminal gave us the thumbs-up sign and yelled: "Right on, Buzz. Don't give them a cent!" Others were less vocal, but the tone of the message was fairly consistent: "We have confidence in the bargaining committee. Just do your utmost to make sure we do not lose our jobs." However, some of the non-union employees and members of other unions were quite vicious, yelling and swearing that we were destroying the airline and trashing their jobs. I could understand their frustration. Most had already succumbed to Benson's demands, and their fate, so they discovered, was no longer in their hands.

A lot of people complained I was being "undemocratic" for not allowing CAW members to vote on the wage concessions. That was the major gripe we kept hearing from Anderson, too. But what those folks did not seem to understand was that we were being ultra democratic.

Our members elect their union leaders by way of a vote, a process similar to the one that elects Members of Parliament. Those same members ratify the terms and conditions of any collective agreement we negotiate on their behalf – a privilege that we, as citizens, do not enjoy when it comes to our parliamentarians.

Anderson reminded the media every few days how undemocratic I was being, but he failed to see the irony in his position. If he was equating democratic action with the right to vote every time an important issue confronts the electorate, why did we need him as a Member of Parliament? Why could Canadians not vote when the Chrétien government reversed itself on the GST? On NAFTA? Or on its decision to reduce the deficit, when the majority of people wanted legislation that would help produce more good jobs in this country?

I asked Anderson once, as he tried to force us to revoke our contract with Canadian, if he would be as enthusiastic if our positions were reversed? "Wouldn't it be interesting," I said, "if, after three sets of wage concessions, we were able to sit here and say: 'Canadian Airlines is now making a lot of money. Thanks to employee concessions, the airline is very healthy. But I just talked to members of our union and, because of the Klein cutbacks in Alberta and the Harris government's attack on social policies, health, and education spending in Ontario, many of them can't pay their hydro bills. They're falling behind on their mortgage payments. Why can we not just reopen the last collective agreement we negotiated with the airline and vote on a further ten percent increase in employee wages?' I wonder what your position would be in that scenario, Mr. Transport Minister."

At the Ottawa airport we learned that there would be a delay in our 3 p.m. flight to Toronto. Fine – it gave us more time to talk with the delegation of concerned employees about the pros and cons of our union's refusal to concede to Anderson's and Benson's demands. Then I noticed that Benson was not at the airport. Strange – he'd told me he'd be taking the same flight.

After we finally took off, our committee was too involved in discussions to notice that it was taking longer than usual to get to Toronto. Over the airport, I realized we had begun circling – once, twice, three times.

The flight crew announced we were being delayed because of a backup in air traffic. I looked out the window. There did not seem to be a lot of air traffic. Down below, it appeared that there were several open gates.

As soon as we landed and the door of the aircraft was opened, a Canadian customer agent, who was also a CAW member, rushed up the aisle and told me I was in for a surprise. "Brother Hargrove," she said, "I've been asked by our Toronto members to warn you that you have quite a delegation waiting for you. They are definitely not friendly. It could get pretty ugly."

Benson, or his people, had been organizing this demonstration all along. They had obtained the cooperation of God knows who – pilots, air traffic controllers, middle management – to make sure we were delayed long enough for them to orchestrate a media event to make me out as the Ultimate Bad Guy. I suggested to the committee members that we sit tight until the other passengers had disembarked. I also reminded them that everyone has a right to demonstrate. The people in the terminal were worried about their jobs. Let's not get belligerent, I said. Let's just explain our position and see what happens.

As we headed up the ramp, the railing above us was stacked with Canadian pilots – members of a union that had voted to give in to Benson's demands. For pilots, a 10 percent rollback was not an act of high sacrifice. Pilots earn anywhere from $90,000 to $200,000 a year. But for many of our members – people earning around $25,000 a year and trying to raise families – 10 percent was a serious blow.

Once we moved into the crowd, I realized that a lot of the throng was made up of non-union office workers at Terminal 3 – as well as members of other unions that had already agreed to concessions. They were accompanied by a large contingent of management personnel. I wondered how the airline's business was being conducted with so many managers given time off (with pay) to protest Buzz Hargrove and the CAW. We later learned that Benson had all but drained the airport of available office and non-union staff to make this staged event as large as it could be. Perhaps I should have been flattered.

The crowd was everything Benson could have asked for. They were loud and angry. They booed the hell out of us as we tried to make our way through. Some were yelling, shaking fists, making threats. None seemed prepared to listen to what we had to say. The main complaint was the one we had heard for the past month: "You're destroying the airline! We live in a democracy, so why don't you let your members vote on wage cuts!"

CAW members tried their best to explain why we did not believe what Benson was saying about the imminent demise of Canadian. But it was futile. The mob Benson had gathered had no intention of listening.

The media like to talk about how much power the Canadian labour movement has, how guys like me – often referred to pejoratively as "union bosses" – can make one telephone call and employees will drop their tools and be in the streets picketing within hours. I'm supposed to be able to wave a magic wand and whole factories and airports close. That's a laugh. It would have taken us days, perhaps a week, to put together a demonstration like Benson's. Where Benson can press a button and make it happen, we have to go through committee meetings and then put the idea to a vote. All Benson has to do is spread the word among his management group that their jobs are in danger and, within an hour, the airport is filled with pilots, non-union personnel, and non-CAW members worried about the repercussions of their agreement to take a wage cut. There are days when I wish I had that kind of power.

No sooner was I home than the vicious, sicko telephone calls began. Worse yet, some freak put my name and former address and telephone number on the Internet and suggested people send messages to me there. It was now the address of my former wife, who lived with my children and my grandchild. This low-life turned their lives into hell. They received a rash of threatening phone calls. The tires on their cars were slashed – in broad daylight. There were bomb threats. A police bomb squad spent days at my ex-wife's home. It is absolutely unacceptable that anyone's home and family – whether a union leader, a politician, or the head of a corporation – should be subject to this sort of abuse. Frankly, I blame Benson and Anderson for making it happen.

ON THE ISSUE of who really has the power to make things happen, even Benson's public demonstration paled by comparison with the other message our bargaining committee had received at the Ottawa airport. A telephone call informed us that, following our unsuccessful meeting in Anderson's office, Chrétien's Liberal government had *ordered* our union to take a vote on the plan to save Canadian with wage cuts. The order, or at least the approval, for a forced vote had to come from the Prime Minister's Office, but it was left to Labour Minister Alfonso Gagliano to deliver.

The decision to force a vote stunned academics, legal experts, and union leaders and members across the country. There was no precedent. As one legal observer put it: "If governments are going to run the unions in this country, why bother having unions at all?"

At the heart of our collective bargaining system is the right of workers to organize and form unions. Workers who decide to join a union are, in effect, authorizing that union to represent their interests in dealing with employers. Canada's Labour Code is clear on this principle: a certified union has "the exclusive authority to bargain collectively on behalf of the employees in the bargaining unit." The CAW had a legal contract in place. The government's decision to force a vote took away the CAW's role of representing our members in dealing with the employer. The government had unilaterally decided that it – not the union – would determine when and on what terms workers would vote. Without debate in the House of Commons, and with no enactment of legislation, the government declared itself the representative for CAW members of Local 1990.

Never before in Canadian history, to my knowledge, has the federal government intervened in this way. It was a violation of section 94 of the Canadian Labour Code, the section stating that employers are forbidden from participating or interfering in the "administration of a trade union or the representation of employees by a trade union." To do so constitutes an unfair labour practice. The Chrétien government encouraged and supported the employer to break the law.

Gagliano tried to put a legitimate face on this miscarriage of justice by saying that the impasse between Canadian and the CAW was a "unique" experience that called for the "employees to be allowed to decide themselves – democratically – on their future...We had to break the deadlock," he continued, "and I believe that democracy must prevail." It was a line right out of *Catch-22* or *Alice in Wonderland*. Democracy was now whatever the Chrétien government said it was.

Our initial response was that we would not accept the government's edict to hold a vote without a fight. We considered challenging the legality of the government's action in the courts. We could easily have sought an injunction, and legal arguments would have dragged out the issue for weeks. The government had no mechanism in place to conduct a forced vote, and it would have taken at least two weeks to organize the ballot across the country. Meanwhile, fewer passengers would have been willing to risk flying Canadian, and Benson would have been desperate about the company's deteriorating financial situation.

By this time, however, many of our members and some of our local union leaders were pressing the bargaining committee to find a way out of the deadlock. "We've made our point," they said. "We got people to recognize that employee concessions are not the answer to the airline's problems. They'll never try this again. Let's find some closure."

Public opinion was also against us. One poll showed that the Liberals had as much as 80 percent support for forcing a vote among CAW members. The Liberals in effect took us off the hook, and we could now say to our members that the union did not cave in. But we insisted that our union still wanted to negotiate the terms and conditions of the final settlement. That is what unions are for, and we were determined to hammer out a deal that would make the best of a bad situation.

Our goal was to get a settlement our members could feel proud of. During the final hours, our bargaining committee was in twenty-four-hour contact with the Prime Minister's Office. Chrétien's chief political adviser, Eddie Goldenberg, was eager to work out an accommodation. The Liberals knew they had bitten off more than they had realized by declaring a forced vote, and now they wanted out of the imbroglio in the worst way.

Someone who was especially helpful at this time was the British Columbia premier, Glen Clark. With an initial offer of $8 million a year, he was the first government leader to put money on the table to save the airline, and he worked tirelessly behind the scenes to convince other politicians and senior bureaucrats to help out. He even travelled to Texas to meet with AMR Corp. officials. His involvement helped pave the way to a settlement.

We got word to Benson that our bargaining committee was now willing to sit down with Canadian management to see if we could settle matters on an employer-employee basis. If we could settle the differences between us, we were willing to conduct our own vote on an acceptable package bargained with Benson and his people.

Now the gun was aimed at Benson's head. He and his management group had a choice: they could let the CAW drag out the forced vote and help drive even more customers away, or they could bargain with our committee over the terms and conditions of any changes to our collective agreement. Benson decided to bargain. As soon as word got out about the negotiations, I received a call from Gagliano.

"You are now saying that the federal government doesn't have to force a vote?" he asked, almost with a sigh of relief.

"Look," I told him, "you do what you have to do and we'll do what we have to do. What our union eventually decides has got nothing to do with you guys."

Needless to say, he was not happy. The heat was now on the Liberals, especially in western Canada, to cough up more federal money to save the Calgary-based airline. Those polls notwithstanding, the Liberals' decision to override the CAW's existing agreement with Canadian was seen by many as extreme. Before this fiasco unfolded, the Liberals had been riding high in the polls and they had expected to gain seats from the Reform Party in the next election. But the airline debacle ate away at their political support in the West. Even the usually right-wing *Calgary Herald* came out against the Liberals' imposition of a forced vote, calling it "offensive." One especially aggravating issue to many western Canadians was that the Chrétien government could find $87 million to make life easy for a profitable company like Bombardier in Montreal, but could not find a buck to save an almost bankrupt western airline. And the Liberals wondered why their popular support out west was falling fast.

The CAW strategy worked. We sat down with Benson's people and put together an agreement that our bargaining committee took back to the members. At the end of the exhaustive talks, our committee chairperson, Anne Davidson, remarked: "Bargaining with employers is a hell of a lot easier than bargaining with the federal government."

Our committee made significant gains for our members. Over the life of the new agreement, the airline agreed not to close any of its reservation offices. To us, this was one of the more ironic things to come out of the airline's financial crisis. The loudest opposition to our union's stand on the wage rollback came from the airline's Calgary employees. Benson's original plan had called for the closing of the Calgary reservation office and the transfer of that function to AMR Corp. The persistence of our bargaining committee saved their jobs. Our committee also bargained job security clauses for employees working in the smaller bases, and substantial severance packages for laid-off employees. But the biggest concession management made was on wages and benefits. The concession package ended up, for most of our members, at about 3.75 percent, less than half Benson's original demand. It called for 7.5 percent off the wages of the highest paid employees, 1 percent for those earning between $25,000 and $30,000 a year, and nothing – no wage or benefit concession – for those earning $25,000 or less.

That $70 million a year for four years that Benson originally demanded ended up as a mixed package that spread the pain more fairly. The key was convincing governments to forgo future taxes on jet fuel. British Columbia raised its original ante from $8 million to more than $10 million, Alberta put in $8 million, the federal government came up with $20 million, and the contribution from employees ended up at roughly $32 million. By fighting back, our committee saved Canadian employees, over four years, $152 million. It was also able to bargain the CAW contribution down to $4 million a year, or about half-a-day's fuel bill for Canadian.

All through the negotiations, Liberal advisers and bureaucrats tried to make life difficult for the negotiators. One of the most juvenile performances came from David Anderson. In a public announcement, he tried to give the credit for this sweeping new agreement on concessions to the pilots' union and the International Association of Machinists –

the first two unions to capitulate. Many of our members had been furious at the pilots and machinists for giving in so easily. It was the CAW bargaining committee, supported by the airline division of the Canadian Union of Public Employees representing flight attendants, that got the wage cuts reduced so dramatically. It was the CAW committee that negotiated new job-security clauses and better work-related conditions, and forced the Liberals to open discussions about airline deregulation.

This same Liberal group then tried to renege on an agreement that a select committee, composed of representatives from government, industry, and unions, would analyze the problems caused by deregulation and recommend policy changes. On December 5, Anderson went on national television to announce the agreement. He waved what was presumably a copy of the letter of agreement and stated, incorrectly, that it was word for word as we had demanded. It was not. We were still negotiating with the Prime Minister's Office on the wording as he spoke. An important issue was whether the committee could recommend changes to federal airline policy. None of that had been settled when Anderson said it had been. He was playing public relations games, trying to get the jump on us.

My assistant Peggy Nash was on the telephone to Eddie Goldenberg, arguing late into the night over the wording of the agreement. At one point I overheard her telling the prime minister's adviser that "if you don't change the wording back to the way we wanted it, we are not in. Our committee will not recommend acceptance and ratification to our membership." The Chrétien government was changing the wording and the intention of our discussions. It was childish. Worse than that, when we did reach an agreement on something our bargaining committee felt it could take to our members, the Liberals denied that they had agreed to it.

The following Monday, December 9, Anderson, despite the agreement, made it clear he would not allow the Liberals' policy on airline deregulation to be debated. Re-regulation was "not in the cards," he said. One reporter asked Anderson when re-regulation might take place. His reported answer was, "When pigs fly." Asked about Anderson's response, I couldn't resist a little sarcasm of my own: "I thought the debate was about keeping Canadian flying, not Mr. Anderson."

MUCH AS I DISLIKE Brian Mulroney, he had a more sophisticated and balanced approach to labour relations than the Chrétien Liberals. For all his faults, Mulroney had worked for years in labour-management relations with the Iron Ore Company of Canada. He understood the need for consistency, fairness, and recognition of institutions for working people. The Liberals do not, and that is what makes them dangerous. To Mulroney, a deal negotiated was a deal made. With the Chrétien government, who knows?

Still, as things began to settle after one of the most tumultuous months in my union experience, the CAW leaders knew we had more wins than losses. The Chrétien government had backed Benson's position to the hilt – until it began to see public opinion swinging away from defence of its airline deregulation policy. Canadians are not stupid: they know a turkey when they see one. Thanks in large part to Anderson's performance, the Liberals took a beating in public opinion polls in western Canada, one that lasted through the 1997 federal election.

The CAW left a strong message for Benson, one that will resonate for a long time within the halls of Canadian Airlines: Don't come back, ever again, and pretend that wages are your principal operating problem, or that wage cuts are the answer to shabby airline management.

The CAW's willingness to fight also sent a message to other employers, in particular Air Canada. While our union was locked in combat with the Benson-Anderson team, it was also bargaining with Air Canada. Instead of demands for wage rollbacks or an offer of pencil-thin annual wage increases, our bargaining committee won major wage and benefit gains from Air Canada: a three-year agreement with annual wage increases totalling 8 percent. The figure was unprecedented in the 1990s, given the tone of labour-management negotiations.

The other important victory our union achieved was a growing recognition that wage concessions are like a form of cancer. Too many unions have succumbed to the demand of wage cuts or loss of jobs. "We need to lower operating costs so we can be more competitive," employers argue. "Keep us competitive by keeping your wages low, and you get to keep your jobs." I hope people now understand that decent wages are not the real issue in business competitiveness.

For the labour movement in this country, the fight with Canadian in late 1996 achieved more on a broader scale than we would have suspected. What happened there was, to some extent, a reflection of the political weakness labour suffers today. There is little support for working people in provincial legislatures or the House of Commons. The Canadian experience demonstrated to many people in the labour movement that, where our political interests are concerned, there are few helping hands at any government level – federal or provincial.

We fought the good fight with Benson, Anderson, and the Prime Minister's Office. We prompted a public debate about the government's policies for deregulation and its negative impact on working people and consumers. We exposed wage and benefit concessions as camouflage for bad management practices. Concessions allow governments to ignore major structural problems in the economy as they coast from crisis to crisis, relying on nothing more than unproven, right-wing philosophies to guide them economically. The real solution for all our economic ills lies in creating jobs – putting an entire country back to work. We were successful in saving tens of millions of dollars for flight attendants, reservation clerks, machinists, pilots, and non-union airline personnel. Most of all, I hope we made it clear to Anderson and Benson that they cannot come back and demand concessions again. A small victory? Perhaps, but small victories are what the labour movement is all about.

2

MORE MEALTIMES THAN MEALS

No man lives without jostling and being jostled;
in all ways he has to elbow himself through the world,
giving and receiving offence.
— *Thomas Carlyle*

My full name is Basil Eldon Hargrove. I picked up the "Buzz" when I got my first job, and I've been Buzz ever since. I was born March 8, 1944, in Bath, New Brunswick, a small village along the Saint John River valley west of Hartland, mid-way between Saint John and Edmundston. I was the sixth of ten children, only two of whom were born in a hospital. My delivery took place in my aunt's house on the main street in Bath, a few blocks from the hospital. We were too poor to afford a hospital delivery. My mother reasoned that if anything went wrong, she could call for a doctor down the street.

Needless to say, no one in the Hargrove household ever gagged on a silver spoon. Our home was back in the bush at a place called Holmesville. The village consisted of about fifty families spread over a ten-mile radius. We lived in a clapboard house with four bedrooms, a big kitchen that served as a family area, and a living room with a large wood stove in the middle. In winter, everybody huddled around the stove because it was the only heat we had, then we raced for our beds.

We might have frozen to death if we had not piled into the beds together. My parents had one bedroom, and my four sisters slept in two beds in two bedrooms. My two youngest brothers, Neville and Cecil, squeezed into a three-quarter-sized bed, and Fred, Lyle, and I shared a larger bed. (Our eldest brother, Carl, had already left home for a job by this time.) Getting out of bed in the morning and having to put your feet on the frigid floor was one of life's great horrors. This torture was surpassed only by an early morning visit to the outdoor toilet.

It was tough times growing up. Occasionally our CAW Council delegates sit around debating the issue of poverty in Canada and what we might be able to do about it. The discussion is usually in the abstract; not everyone can relate to the real thing. I know what poverty is because I lived it.

I recall a whole lot more mealtimes than meals. Often our lunch for school consisted of a piece of white bread with sugar sprinkled on it. No one whined because that was all we had to eat. Our principal food supply was what we could grow and raise. We usually had a few chickens, some pigs, and two or three cows. Milking the cows and cleaning the barn were the boys' chores after school. We had a barrel in the cellar where pork was stored in salt. That would be our meat supply for most of the winter. We always had a large garden, and our job as kids was to keep it weeded. My mother preserved the vegetables and made jam with the berries we picked in summer. My brothers and I spent a lot of time fishing for brook trout. I got quite good at it. But even with nature's larder close at hand, it was hard to make it all stretch to feed and nourish twelve people. If the winter was long and fierce, we would run out of almost everything, and be back to sugar sandwiches again.

We never had running water. We used to lug our drinking water by hand from a spring a quarter mile from home. Our washing water came from a brook. I can remember struggling with the galvanized steel pails, spilling half the water over myself on the way home, and arriving covered in ice. We had no electricity until the mid-1950s. My mother did her ironing by setting the iron on the stove to heat and then pressing the clothes with it. We cut and piled our wood for the stove. Every night after school our chores included a couple of hours sawing and splitting logs.

All things considered, we were pretty lucky. My dad always had work. He was a carpenter in the summer and he worked in the woods in the winter, cutting pulp and lumber for a company owned by the former premier of New Brunswick, Hugh John Flemming. My father was a good carpenter and spent a lot of years working on projects like the Beechwood Dam on the Saint John River and the Hugh John Flemming Bridge at Hartland. In fact, Dad died on the job while working for the Flemming family.

He died of a heart attack in the bush in the winter of 1961. He was fifty-three years old. There was no medical care available for the workers then, no ambulances and no rescue helicopters. The only way out of the woods was by horse and sleigh. A pickup truck would meet the sleigh and take the injured worker to civilization. Many people today survive a heart attack on the job, but there was no surviving one then.

I often ask myself if my father would have lived had someone in the lumber camp been trained in cardiopulmonary resuscitation. Would it have been too much to ask, in the early 1960s, for companies to be required to have medical assistance or training for some of the staff in the lumber camps? It was years before unions were able to force companies to provide even the most rudimentary safety provisions for their employees.

Working for Flemming and other companies was, for my father, like going to prison every year. The men rarely got home. Their cheques were delivered by the company to their wives. Each November, when freeze-up began, my dad packed up his gear and headed into the woods. He worked six days a week, ten to twelve hours a day – until the spring thaw came – all for a few dollars. The only break the workers had was a few days at Christmas, and then it was back to the woods. Sunday was supposed to be a day of rest, but after playing a few hands of cards they still had to clean out the stables, feed the horses, and do other chores until bedtime.

My dad was a hard-working guy, but he was a miserable son-of-a-bitch. He had the personality of a mud turtle. I never could understand the man or get close to him – none of us could. He showed no warmth or affection to any of us and seemed intent on isolating himself from everyone. I can never remember him ever hugging me. He came with the belief that fathers were the kingpins of the family and that everyone bowed to them. He had his spot at the table, and no one ever tried to sit there. He made sure he was fed first, before the kids, and then he left the table. We got more warmth from that old wood stove than from my father.

He always seemed to be mad at something. The only time I saw him relax was at Christmas. He had a few beers – he never drank much because there was no money – but when he did he got abusive, especially with my mother. The other thing I remember is that he was tight as a fiddle string. As we were growing up, when there was a bit more money around, Dad always found enough to have an old car or truck. But he was still cheap. He used to try all sorts of things to save gas. He would drive to the top of a hill and put the car in neutral, turn off the ignition, and glide down the hill. Halfway up the next hill he'd turn the engine back on. He never seemed to take into account all the wear and tear he was putting on the starter and the generator.

On Sundays he would shove us kids into the car and drive along the roads, getting us to search in the ditches for pop and beer bottles from the Saturday night revellers. He would get one or two cents a bottle. I used to be embarrassed when the neighbours passed us on the road, watching the Hargrove boys scrounging for bottles. But the most embarrassing thing was collecting bruised potatoes from farmers' discard piles. There, in full view of anyone passing along the highway, we picked through the culls, throwing the best ones in bags to take home to eat.

Dad was born in the same general area, around Holmesville, but he was brought up in the bush. If I thought I was raised in wilderness, Dad was six or seven miles farther on in a place called Moose Mountain. My brother Cecil and his family now own the property and live there in the most rustic conditions imaginable. But growing up in that isolation might explain why Dad was the way he was.

My mother, Eileen, was the opposite. She was a warm person with an outgoing personality. She was born in New Brunswick of French and Irish stock and celebrated her eighty-first birthday in August 1998. She has been a strong influence on my life. It was my mother who taught me the two basic rules I try to follow: be honest, and stand up for what you think is right.

As hard as my father worked and as tough as he was, I think my mother worked harder and was just as tough – tougher, maybe. They separated when I was about thirteen years old. She left and went to work in a hospital in Woodstock, New Brunswick. She got involved with the union there and helped organize the hospital staff into the

Canadian Union of Public Employees. So my union organizing roots are close at hand.

I was supportive of her leaving Dad. I might have been young at the time, but I remember saying I could not imagine why she had stayed with him as long as she did. In fact, it was always a relief for us in November when he headed out the door with his bag. Knowing he was gone for a couple of months raised everybody's spirits. I shake my head when I think how hard he worked to put what little bread he could on the table. He tried to provide for us, but it was an impossible task. So my mother ended up – between having ten kids – working as well.

Mom worked on the farms around our area. In the spring she "cut seed" for potato farmers. She sat for hours in the cold and damp of the potato house, cutting the seed potatoes into four or five pieces with "eyes," filling barrel after barrel. The tedium, the drudgery, the cold, and the dirt were awful. If she was not cutting seed, she did "tubular seeding" – which was even harder. With a burlap bag full of high-priced seed potatoes on her shoulder, she cut the potatoes and planted them in the field as she walked: cutting, stooping, planting the seed, lifting the bag, moving on to the next plant, on and on for hours. The scene was much like those bleak paintings of seventeenth-century Dutch farms, with the workers permanently bent over.

We kids all went with Mom to the fields, helping out here and there. In the fall we did our share with the harvest. I remember picking potatoes – I cannot recall how young I was. Mom crawled along on her hands and knees, filled a woven Native basket, and dumped it into a barrel. God, it was heavy work. Her pay was about fifteen cents a barrel.

That was how my mother made money to buy us winter clothes. From her work in the potato fields, each of us would receive one pair of blue jeans, two pairs of long johns, and two plaid shirts. They would have to last us until the next year. Before the harvest, my mother began knitting mittens and socks as well. She worked at it all summer. We sure needed the socks and mittens, but I think the knitting was her way of relaxing. Through it all, year after year, she never complained.

As bad as things seem in retrospect, I thought at the time that our family was well off, compared with others that really struggled. At least my father had two good jobs. He was a skilled carpenter and was paid more than the unskilled labourers. Everybody had big families in those days. The Catholics had the priests after couples to have more children because, if they did not, the Protestants would dominate the community. When the Protestants heard that the Catholics were gearing up for more kids, they had more too. Even if parents wanted to limit the size of their family, no birth control pills or information was available. So everybody ended up poor.

Although religion was not a big thing in my life, there was always church when we were growing up. We were United Baptists and we went to church every Sunday. We also had to attend prayer meetings. Between sermons on Sunday, one of the local laymen visited the homes in the area and led us in prayer with all that fire-and-brimstone stuff about going to hell. I'm reminded of him sometimes when I listen to the Liberal government extolling the virtues of its high interest rate policies, and telling us we should all be prepared to sacrifice so Canada can be globally competitive. As with the Liberals' catechism – you give, we get – we were told in church to be patient and to wait for our turn to come. Well, I was not very patient.

I used to watch the preachers closely, as they pounded the pulpit and chastised the congregation for being sinful, telling us to sacrifice now for a place in the Great Hereafter. I could never accept their logic. Just across the aisle were all the well-to-do people of the community – they had food on the table, money in the bank, fine clothes, new cars and trucks – and then there was the rest of us, who had little or nothing. Why the hell did I have to wait for my rewards when these other people had everything? Not surprisingly, I turned off religion at an early age.

AS TOUGH AS THINGS WERE, and as much as my dad's personality could put a damper on things, we were a tight-knit family. I was very close to my brothers Fred and Lyle. Fred was born a year and two days before I was, and Lyle was born less than two years after me. Our family was like a stepladder: just one kid after another, it seemed.

Growing up in the bush, we had to rely on each other a lot. There were no facilities for play – no organized sports, for instance. We didn't have to worry about not having a baseball glove because there was no baseball. We had no skates, but there was no hockey, either. Our days were made up of school, chores, and fishing, when I could sneak my dad's fishing pole out of the house. Like most kids growing up, my brothers and I wrestled a lot. My mother's brothers, Uncle Alvin and Uncle Emery, used to visit occasionally. They would offer Fred and me a nickel to see who could whip the other. A nickel in those days was like a million bucks.

I recall getting into one scrap with a neighbour, Brian Doherty. Brian was a friend, but this day we went at it and Brian, who was older and bigger, was winning. Fred stepped in to defend me and ended up with a broken arm. Dad tried to set the arm, but infection set in and Fred was laid up for two weeks. Of course, there was no national medicare system then. The doctor and hospital bills kept the family in debt for a year.

We had the usual fights and arguments among ourselves, of course. My two eldest sisters, Roma and Joan, could be tough on the younger ones, especially when they had to babysit on Saturdays while my parents went to Woodstock to buy groceries. But other than that, we were all quite close. I was – and still am – especially close to my sister Mildred, who is a couple of years older than I am.

Mildred had polio as a child. She was constantly being taken to Fredericton or Saint John for operations – the expenses must have been a terrible burden for my parents. Mildred seemed always to be in a cast – her leg, her arm, or most of her body. She went through great pain with incredible courage. Later, she would marry and, with the use of only her left arm, raise five children. Even today, she suffers from a form of post-polio syndrome and the pain has returned. She has also had one of her hips replaced twice. She is a courageous woman. Last year she took it upon herself to redecorate my apartment – painting, papering, climbing up and down the ladder – and thrived on it.

People sometimes ask where I got my sense of commitment, my sense of social responsibility. Well, I watched Mildred for many years – how she struggled, how she dealt with being shunned because she was different. I learned that we have to recognize that there are people in our society who are different and who must be treated in a way that helps make their lives easier. Mildred has certainly helped me in my thinking about how we in the CAW must deal with people with disabilities, with workers of colour, with Aboriginal people, with gays and lesbians, with women. When our leaders struggle with these issues, I try to remind everyone that the easiest thing to do would be to ignore this stuff – to say that these matters have nothing to do with labour-management relations and collective bargaining, that it should be left to governments or somebody else to deal with. That's a cop-out, one that the leaders of the CAW are constantly challenging ourselves and our members on.

No man will ever know what it is like to be a woman, but we have to recognize the differences and work to provide equality. No white person will ever know what it is like to be a worker of colour. No Caucasian will ever know what an Aboriginal person might be up against. But if you have a terrible car accident or you slip on the sidewalk outside your house, you can be disabled in a heartbeat. Then you'll know what it's like to be different. Mildred taught me that.

WHEN MY PARENTS SPLIT UP, we Hargrove boys moved with Dad to Hartland. That was a traumatic time for me. I did not want to leave home. That homestead was all I knew. We had gone to school in Bath on the bus, and occasionally we walked the seven miles into town to see a basketball game. Other than that, my world ended at the outskirts of Holmesville.

The upset of moving to Hartland was one of the reasons I could not settle down in school. All the faces around me were new and strange. I was a very shy kid and my schoolwork suffered. I had taken grade nine in Bath, but I failed to finish grade ten in Hartland. I was going through a sulky and rebellious period. I bummed around and spent more time in the poolroom than I did in school. Next year I went back to take grade ten again, but after a couple of months I dropped out.

A block down the street from our apartment lived an old family friend by the name of Bill Clark. I was chums with his son, Cyril, and I just kind of moved in with them. My brothers soon followed. Bill lived on the second floor of an old building in the centre of Hartland. He never had anything in a material sense. He worked hard every day of his life, on a farm in the summer and in the woods in winter. There was no union to make sure he got a decent wage or decent working conditions. Men like Bill and my father were little more than serfs for the Flemmings, the McCains, and the Irvings.

Bill's wife had died before I moved in with him. They had, I think, seventeen children, six of whom had died at birth. After his wife's death, Bill got a job working with an undertaker. He learned the profession, including embalming, as he went along. On the odd occasion, I went with him to pick up a body and help carry it out to the ambulance and into the embalming room. I always declined Bill's cheery invitation to prepare it for burial.

Bill was incredibly generous. He did not have much, but you could always get three square meals. One particularly nasty winter he looked out the window and saw a guy shivering on the street corner. "Who is that?" he asked. "He must be new here. He looks pretty cold. Do you suppose he's had anything to eat? Why don't you go down there and ask him?" It was always like that. If the guy had no place to go, Bill would invite him to stay with us. He had only two rules: stay clean and don't steal. He was an amazing human being. I still have a picture of him in my office today.

When I finally gave up on school in 1960, Cyril Clark and I took off with no idea of where we were going. It was like a scene out of Don Shebib's film *Going Down the Road*. Cyril and I ended up in Toronto and rented a room with board for $15 a week from a lovely old couple originally from Hartland, Roy and Edna Cannon. I got a job warehousing in a little factory called Beekist Honey for $1 an hour. But I quickly got the urge to move on, and over the next couple of years I travelled all over Ontario, taking whatever job came along. I hitchhiked back to New Brunswick a few times and stayed with Bill Clark. My father lived a block away, but I never went to visit. I picked up some work around town, saved a few dollars, and headed west to Calgary, where Mildred and her husband, Edward (another of Bill's sons), were living. Edward got me a job with Alberta Government Telephones. It was a good job, but tough.

AGT was in the process of converting its lines from overhead to underground. My job was to operate a jackhammer. I would go down each manhole and lift the jackhammer – which was probably heavier than I was – shoulder high, holding it there for hours at a time to cut a 12-by-18-inch hole in the wall of the concrete so the cable could be run through. The constant vibration and the weight were bad enough, but the racket in that confined space was terrible. When I finished one hole, I moved on to the next. It was like operating a jackhammer in a tiny, concrete bathroom all day.

It was my first lesson in how employers did not give a damn if your job was affecting your health. Before unions fought for safer working conditions, the average worker was treated like a piece of Kleenex. Once employers had used you up, they tossed you in the corner and replaced you with someone just as dumb as you had been. Companies like AGT did not hand out ear plugs in those days, and the jackhammer permanently damaged my hearing. Today I have a significant hearing problem because of one short-term job I took back in 1962 for the princely sum of $1.89 an hour.

I graduated out of the manhole into driving a truck. It was a union job, so I was making more than I ever had on an hourly basis. It lasted only eight months, but I learned first-hand about "consolidation" and "downsizing" – the process employers use so effectively these days to get "competitive" or "improve productivity." At the time, AGT was con-solidating its operations with Edmonton Telephone. These moves to achieve "efficiencies" meant they needed fewer employees. I was one of the junior people, so I was laid off first. That did not particularly bother me because the supervisor was a good guy and promised to take me on as a temporary while they moved the crew from Drumheller to places like Red Deer.

In fact, I ended up having a wonderful time following the crew around and picking up work here and there. I even visited Banff National-al Park. The company paid expenses and they put us up in good hotels. The scenery was great and the late-night parties were terrific. But when my brother-in-law said he was heading into northern Alberta and British Columbia to work on the pipeline, I decided to move on, too.

My first job on the pipeline was cutting bush. It is hard and dangerous work, but I paid close attention to what my chain-saw was doing. It can reach up and kiss you when you least expect it. I had worked one winter in New Brunswick with my dad for a few weeks cutting wood, so I had some experience. But in northern Alberta we were working on frozen muskeg, and every now and then there would be a soft spot. One day an old Danish guy was cutting next to us. One of his feet sank through the muskeg down about two feet. The chain-saw swung around and cut him across his knee, slashing through muscle and ligament down to the bone. I could feel the pain just watching it happen. Two days later, after they patched him up, the old buzzard was back at work, as crazy as ever, throwing his chain-saw around as if nothing had happened. But it was a lesson for me.

I eventually got work driving what they called a skid truck – delivering wooden skids to set the pipeline on while they welded the sections together. I lasted only about six weeks before they fired me, but I was learning lessons all over the place. If you did not have a union to protect you, you could count on employers to treat you like dirt.

We were a long way north, laying down pipe called "yellow jacket" – a ten-inch pipe used to run water to oil drilling sites farther south. Water pumped into the area surrounding a drill hole helped bring the oil to the surface. One day, in mid-winter, we were laying the pipeline across an open, rushing creek. Draglines dug a trench across the creek bottom deep enough for the pipeline to rest below the frost line. When the trench was ready, huge concrete blocks were attached to the pipeline to sink it. But this time the engineers underestimated the weight needed and the pipe would not sink.

The supervisor was a tough SOB if ever there was one. He began barking orders at the men standing nearby: "You, you, and you, get on that pipe, grab those big bolts, and when they lower the concrete, bolt it onto the pipe." That meant workers had to sit on the pipe in freezing water with the temperature close to minus 30 degrees. They had to tighten the bolts and then find a way out of the freezing water. I said, "No way. Not this kid!"

It was not that I was scared. As a youngster, I'd contracted tuberculosis and it scarred my lungs. I'd had pneumonia three or four times.

Even today, I wear warm clothes in cold weather, especially turtleneck sweaters, because I am so susceptible. The supervisor fired me on the spot. I thought he was going to grab me and throw me into the creek. As romantic as his toughness and work ethic might sound, these guys were nineteenth-century throwbacks, leftovers from the days when the employer's word was law.

I recall two young guys showing up one morning looking for work at the camp. After the supervisor talked with them about jobs, he said: "All right, stow your gear. Tell the cook you're on the payroll. Get a bite to eat and be ready to go to work in the morning. And by the way, clean up and shave off those beards."

The labourers looked at him kind of funny. When they came in for breakfast the next morning, they still had their beards. The supervisor walked over and said, "I guess you two don't want to work after all, eh?"

One guy asked him what he meant. The supervisor said, "I told you to shave your beards off."

"I'm not shaving my beard off," the other replied. "The beard has got nothing to do with how well I work. I'm a good worker."

"I told you to shave your damn beard," the supervisor roared, "or you don't work here!"

One of the guys jumped to his feet and, in a flash, the supervisor cold-cocked him. He turned and dropped the other kid where he was standing. Bang! Bang! I could not believe it. We were hundreds of miles away from civilization in the dense bush of northern Alberta and the supervisor insisted on a no-beards policy, backed up with fists.

After returning to civilization I called Al Muldoon, a friend from AGT days, to ask if he knew of any work I might get. Al was a wonderful, down-to-earth, jolly Irishman who always had some cockeyed scheme to make a million dollars but never did. He was living in Calgary and said he was headed for a job on the South Saskatchewan River dam project. He called to see about getting me on and, in no time, I was heading for Outlook, Saskatchewan, to work on a survey crew.

I worked there as an assistant through the fall and most of that winter of 1963–64. I headed back to Calgary to wait out the freeze-up and Al insisted I meet his daughter, Linda, who was from Ottawa. He said she was my age and an attractive young woman. I did not have a girlfriend at the time, and we began a relationship that got pretty serious. She ended up getting pregnant, and in December 1964 my first daughter, Karen, was born.

At the time, there was no way I was getting married. I was barely nineteen. I had no sense at all about what I wanted to do with my life. Given what I had witnessed growing up at home, marriage was not an institution that appealed to me. So I decided that until I was called back to the dam project, I would head back to New Brunswick to visit my mother and the rest of the family. I bought a 1958 Ford Fairlane convertible – red and white interior, black outside with a white top. I was pretty proud of that machine.

Mildred decided she wanted to go back and visit our family as well, so I loaded her and her three kids into the convertible and headed east. We drove to Windsor, where Mildred wanted to visit our oldest brother, Carl. The Hargroves are a pretty tight clan. We like keeping in touch and we enjoy each other's company. Carl talked me into putting in an application for a job at the three major automobile manufacturers. I had a job waiting for me back in Saskatchewan, but I put the applications in to get him off my back. I had no desire to work for a car company. But that job application changed the direction of my life.

THE LATE 1950s had been a disaster for General Motors, Ford, and Chrysler. The early 1960s were hardly better. The car companies were not doing a lot of hiring, so I was confident I would never hear from them. But no sooner was I back in New Brunswick than Carl called to tell me Chrysler had phoned and wanted me to go to work. I said, "You've got to be kidding. I just got home, I'm young, and I'm having a hell of a time partying. Besides, I have a good job waiting for me in Saskatchewan. Who needs a job on a production line at Chrysler?"

Well, Carl is a persuasive guy, and in April 1964 I started work in Chrysler's maintenance department doing cleanup. The work was dirty and hard, but the money was good – the best I had made anywhere. There was also a mood of optimism around the plant because the United States and Canada were deep into talks on something called an Auto

Pact. There was a general sense that this would be very good for Canada and that, if the agreement was signed, extra shifts would be put on the lines at all three plants. There would be even more jobs. It was not a bad time to be signing on at Chrysler.

The Auto Pact was implemented in 1965. This trade agreement allowed auto manufacturers to ship vehicles and components duty free across the Canada–U.S. border. U.S. auto companies were required to produce roughly one vehicle in Canada for every one sold in Canada. It was a major boon for this country. Employment in the Canadian auto industry sky-rocketed.

Chrysler immediately expanded its operations. A new shift was put on, meaning that as many as 2,000 new workers were hired within the year. I went from being a temporary hire for a job that might last six weeks to one of the senior people in the plant. Talk about being in the right place at the right time! At this point, I did not care about the union. My main problem was that the maintenance position turned into a night-mare for my social life. I was working afternoon shifts. If the plant worked five days in a week, maintenance worked six and sometimes seven days. I was getting off work at 2 a.m. – when the bars were closed – and going to work at four in the afternoon. I said to my shop steward, Ron Sweeney: "I gotta get off this shift. It's killing me."

Ron pointed me in the direction of Ken Gerard, the union's plant chairperson. He and I would later be close friends. I consider him the first of a number of mentors I've had in the union movement. But back then, all I wanted was to get off afternoon shift.

I was beginning to respect the way the union looked after its mem-bers on the shop floor. About the time I was after Ken to help me find another job on the day shift, I witnessed what would now be considered an insignificant event. I watched the union and management go toe to toe over the size of the plant floor area a sweeper would be required to cover if he wanted to keep his job.

The sweeper's name was Gino. He was a short, stout, bald-headed Italian guy whose job was to keep a certain floor area clean of dust and debris. Gino could sweep his area in four hours out of an eight-hour shift. The rest of the time he would read pocketbooks. Well, given that he could get through his day's work so quickly, management started pushing for him to sweep a larger area. But when they came with their stopwatches and clipboards, Gino would sweep exactly his area of responsibility and make it take eight hours.

Management knew he was capable of sweeping a larger area and was challenging their authority. They suspended him for a day. If he continued to ignore their order to sweep a larger floor area, they would continue to suspend him. In no time Ken Gerard was facing off with a big, tough-looking plant superintendent by the name of Ed Charette. These two had earlier had it out in a bar over another plant issue and Ken had beaten the stuffing out of Ed. So management now backed off. Under supervision, Gino swept his floor area for the next three nights in exactly eight hours. Ken stayed around and made sure Gino was not hassled by management. In a few days, Gino was again sweeping his area in his usual four hours. Management was nowhere to be seen.

For a young buck like me who had never had anyone in any job come to his assistance, I was fascinated that the union could play that kind of role. I thought of that supervisor in the pipeline camp in Alberta. If there had been a union steward standing up for me at that creek in minus 30 weather, I would have been able to say "no way" and still keep my job.

I know people will jump on the Gino story to show how much boon-doggle unions support, how lazy workers keep employer costs high. But that is not the point here. What we are talking about is power. If you do not fight, you lose. The company holds the power. The amount of power a union has depends solely on the extent to which we can build solidar-ity with our members. Gino's fight was not over the size of the floor he would sweep. It was over who had the power to demand what a worker had to do. The larger issue becomes, how many workers can you get rid of if you can force employees to do more work for the same wages? For me, power, at that moment, was clearly in the union's hands. The union accepted the challenge laid down by management and it won. A small victory, to be sure, but a victory nevertheless.

A union's survival depends on how it uses the power it has. Ken Ger-ard was a hell of a strategist in that respect. He always had the company back on its heels. You always have to be on the offensive, he said. If your union is sitting back and not putting the pressure on at every opportunity, the company is quietly winning.

I HAD BEEN AT CHRYSLER less than a year when I was asked to act as a shop steward in the United Auto Workers. I did not know much about how unions worked, but by the next year I was elected shop steward and stayed in that position for seven years. Thanks in large part to the Auto Pact, a lot was happening at Chrysler's Windsor plant. The place was full of young workers new to their jobs and to the labour movement. The atmosphere was highly charged with politics, both internal and external, and rebellion against authority was the order of the day. If we were not fighting the company or the government, we were fighting each other. We formed a political caucus, called the blue-white slate, with Ken Gerard as our leader. Our aim was to take over the local union, with Ken as president.

At the time, Local 444 was led by Charlie Brooks. Charlie was a passionate, veteran labour leader and community activist. Politically, he was known in the union as a real progressive. He believed workers had a responsibility to agitate for social change as readily as we fought for improved wages and benefits. He also believed that we owed a big debt to our communities. We did not just exist for the shop floor. Under Charlie's leadership, the Chrysler plant in Windsor held the most successful United Way canvasses in the entire country. Charlie taught me my early lessons in social unionism. He was the first person I heard talk about equity for women workers, and he encouraged workers of colour to run for leadership positions in the local. Eventually, Glen Watkins, a black, became our local vice-president.

Still, we younger members worked our butts off to defeat Charlie and his caucus slate because he represented another generation, not as radical in its thinking as we would have liked. He had less time for in-plant debates and confrontation with management – which is largely what fuelled our enthusiasm. Of course, this was the mid-1960s and everyone wanted to claim ground on the political left. But to do that you had to be a well-grounded thinker. In Local 444 you did not just sound off with any sort of opinion. There were too many people around who knew their politics and knew what the union bylaws and constitution meant. These were people who understood what was happening on the provincial and federal political scene.

It was an exciting time for a young kid from rural New Brunswick, and a great opportunity to learn about the union's history. Many a night we sat up until 3 or 4 a.m., drinking beer and talking about the struggles the union had gone through, the politics of the various factions. We would crawl into the sack for a couple of hours, then be at the plant gates as the sun came up, handing out leaflets for our caucus.

I enjoyed working the shop floor as well. As a shop steward I was responsible for about 250 workers. I enjoyed dealing with their problems. I was still pretty shy in those days. I was okay one on one, but if I had to speak to a meeting of two dozen people I would choke up. The union was a real growth experience for me, not just as a trade unionist, but as a democratic socialist and a thinking person.

As a young man working at Chrysler, I was going through a drastic change. Outside work, I was totally undisciplined. I raised hell and was my own free spirit. At work, I was in an environment where I could stand up for my rights and the rights of other workers, and the union would be there to back me up. I had lots of company. The Chrysler plant was overrun with young hotheads full of their own ideas and not willing to take orders from authority figures – company or union. We were rebellious and we took advantage of our collective power and the protection the union offered us. Between 1965 and 1968 we had more wildcat strikes in our section – the cushion room – than at any other time in the plant's history. It was a war zone.

In the 1986 National Film Board production *Final Offer*, about the 1984 UAW negotiations with General Motors – which explains in graphic detail why the Canadians split from the UAW and started the CAW – the cameras recorded the run-ins between GM supervisors and the union stewards and line workers: supervisors and workers yelling and screaming in each others' faces, threats, swearing. These were the good days! Back up twenty years and, by comparison, those raw conflict scenes in *Final Offer* were like watching a Bugs Bunny cartoon.

The toughest battles with management on our assembly line were over workload. The company wanted to give every worker more work so it could lay off other workers. Fewer workers meant lower costs and higher profits. The question was, how much grief, stress, and pressure the company could place on our members in the interests of enriching its investors. If the company wrongfully disciplined a worker, we would not only grieve but put on a show or a work stoppage to get management to back off. Many of my friends and co-workers were suspended, and I myself was suspended three or four times on work standard issues. When the company went on a campaign to make workers do more work for the same pay, we brought the plant to a halt with a wildcat strike.

Sometimes it became an adrenalin show. Both sides would be pumped up. The workers would be rooting for you, yelling, "Go get him, Buzz!" Most of the disputes were out in the open and had to do with manpower reductions or safety problems. The company did not put any emphasis on health and safety for its workers. Trying to get it to pay attention to safety problems was like whistling in the wind. The supervisors were under intense pressure to get more cars out and to drive costs down. They had to keep the line moving. As a result, people got hurt. Management didn't care. It simply grabbed a worker from another department to replace the injured one.

One time, management was about to suspend a worker for refusing a transfer to another department to fill a job vacancy. The refusal was costing the company because it slowed the production line. I was informed that a real hard-nose of a foreman was going to suspend the worker who refused the transfer. I got into a big argument with this foreman on the shop floor. I was smoking in those days and I fired my butt to the floor and stomped on it. When he ordered me to pick the butt up, and I told him to "f" off. He suspended me on the spot for six days for refusing a direct order – as if the plant was Stalag 17. He figured that if he suspended me, it would scare other workers into accepting transfers. The company's attitude was that once you punched in your time card, it owned you – body, soul, and keister – until you punched out.

IN 1972 I RAN FOR CHAIRPERSON of the roughly 120 stewards in Local 444. A chair has a seat on the executive council of the local. I was becoming more entranced by the politics of unionism than by the cut-and-thrust of shop floor unionism. I enjoyed my time at the local: my fights in the plant with management, my experience on the executive council, my role as part of the caucus. But I was becoming more aware of what we could achieve if I focused my energy on union politics.

I had a lot of friends and supporters urging me on, particularly Ken Gerard and Jim O'Neil. Jim and I had been hired on at Chrysler within days of each other. He's now the CAW's national secretary-treasurer and is always there for me when I need him. Ken and his wife, Beatrice, were great friends as well. I spent many hours in their home, and, on summer nights, barbecuing at the beach. Bea was a sweetheart, warm and gracious, but she could be tough. I remember showing up at their house with Ken after celebrating a successful cancer fundraising campaign sponsored by our union. In an inebriated form of apology for our lateness, we brought Bea a cold pizza. She threw it out the door and called the police.

One night in 1974 a few of us, including Ken and Jim, were sitting in a bar at the UAW's leadership school in Black Lake, Michigan, talking about the UAW. We felt that the fierce passion for unionism, especially the social unionism of the left wing, was evaporating. The younger members, who had fought their way through the 1960s, were getting frustrated as the times became less radical. We felt blocked by an aging union administration. There seemed less chance for pushing through more progressive ideas. That was especially true at the international staff level. Local 444 had no presence, no representation there, and that bothered us. Our local had not had an appointment to a staff position in more than thirty years. We had paid a lot of dues to the international union and felt we deserved representation. We told Dennis McDermott, the UAW's Canadian director, our concerns, and he arranged for the creation of a new international staff position in Canada. I eagerly threw my hat into the ring for the job.

A number of people warned me that I'd end up frustrated and bitter, just another bureaucrat caught in a job away from the real action at the local level or on the shop floor. I could see only the upside: I would be in a place where I could help build the social democratic movement as well as strengthen the union. I could bring a younger and fresher perspective to bargaining, organizing, and policy work. And perhaps, most of all, I could continue my education in the labour movement under the likes of some of the best teachers our union has ever had: Dennis McDermott, Bob White, and Sam Gindin.

When I came on staff, I was as green as grass, a relative unknown in UAW staff circles. I was barely thirty-one years old. I knew Local 444, but there were huge chunks of the UAW I knew little about. People had to introduce me to the union leaders in plants I would be responsible for serving. Yet any intimidation I felt quickly disappeared. There was so much to do.

I joined the staff in August 1975. No sooner had I hung up my jacket than an issue arose that would occupy us for months. The Trudeau government had been re-elected in 1974 on a promise to solve the country's economic woes with something other than wage and price controls. But inflation was running at more than 10 percent, and one of the first things the government did was to renege on its commitment. Under the Anti-Inflation Act of 1975, wage and price controls were to come into effect on October 14, 1975 – Thanksgiving Day. We busied ourselves in mounting a widespread attack against the Liberal government.

We knew from the brief experience of wage and price controls in the United States that we would end up with controls on wages, but no real controls on prices or corporate profits. Wage controls constituted a direct attack on labour. They put a lid on what unions could bargain for and marginalized the leadership. As expected, the Trudeau government made no attempt to control prices, or determine where capital investment should be focused to strengthen the economy. The struggle over wage controls was ultimately about worker concessions. Over the three years of their implementation, wage controls cost the average Canadian worker $2,200 – $20 billion for the country's workforce. In the meantime, corporate profits soared. Between 1978 and 1979 (when wage controls were at their most effective), corporate profits surged 58.3 per cent.

If we were to retain the confidence of our members, we had to avoid any role in endorsing the government's controls and mobilize our members to fight them. I had a hell of a time convincing our people we could defy wage controls. Not many of our members believed you could actually fight a law. They thought what I was suggesting was illegal.

Our plan called for a two-pronged assault. We let it be known that our union had no intention of bargaining within the 6-and-5 percent guidelines. Instead, we would ignore the restrictions and bargain for whatever we could get. If the settlement included a wage package in excess of the 6-and-5, that was a problem for the Anti-Inflation Board. Our goal was not to break the guidelines, but to ignore them. We were simply not prepared to sacrifice our members' gains.

The strategy also made political sense. By forcing the Anti-Inflation Board to strike down a duly negotiated settlement, the board – and, by association, the Trudeau government – became the bad guys. If we agreed to accept the guidelines and negotiate under a ceiling, we were doing their dirty work for them. If we ignored the guidelines and the board stepped in and took back some of the wage gains we had negotiated for our members, the Liberals were on the spot: the union put money in your pocket and the government took some away. If you were going to get mad at anyone, it would be the federal government. The UAW went on to stage about a hundred strikes during the controls period. We won wage gains in excess of the guidelines in 75 percent of the cases.

Working with the Canadian Labour Congress, we also took an active part in a nationwide Day of Protest on October 14, 1976 – the first national work stoppage in North American history. It was exhilarating to think that we were organizing what could turn out to be a national protest. On that day, about one million workers took the day off and marched and picketed in protest over wage and price controls. Others made their way to Ottawa, where a gathering of more than 100,000 workers made a strong public statement about how labour felt about this "tax" on their wages. The Canadian UAW chartered a train to leave Windsor and pick up passengers along the way. The train was full before it left Windsor. We had to hustle and arrange bus and car caravans to get our protesting members to Ottawa and back again. All in all, it was quite a day.

I LOVED THAT STAFF POSITION. There were times when I was involved in five or six contract negotiations at once. The days and nights blended together into one long string of bargaining, strategy sessions, more bargaining, committee meetings, membership meetings, and, finally, settlements – or strikes. It was an exciting time, but there were drawbacks. Although I made a point of spending as much time as I could with my family, union staff work can be a family-killer. When you're organizing a new bargaining unit, you might be away for weeks and months. My whole family ended up paying the price.

I'd married Linda Dupuis in July 1972 and she moved with me to Toronto when I took the staff position. We'd settled in a small house in Georgetown, fairly close to my office, and started to plan for a family. This responsibility was new for me. I liked to party back then and I was quite a gambler. I was heavily into poker in my early Windsor days, sometimes playing all night in a little bootleg joint owned by a friend who had been fired from Chrysler. More than one morning I saw the sun come up as I made my way from his shop to the Chrysler plant. I had a lot of energy in those days, and sleeping was something that did not excite me.

Once the racetrack opened in Windsor, I expanded my wagering horizons and started on the ponies. Sometimes luck came my way, but most often it did not. I was drinking at the time as well. I could drink a huge amount and not get belligerent or stupid, but alcohol is hard on your health, and over the years I scaled way back and began a fairly strict jogging and workout regimen.

I did my share of womanizing when I was young, too, and out of those liaisons had come a number of children – in addition to my daughter Karen, a son, Kevin, who lives in Victoria, and another son, Cory, who lives in Holmesville, New Brunswick. I love children, but I did not, when I was younger, believe in this thing called "love." I used to feel that relationships had more to do with desire than love. Was this a hangover from a broken home when I was a kid? Probably. Eventually, though, even sceptics can change. All my children have helped me, in one way or another, to understand better what love is. A child's love is unquestioning love, and my children have helped me come to appreciate what love really means between adults.

Linda and I had two daughters – Jaime Lynn, born in May 1976, and Laura Lee, born in August 1977. Linda and I separated in 1981. The marriage was not working and we both knew it. We had reached a point where we argued over everything – or at least Linda argued. I chose to make my case and then sit on it. But it was not a good environment in which to raise children. I moved out and took an apartment near the airport. I was travelling a lot and I wanted to be close to the girls when I did return to Toronto. I missed them unbelievably. It was one of the lowest periods in my life.

Eventually I called Linda and we agreed to give marriage another try. I moved back to the house in Georgetown. I had not been a part of Karen's, Kevin's, and Cory's lives as they were growing up, and I regretted that deeply. I was determined, somehow, to be an important part of Jaime's and Laura's childhood.

In 1984 Linda decided that we should move to Pickering. It turned out to be a disastrous move. The girls had been doing well in school in Georgetown, but the relocation to a strange environment frustrated them and, young as they were, they became rebellious and difficult. I was travelling a lot, which annoyed Linda, and soon you could cut the resentment with a knife. Our relationship began to deteriorate even further.

We bought a rustic little cottage on a small lake near Parry Sound. I acquired a boat so the girls and their friends could water ski, and a canoe so we could take marvellous morning paddles around the lake. Although Linda seldom stayed more than a few days, the girls loved the cottage and we spent weeks there. Those were the times we enjoyed the most. But the bickering and arguing continued at home. It was especially hard on Laura. She was such a bright child in so many ways, but she had trouble mastering school work. As time passed, she grew more frustrated.

We made a major mistake when we decided to hold Laura back to repeat grade one. It had a devastating effect on her self-esteem. She all but gave up on school. By the time she'd entered her teen years, she'd begun to take out her resentment by turning to her friends and becoming even more rebellious. The atmosphere in the home became sour. There was no real relationship between Linda and me. I was around because of the girls, who now argued regularly with Linda. I came home one

Friday evening and no one was home except Laura. I asked her where Jaime was and she said she was on the train to Windsor to live with her grandmother. When I heard that Jaime had taken her pet turtles with her, I knew she was serious. Laura then informed me that when she turned sixteen, she would move out too.

I asked myself, what the hell am I doing here when everyone seems to be taking off? If the kids wanted to leave, what could I possibly do to change their minds? They were not happy, Linda was not happy, and I was sure no bundle of laughs. That night I told Linda I was leaving and that I would file for a divorce.

When Laura was about thirteen, she began hanging out with a group of kids who found more excitement in trouble than in school work. They got into stealing cars for joyrides, doing dope, fighting, and threatening other kids at school. I was at the police station more times than I can remember. It was a really tough stage for her, and I felt miserable and helpless. There did not seem to be any way I could reach out to her and reaffirm that I loved her and cared for her dearly. I was at a loss.

Then she took up with a white supremacist group. The kids in the group were led by a sort of Heritage Front guru about my age who preached vicious anti-black, anti-Asian, anti-Jewish rhetoric to these susceptible kids. I had spent most of my life promoting tolerance and understanding, talking about the richness different cultures bring to our country, and to discover my daughter distributing hate material and practising racism was more than I could bear.

Jaime was in many ways the opposite of Laura. She was always willing to reach out and embrace people of other cultures. She had black friends and Indian friends, and was comfortable with people of diverse backgrounds. I was at a meeting one morning in the Royal York Hotel when I got a call from Linda informing me that the girls were having a terrible fight. It had been triggered by Jaime's discovery that Laura and her skinhead acquaintances were preparing to hand out racist leaflets at Jaime's school. The two were going at it fiercely. Linda wanted me to get back to Pickering and sort things out. I felt totally helpless. I was miles away. There was nothing I could do at that moment. The best I could come up with was to encourage Jaime and her friends to stage a counterdemonstration – to hand out leaflets that opposed the claims of the supremacists. Laura ended up in a training and detention centre.

She put us – and herself – through some torturous times. It took a major tragedy to make her understand that life is too short to waste on hate. When she was seventeen years old, six of her male friends were partying one night and decided to steal a small boat from a Pickering dock and go for a joyride with some beer. It was late autumn and the water was like ice. They were never seen again. The gas tank from the boat was found later, but there was no sign of her friends. The drowning shocked her. I suspect it brought home the message that none of us is immortal and that time on earth is not to be wasted. She's in a good relationship now and her intolerance has disappeared, as I suspected it would. We talk much more than we ever did.

Jaime and I still find it difficult to be open and frank with each other. She also has her share of personal challenges. In her teens she was stubborn, defiant, and certain she knew the answers to everything. She's twenty-two now and has a baby. Linda is helping her cope with mother-hood, and Jaime is working out her new responsibilities. I know she'll be all right, and I'm proud of the way both she and Laura have hung in there.

Why do I share this painful history? Well, I may not be a person who spills his guts easily, but I don't hide things, either. I believe that when you take on a public position, as I did, you give up your claim to a completely private life. In that case, full disclosure is the only route. My daughters are aware of what I've written here, and encouraged me to be candid. I also feel it's important to be candid about life experiences because a lot of people carry huge personal problems and feel alone in their struggles. In truth, of course, we've all screwed up at times, and we've all suffered, and caused others to suffer, in one way or another.

I was rebellious when I was young, just like Jaime and Laura. I had a lot of energy and I was not at all clear where I was going. My teen years were a fight for survival. I did not have many options: I could steal and, probably, go to jail, or I could find a job. As I got older I still had a lot of energy, and the union became an outlet for me. It provided me with more options than I thought I had or deserved. It helped me see more clearly how the deck is stacked against the poor and the disadvantaged. And it gave me a chance to put into practice the values and lessons that life has taught me.

3

UNION DUES

Nothing can preserve the integrity of contract
between individuals, except a discretionary authority
in the state to revise what has become intolerable.
The powers of unintended usury are too great.
— *John Maynard Keynes*

The Canadian Auto Workers union – along with its predecessor, the United Auto Workers – became the second family I needed as I grew out of my twenties. It was a place where I could invest my energy and passion and, in return, see the work we were doing result in impressive improvements in the standard of living for our members. The strength of our union lay in the strength of our leaders. I was fortunate to develop as a staff member under three of the most impressive leaders in our union's history: Ken Gerard, Dennis McDermott, and Bob White.

Ken Gerard's personal story is one of overcoming tremendous odds. As a young man, he was struck by lightning, suffered paralysis, and almost died. Like most working-class families in the days before universal medical care, the Gerards were poor and found it impossible to pay the bills for Ken's care. Strangely enough, like a scene out of a Hollywood movie, an unnamed benefactor came forward and took responsibility for his mounting medical bills. No one knew why this philanthropist did what he did, but we have often wondered what that Good Samaritan might say if he knew that his charity helped turn Ken into a politically active member of the left.

Ken was an important role model for me. The only time I ever gave up on the union movement was in the early 1970s when he was defeated for plant chairperson by a fellow caucus member. I was disillusioned. Here was a man who had made a lifetime commitment to workers being turned upon by the very people he was fighting for. I began asking myself if the union was worth it.

I was a candidate in a runoff election at the time, but I was so depressed that, instead of campaigning, I went on a week's booze and gambling spree. Friends covered for me and I won the election anyway, but I was so rattled by what the members had done to Ken that I did not care what happened. I returned to my job as shop steward, but when Ken heard about my reaction he took me aside and gave me some advice. He shrugged off his loss and made his point: if you are going to let a little incident like this deter you, you're in for some bigger setbacks. I returned to the shop floor more determined than ever to keep fighting. Ken went on to become president of the local. Under his leadership, we took on Chrysler during the late 1970s and early 1980s in some of the most important battles in the Canadian auto industry's history. We won more than we lost.

Dennis McDermott was the Canadian director of the UAW for a decade before he became the head of the Canadian Labour Congress in 1978. He taught me there was more to unionism than wages and benefits. He learned at the feet of the most progressive union leader in North America – Walter Reuther. Dennis carried Reuther's belief in social unionism into the Canadian section of the UAW, challenging us to think about our responsibility to the poor, to ponder the inequitable situation of women workers, to consider the plight of workers of colour, and to show respect for the communities in which we lived.

Education of our members was at the top of Dennis's priority list. He knew the value of teaching labour history. He wanted our members to study the political and economic systems that confronted them. He insisted we understand where our adversaries were coming from. He also showed our members that he had a deep, fundamental respect for them because he believed they were capable of learning and adopting new ways of thinking.

Where Dennis was concerned, educating a worker in the union's struggle was always easier than trying to teach an employer something new. The consciousness of corporate executives is fully developed by the time they sit down on the other side of the bargaining table. But workers are usually still trying to formulate a package of philosophies they can be comfortable with. To Dennis, education was never wasted on a union member. It was like an investment with a guaranteed return.

He also taught us, as Reuther preached in the United States, that our members should look at politics as a logical extension of unionism. Unions always need someone at that political table to work in their interests. I joined the New Democratic Party in 1966, shortly after I was elected as a shop steward. That was one of the first things we were taught in our local. If our movement was to go forward, we had to have a political ally, and that ally was the NDP. We became active in the party, working to elect NDP candidates in the Windsor area. We knocked on doors, solicited donations, campaigned, and handed out leaflets.

If Dennis McDermott was responsible for laying the foundation for the most successful union in Canadian labour history, Bob White was responsible for building our own strong house upon that foundation. Bob came into the Canadian director's chair just as the North American union movement was beginning to sag. The 1970s combination of high inflation, rising prices, and falling wages took a lot of spark out of the movement and dampened its sense of militancy. The air was full of talk about the need for unions to make concessions to employers, and too many unions were quick to oblige. Some mused about forming tripartite "pacts" or coalitions – government, employers, and labour – working together in what was presumed to be fairness and harmony for a stronger national economy.

Bob marched in and took a firm stand. The golden era might be over, he argued, but unions still had to play their traditional role. Bob made us understand that giving in to employers' demands for concessions was ultimately destructive and divisive for labour. Workers needed unions to be independent organizations that represented only them and their interests. Unions had no business trying to be the industrial relations arm of corporations.

Under Bob White, the Canadian UAW refused to reopen agreements and make concessions to employers. Our American brothers took the opposite tack and are still, to some extent, paying the price. The Canadian UAW opposed wage and price controls. Other unions did not, and many still have not caught up to the CAW in terms of negotiated wages and benefits. Later, after we split with the UAW and formed the CAW, our union opposed free trade with the Americans and captured an important nationalist high ground that even the federal NDP was unable to occupy during the debate. Under Bob's leadership, we refused to be controlled by an international union with headquarters in Detroit. Those were critical events that helped build a stronger, more influential union.

I first met Bob around 1968 when he was director of organizing for the UAW. We did not know each other well, even when he was appointed McDermott's assistant in 1972. After I moved to the staff job in 1975, we became better acquainted. During Trudeau's imposition of wage controls, we were negotiating with a plant called Milrod Metal, a company owned by ITT Automotive – a big conglomerate. The environment was scary. Bombs had been planted under cars and there were confrontations all over the place. The three hundred employees were mostly from the Caribbean, East Asia, and Africa. Management was all white.

When I got to know the workers, I thought they were great guys. They were a little loose living, even for me. They would think nothing of breaking out the booze at 9 a.m. membership meetings. They did not care much about authority. The atmosphere in the plant was so bad that even Dennis McDermott thought the workers were nothing but a big dose of trouble – a bunch of flaming Marxists and Leninists.

Bob called me one day and asked if I would go into Milrod, work with the local bargaining committee, and help them get a first contract. It was a big pat on the back for me because I was just thirty-two years old and a relative novice. The main issue turned out to be ITT's refusal to implement our settlement, which was above the Anti-Inflation Board's guidelines. I could see we were heading for a war if we did not get an agreement. There was going to be violence, and people were going to get hurt. Given its nasty reputation, ITT was not about to back off, either. I sought Bob's advice. "I am not trying to skirt my responsibilities here and get you to make the decisions for me," I said, "but I wanted to let you know we're heading for a bloodbath."

Bob gave me his poker stare. "Just so you know, my friend, once you bring me a problem, it belongs to me. I will now make the decisions about what we will do with ITT. Our policy is to negotiate as if the wage and price controls and the AIB did not exist. With an employer like ITT, that is damn tough to do. I agree that it might not make sense, but if the negotiating committee wants to strike we will support it. And then we'll see where we all end up. Your job is to force the company to bargain whatever you can. If they won't implement our wage settlement, we'll strike them and take the consequences."

To my surprise, the bargaining committee eased up and agreed to the company's 6-5-and-5 percent increase over three years, if the balance they wanted – an extra 2-2-and-2 – was submitted for AIB approval. The committee went with the company to the AIB and won the rest of those extra wage percentages. So everyone – except perhaps ITT – was happy with the way it was settled.

It was a learning experience for me. It taught me that the deal is paramount. Some of my critics like to call me "the labour boss who rattles the boardrooms" – as if my only intention is to be stubborn and force a strike on management. That's absurd. I'm better known in labour-management circles as a person who knows how to reach a settlement by reading the situation and moving demands around on the table until the deal begins to look too sweet for the employer to pass up. Our goal is always to get a deal our members can be happy with. I learned that from people like Gerard, McDermott, and White.

Bob was elected to replace Dennis as Canadian UAW director in 1978 when Dennis moved on to the Canadian Labour Congress. Bob phoned me the day after his election and asked if I could meet him for breakfast. When he asked me to be his assistant, I went into shock. I was thirty-four years old and one of the junior people on the staff roster. There were lots of older guys who felt they should be given a shot at the job. But Bob wanted more aggressive leadership than Dennis had provided, needed people with energy and commitment, and assumed I could fill that bill. Our Local 444 in Windsor had a track record of activism, and Bob liked that. It was the direction he wanted the Canadian section of the UAW to head in. When we began the journey, no one could have anticipated the many storms we would have to ride out or how they would change our union: who we were, what we stood for, and our impact on Canadian society.

THERE IS A NEAT LITTLE PROMOTIONAL STICKER I've seen floating around the labour movement these days. It reads, "Unions: The People Who Brought You the Weekend." It could also have read, "and Higher Wages, Pension Plans, Vacations, Safer Workplaces, Workers' Compensation, Pay Equity, the Minimum Wage, and Social Housing" – to name just a few of the benefits Canadians have inherited from the persistence of unionists in this country.

It should not be forgotten by the millions of Canadian workers who do not belong to unions that the wages and compensation they enjoy did not come about by virtue of a sixty-year streak of management benevolence. It was the union movement – not management, not corporations, not government – that identified the need for better conditions and brought about this revolution. If you're a non-union industrial worker, a white-collar worker, a supervisor, or even a manager, you owe your good fortune in the workplace to the fight carried out by unions at the bargaining table. Without their effort in forcing employers constantly to improve pay and working conditions for their members, there would be no benchmark to pay non-union workers a decent wage.

None of the benefits we enjoy – statutory holidays, health and safety regulations, the forty-hour week, workers' compensation – would have passed into legislation without unions. The labour movement built the foundation for worker benefits that many people now almost take for granted. Union members challenged governments and employers. The results of their sacrifices are the social benefits, relatively affluent wages, and high standard of living many of us enjoy.

Yet the Canadian labour movement today is under attack as it has not been since the 1930s. Unions are threatened from a number of powerful sources: the business community, federal and provincial governments, a conservative and reactionary media, influential right-wing "think-tanks," even a generation of young people made sceptical by an education system devoted to teaching the pre-eminence of business, market competition, and the joys – however illusionary – of individualism compared with collective action.

We face demands, as we did at Canadian Airlines in 1996, to roll back wages and make concessions, allegedly to solve the financial problems of our employers or to improve their global competitiveness. With most of Canada's newspapers and television and radio stations owned by pro-business interests, we are assaulted daily by a nationwide propaganda campaign that routinely portrays workers as overpaid and their unions as costly anachronisms. We face government attacks on the union's right to organize and bargain collectively. We endure growing pressure to sign long-term agreements that handicap bargaining flexibility, but keep the lid on employer costs.

We're told we must help employers improve productivity by accepting wage rollbacks, layoffs, and benefit concessions. With Canada's two major railroads – Canadian National and Canadian Pacific – productivity meant the layoff of thousands of rail workers and longer hours for those with jobs. Understaffing led to accidents and injuries. As railway productivity increased 117 percent between 1986 and 1997, real wages for railway workers fell by 4 percent.

In Ontario, unionized workers face punitive legislation from the Harris government, which has taken the province back to the anti-labour days before the 1930s. What's next? Legislation allowing for child labour, the six-day work week, Pinkerton detectives to keep track of labour "radicals," and goon squads to straighten them out?

I never thought I'd see a time when every hard-fought benefit dear to working people would be under attack from the very governments they helped elect. The list is astounding: from education to medical care, from social assistance to pensions, from Old Age Security to Workers' Compensation, from wages and benefits to the right to strike. It is not as if we, as a nation, cannot afford to pay for these rights. We are going through a period of incredible wealth creation, yet we make life harder for workers and their families.

Hundreds of Maple Leaf Foods workers in Alberta lost their jobs because they refused to accept the employer's final offer. Maple Leaf shut the plant, then told their workers in Brampton, Ontario, that they, too, would lose their jobs unless they agreed to wage concessions. By a narrow margin, the employees voted to accept the employer's offer – up to a 40 percent cut in wages and benefits. Then, on the first business day after forcing employees to accept the cuts, the company announced that it made a profit of $47 million in 1997, an 11 percent increase over 1996.

As I write in early 1998, these attacks on workers are happening in what is said to be the best economic climate this country has had since the 1960s. We live in a so-called golden economic age, and a million and a half people are out of work. Unemployment among the country's youth is officially about 17 percent, but many peg the real number, when taking into account kids who have given up looking for work, at around 30 percent. If these are the golden days, God help us when things turn sour.

What's going on in this country? Why is it that things we took for granted in less prosperous periods – the right to organize and bargain, universal medical care, national pension plans, unemployment insurance – are now under attack? Something overwhelming has happened to our society since the early 1970s. It has changed how we live and what we expect, but we do not seem to have grasped the full scope of this change – or who exactly is orchestrating it.

Economists generally divide the half century since the end of the Second World War into two periods. The first twenty-five years is often referred to as the "golden era." The second might now be called the "era of permanent recession." Within one generation, at the start of the second period, our rate of economic growth fell to half its previous level, unemployment rates doubled, budget surpluses turned into chronic deficits, and social programs were dismantled – slowly at first, but then at a frighteningly accelerated pace.

The stunning thing is that these changes happened in the face of other trends that should have left us better off rather than worse. Our work-force is better educated than ever before. Because of the widespread entry of women into the workforce, families are now contributing more hours of work than ever before. Thanks to technological innovation, we work with the most productive tools and machinery man has ever employed. Reorganization of the workplace gets more out of every worker.

Why, if we're working longer hours, bringing more education to our work, and doing it more productively, are things getting worse for workers? Why are corporations now demanding that we work even longer hours and put in more overtime? Why are businesses demanding, and getting, wage rollbacks and concessions while they pocket record profits? Why do we have permanent, double-digit unemployment? Why are the number of full-time jobs in our economy declining? Why have wage gains made by employees been less than the rate of inflation?

This human tragedy is happening not by accident, but by a program of planned inequality. Government spending for health care, education, and social services has been slashed. Funding for social housing has been eliminated. Minimum wage protection has been seriously eroded. Deep cuts have been made to welfare benefits for the poor and indigent, unemployment protection, seniors' pensions, workers' compensation, women's shelters, support for job retraining, child care centres, and immigrant and refugee services. Now the attack is focused on changing laws that defend the rights of the labour movement to organize, to bargain collectively, and to preserve the gains made over the years.

In March 1995 the Chrétien government imposed a contract on railway workers after a series of strikes that brought howls of indignation from the business community. In 1997 postal workers were forced back to work by federal legislation. Why have laws on the books if you persist in taking them back whenever the business community cries out? When is the right to bargain collectively a law and when is it not?

Defending collective bargaining is not an abstract principle. It is essential to the establishment of greater workplace democracy, safer working conditions, and a fairer distribution of income throughout the economy. Collective bargaining is more than a way to attain better wages and working conditions. It is a way for working people to exercise a progressive influence over their lives. Collective bargaining rights did not appear one day, as if written in the Magna Carta. They had to be won through long and bitter struggles with employers and with governments. Today we are faced with an unprecedented attack on those hard-won rights.

The first serious item on the agenda when the Harris government came to office in Ontario in 1995 was Bill 7 – a piece of anti-union legislation that, in some areas, set back the province's union movement fifty years. After five decades of tough slogging to convince several

Ontario provincial governments to liberalize labour laws, we were able to achieve automatic certification if 55 percent of employees in a workplace signed union cards. Management had no right to interfere. The Harris government changed that, allowing employers to force votes on union membership, including allowing employers to interfere in the process and threaten workers' jobs, change work conditions, even bribe employees not to vote for a union.

The Harris government removed anti-scab legislation, attacked the rights of public service employees, and used injunctions and police intimidation to end disputes. This behaviour discouraged many workers from joining or even thinking of forming a union. Labour Minister Elizabeth Witmer was gleeful when a 1997 ministry report showed that union certifications were down 50 percent from the days of the Rae government. She used the statistic in her speeches to business, bragging that it was one of the major "accomplishments" of the government. This would be more understandable if public opinion was solidly behind the Harris Tories, but it is not. Surveys show that a majority of citizens – more than 60 percent – support unions in their fight with the government. Among young people, the percentage is even higher.

Together, the troubling moves by these anti-union, right-wing politicians are further polarizing our society into those who are secure, wealthy, and powerful and those who are not. The only effective counterbalance to corporate power is the labour movement. Corporate leaders, with the support of governments, urge Canadian workers to make more sacrifices so our economy can remain globally competitive. But global competitiveness has become synonymous with greed, poverty, homelessness, and unemployment. In country after country, "competitiveness" is used as a battering ram to lower the standard of living of working people, to crush unions, and to obliterate agreements bargained for legally and collectively.

Over the past decade, employers have been shedding workers – union and non-union, public sector and private sector – at an alarming rate, a tactic that inevitably makes it harder for unions to organize and maintain their numbers. Union membership in Canada now stands at roughly 3.5 million workers, down from 3.8 million in 1990. Although better than one-third of all workers in Canada are unionized – compared with roughly 15 percent in the United States – two out of three new jobs created since 1990 are non-union. In the United States, labour union membership is plummeting. Since the 1970s, 7.5 million union jobs have disappeared. Only 10 percent of the private sector is now unionized. It is predicted that by the year 2000, only 7 percent of Americans in the private sector will be union members. This decline is primarily due to the relentless pro-business pressure to extinguish the rights of workers to organize and bargain collectively.

Canadian governments seem to have decided that they do not need to talk to the labour movement or take its views into account. They have tested the political waters and feel confident they can largely ignore the labour movement, even alienate it, without fear of wide reprisals. Our union, and the labour movement in general, had more access to the Mulroney government than we do to the Chrétien government. This treatment effectively disenfranchises three and a half million Canadians.

In more civil times, organized labour was regularly invited by government to voice its opinions on future legislation and government policy. Now the Liberals listen primarily to corporations and the Business Council on National Issues. In today's labour–management environment, there is no pressure on the federal government to improve the lot of unionized workers, who represent more than a third of Canada's workforce. More than ever, this government represents Bay Street, not working Canadians. The business community is an incredibly powerful force on Parliament Hill. Today's Liberal government – as right wing as any Conservative government we have seen, and on some issues not far away from Reform Party thinking – caters to the business community and provides it with virtually whatever it wants: tax relief, elimination of regulations, grants and low-interest loans, and an open regulatory door to mergers that make shareholders and CEOs wealthier while saddling Canadian consumers with higher prices and fewer jobs. What a deal!

The Liberal government and the Canadian business community could not work more closely together. The head of the Business Council on National Issues, Tom d'Aquino, can be considered a de facto member of cabinet. He may be the most powerful person in Ottawa today, after the prime minister and the minister of finance. And no Canadian voter has ever cast a ballot for him.

Together, the federal government and the business community use the stick instead of the carrot where labour is concerned. They have shrewdly manipulated public opinion so that many Canadians accept, as a matter of course, unemployment rates higher than those in most other developed countries. Keeping unemployment high and workers fearful of losing jobs is their way of "disciplining" the workforce to the inevitability of permanent recession. This is madness, right out of the movie *Dr. Strangelove*. It's like listening to talk about the logic and efficacy of a plan for Mutually Assured Destruction. In this day and age, the fact that we can pretend, rationally, to discuss a course of government economic policy that ensures that more than a million Canadians will be permanently unemployed is insane.

In this environment, where so many working Canadians are assigned to the economic trash barrel, some unions are signing collective agreements with no improvements whatsoever. They sign not for increased wages or improved benefits, but just to keep their members working. This self-disciplining of workers in the permanent recession works beautifully because it also leaves a highly vulnerable public sector confused and demoralized. It makes it easier for governments to implement deregulation and privatization policies and to shift more government responsibility, along with those once-valuable public assets, to the private sector.

We have to put these attacks on unions into historical context. From the time when unions first began to organize successfully in the latter years of the nineteenth century, collective bargaining has been portrayed by business and by many governments as a menace to society. Unions were initially outlawed. It was argued that they constituted a "monopoly" on the "sale" of labour. Therefore, unions could wield unfair economic power and inflict untold damage on private enterprise.

These were not merely the days of "them" versus "us," a time when angry words and demands were hurled back and forth across bargaining tables. This was war, a war declared by business and governments on organized labour, on individual workers, their families, and, indirectly, on all Canadians not wealthy enough to protect themselves. Tens of thousands of workers were arrested, jailed, or beaten. Many died in the fight to be able to organize legally and to bargain with employers. It was a right not enshrined in North America until a wave of enlightened legislation made its way into law in the late 1930s and 1940s – less than sixty years ago.

Even today, particularly in the private sector, the right to bargain collectively is at best tolerated by employers. That right is always vulnerable. Employers work politically through their business associations and lobby groups, business councils, Chambers of Commerce, and right-wing organizations like the Fraser Institute to pressure governments to pass legislation undermining labour unions. They portray unions in the news media as unnecessary, awkward, and costly. They accuse us of not changing with the times.

Preston Manning calls the right to strike – the only strategic weapon a unionized worker has – "an obsolete tool." Right-wing columnists, such as the *Financial Post*'s Diane Francis, have called for the abolition of the Rand Formula – the only fair form of legislated security organized workers have at the moment. Hardly a week goes by without the *Globe and Mail*'s Terence Corcoran blaming unions for practically every economic and social ill mankind suffers – from the effects of El Niño to the collapse of the Asian Pacific economies.

People often ask what keeps me fired up, willing to fight against what seem at times to be insurmountable odds, given the scope of the attack on unions these days. "Well," I tell them, "I get up in the morning. I read the *Globe and Mail,* and if I'm not mad as hell by the time I finish the Report on Business, I read the *Toronto Star* and the *Financial Post* – then I'm mad enough to keep going for the whole day!" No doubt when Conrad Black gets his national newspaper on the streets, I will have enough stimulation from a single day's reading to keep me going for weeks.

Francis and Corcoran, along with the Fraser Institute, applaud the introduction of American-style right-to-work laws in Canada. By stripping away what remains of any pro-labour legislation, these pieces of antiquarian legislation make it virtually impossible to organize effective unions. All you have to do is look to the poorer southern states where right-to-work laws are in place. There you will find low wages, poverty, corporate abuse, and social neglect that makes you think of Charles Dickens. That is what many of these right-wing politicians, columnists, and institutes are prepared to tolerate – workers in eighteenth-century destitution while owners and shareholders prosper.

Like most of the business community, these people claim that the unions "have too much power" through the right to strike, even though the incidence of strikes in Canada has been extremely low for more than a decade. But who really has the power in modern employee-employer relations? Employers hold the purse strings and pay workers as little as possible. They own the workplace. They decide who will be hired and how the work will be performed. They decide what will be produced and where it will be marketed. They look for ways to produce more with fewer employees. Fair enough. Their goal is to make profits. The only power workers have is to organize, bargain collectively, and withdraw their services – a decidedly costly alternative that is never undertaken lightly. In many instances, employers simply get sympathetic governments to force employees back to work. I repeat: Who really has the power?

The media like to speak of Big Business and Big Labour as if each holds equal power. The CAW's strike fund is about $50 million at the moment. The profits at General Motors of Canada in 1997 were thirty-five times that. The total dues gathered by the CAW are about $100 million annually. In 1996 Frank Stronach, the CEO of auto parts manufacturer Magna Inc., was paid just under $40 million in salary and bonuses. The CAW strike fund exists to ensure that 200,000 workers and their families do not starve or lose their homes during a strike. To someone like Stronach, our strike fund is little more than pocket money. So much for Big Labour.

MOST OF LABOUR'S CRITICS seem to think the right to strike is some diabolical invention of modern unions. They seem to believe that out-lawing the right to strike will ensure labour peace – that animosity and conflict between management and labour will suddenly disappear.

What they don't understand is that there has never been a time in human history that was free of strikes. Strikes pre-date modern unionism by more than 8,000 years – ever since man was required to earn a living working for others. The first recorded strikes took place during the building of the Egyptian pyramids. References to strikes have been discovered in civilizations long since vanished – Sumeria and ancient Persia, for two. The history of the Roman Empire is a five-hundred-year history of strikes by tradesmen. Craft guilds in Europe struck employers during the thirteenth and fourteenth centuries. In England in the sixteenth century, priests went on strike. The first strike in Canada took place in 1794 at Rainy Lake – in what would eventually become Ontario – when voyageurs demanded higher wages.

The relationship between workers and bosses is always strained, always headed towards conflict. It is a natural conflict built into the free enterprise system. But if anyone thinks that unions take pride in striking an employer, think again. Unions do not strike on whim or use strikes to show off their power. They look on strikes as costly and disturbing, especially for workers and their families. Strikes are called as a last resort.

Unions probably prevent more strikes than they precipitate. Given our adversarial system, where it is often assumed, incorrectly, that every gain by the worker is a loss for management – it's surprising there are not more strikes. The fact is that unions are an essential vehicle for lessening the frustration many workers feel – three out of every four workers say they don't trust their employers. Good unions work to defuse that anger – and they do it effectively. Without unions, there would be anarchy in the workplace. Strikes would be commonplace, and confrontation and violence would increase. Poor-quality workmanship, low productivity, increased sick time, and absenteeism would be the preferred form of worker protest. By and large, unions deflect those damaging and costly forms of worker resistance. If our critics understood what really goes on behind the labour scenes, they would be thankful that union leaders are as effective as they are in averting strikes. In my view, the wonder of the collective bargaining process in Canada is that we have so few strikes.

Another frequent assertion by corporate spokesmen is that unions make doing business more expensive than it should be. Unions, they say, lower productivity and add huge costs to a company's bottom line, making companies uncompetitive and reducing profits. In our experience, especially in the North American auto industry, unions improve productivity and help make it one of the most profitable manufacturing industries in the world.

CAW auto workers are some of the highest paid and best compensated workers in Canada. Instead of being a drag or a "cost" on General Motors, Ford, and Chrysler, however, our members have been the principal reason why the Big Three have drastically improved productivity and output this decade. Profits for 1997 were the highest on record. In Canada, the Big Three made estimated after-tax profits of $1.25 billion. By the end of the third quarter of 1997, the U.S. parent companies were sitting on a staggering pile of cash – $32.6 billion. GM Canada made so much money in 1997 that, for the first time in twenty-five years, it refused to break out the Canadian profit numbers.

If unions are such a costly proposition for Canadian corporations, why did a study undertaken by the Department of Foreign Affairs and International Trade in 1997 find that Canada is probably the best place in the world to set up a business? The study surveyed costs of doing business in Canada, the United States, and five European countries. Based on comparisons of land, construction, transportation, fuel, services, and manpower, the study concluded that the cost of starting up a business – including unionized wages and benefits – was lowest in Canada. One further finding from the study blows holes in the arguments of the right-wingers: corporate taxes in Canada – the ones politicians like Preston Manning like to claim are too high – were the second lowest of the seven countries. Only Sweden's were lower than Canada's, and then only marginally.

A recent study at the Massachusetts Institute of Technology compared productivity, quality, and profits in the manufacturing industry in the United States at union and non-union plants. It concluded that unionized workplaces were, on average, more productive, produced higher quality products, and made higher profits for their employers than non-union operations in the industry. The right-wing rhetoric simply does not match reality.

Every employer says it cannot afford unions and collective bargaining. That's because employers would rather pay lower wages and dictate terms of employment. They would prefer not to pay for employee benefits. Almost every employer looks to its labour costs first, as the simplest way to improve the bottom line when times are tough, instead of undertaking more complex analyses of the problem. For a private sector employer, such analysis might suggest a need for more innovative products and services, new manufacturing processes, and more investment in research and development. For a public sector employer, it might mean figuring out why revenues have fallen, how to rebuild them, and how to improve efficiency and control non-labour costs. These are all expensive, difficult, and risky tasks. It is always easier just to look at the most visible number on the cost side of the ledger – wages and benefits – and demand concessions.

Good employers know that you do not turn on your employees and demand rollbacks when the business runs into problems. When he ran into financial difficulties in the early 1990s and was facing bankruptcy, Magna's Stronach could have forced a wage cut on his non-union workforce, but he knew how valuable his employees were to him in the competitive auto parts manufacturing business. True, he had to close down some plant operations, and jobs were lost as a result, but he did not ask or force his workers to take pay cuts. There are too few Frank Stronachs and too many Kevin Bensons running businesses in Canada these days.

When the CAW is negotiating with an employer who says he is losing money and needs the union to back off in its demands, we are often asked by reporters: "Why don't you give this guy a break? Why don't you accept wage cuts to help him get back on his feet?"

First, as with Canadian Airlines, labour costs did not cause the company's problems. They never do. Poor management, severe market deviations, or normal business cycles are usually the cause. Second, the wages and working conditions embedded in a collective agreement are the result of years of struggle. If we give them up just because an employer is losing money, we'll have to start all over again when his financial situation improves. Human nature being what it is, that employer will bargain tenaciously to make sure he does not have to give back anything the union lost in the last negotiating round.

And third, experience tells us that if we make a concession to one employer, almost instantly there will be a long line of other employers demanding the same consideration. Unions cannot base gains negotiated over decades on the short-term financial circumstances of one employer. Workers and their families can't adjust their living expenses simply because their employer is not doing well at the moment. The view on both sides must always be long term. Fair wages and reasonable working conditions are too embedded in a long-term struggle to be tossed away every time a company finds itself in a financial bind.

In late 1981, when our union was still part of the UAW, our Detroit office began making noises about reopening our contracts with the Big Three. The industry was being hit by a serious recession and the companies were crying poor. They had not responded to consumer demand for smaller, more fuel-efficient cars, and they were getting killed by Japanese car companies. The Big Three convinced the international office of the UAW to reopen the contracts and give back wages and benefits to keep them afloat.

Bob White, the Canadian UAW director at the time, gave a brilliant speech at the international executive board meeting that year informing the members that it would be a dark day in hell before the Canadians made wage and benefit concessions. The problems the companies had were not caused by unionized wages and benefits, he argued, but by the desperate need for restructuring. Concessions would only postpone the tough strategic decisions that were essential to turn the industry around. Even more important, concessions by workers would get the U.S. and Canadian governments off the hook for allowing massive increases in Japanese imports into the North American market. Bob was blunt in his refusal to consider concessions. "Workers don't need a union to walk them backwards," he said. "They can do that on their own."

The Canadians won that battle against concessions; the Americans did not. It took the UAW the better part of fifteen years before it figured out that you never win back what you've conceded. That decision cost the UAW in wages and benefits and, when the Big Three started unloading UAW members as redundant, it cost them in numbers and in loyalty too. Only recently have UAW members south of the border discovered these essential truths. Only now are they fighting back against the Big Three – witness the GM strike in the summer of 1998.

Because of our hard stand against concessions, the newly formed CAW went on after 1985 to become the strongest union in the country. True, in some cases we had to go on strike to beat concessions – even though our employers, the federal government, and the media all predicted that our resistance would destroy Canada's auto industry. Our stubbornness, it was said, would drive the foundering Chrysler Corporation into bankruptcy. Unable to pick its workers' pockets, Chrysler was forced to redesign its operations and its cars. Once those fundamental problems were addressed, Chrysler was back on its feet. Today the Big Three are booming as never before.

IT USED TO BE RADICAL to say that we live in a class society. Today, thanks to the corporate agenda that has been adopted by our governments, talk of class inequality is commonplace. Less than 10 percent of our population controls more than 80 percent of the nation's property, factories, and farms. The right to be part of a union is, or should be, a citizen's fundamental right in a society where there are such huge distinctions in wealth, status, and power. Nothing in our lives consumes more of our time and our thoughts than our work. Why, then, is the right to work and bargain for our labour not enshrined in the Constitution Act of 1982?

Without the right to organize and bargain collectively, many workers have no voice, no influence over their incomes, no base from which to oppose the power of business. The right to belong to a union, to counterbalance the power of employers, is only a right on paper if it does not include the right to bargain and, collectively, to withdraw our labour. In our experience, that paper right can be brutally, almost whimsically, withdrawn.

Take the example of the CAW's fight with an Ontario company called PC World in September 1997. The Harris government helped trigger this confrontation by ripping up the existing Labour Code and giving companies the right to hire scabs to replace legally striking workers. Because of the double digit unemployment we had been living through, there was no shortage of desperate people willing to be hired on as scabs at PC World.

Scabs give employers a huge advantage during a dispute. They keep plant production going while striking workers cool their heels on the picket line. The first anti-scab legislation was introduced in the late 1970s by Quebec's PQ Lévesque government. British Columbia introduced its version in 1992. Ontario's NDP Rae government passed similar legislation in January 1993, but it was reversed by the Harris government in 1995. To striking workers, scabs are like thieves who enter their houses, take their furniture, and threaten their families. Scabs also make it impossible for a union to negotiate a settlement. Employers have little interest in bargaining while the plant is operating with scabs.

At PC World, a tentative agreement had been reached, but the workers – mostly new Canadians and workers of colour – refused to ratify it. They went on strike, positions hardened, and the dispute dragged on for eight months. With little movement in sight, I challenged our staff and local union leaders to occupy the plant as a way to stop the use of scabs, stop plant production, and get negotiations back on track.

At 5 a.m. on a weekday morning, thirty CAW activists seized the PC World plant, released the security guard and a few scabs without incident, and ensured that production came to a halt. Over the next few days, hundreds of strikers were joined on the picket line by CAW activists from as far away as Windsor. The tension on the line increased. On one occasion, one of the PC World's owners leaped out of a truck and swung a steel bar at our picketers.

By the third evening of the occupation, police began gathering in the industrial park where the plant is located. There were several hundred: SWAT teams, cops with horses, cops with water cannons, cops with billy sticks. An army was massing against us. As I met with our people inside the plant I realized how vulnerable we were to a police attack. Tear-gas canisters would easily shatter the floor-to-ceiling windows and it would be over quickly, except for the clubbing.

I met with the police outside. They were adamant that our people leave the plant. I said there was no way our members were going to allow scabs to take their jobs again. The police were insistent, but what they really wanted was our occupying group out of the PC World plant.

"Are you saying that if we get out of the plant, we can continue to picket around it?" I asked one cop.

"The people occupying the plant are breaking the law," he said. "Our instructions are to clear the plant."

No one was saying that we could not continue to picket and keep scabs from crossing the line. We would still be able to stop production, our primary goal. I went back inside and told our members. Many were disappointed and were willing to stay and risk their well-being. Some saw it as a defeat. "I'm still the president of this union and I'm not going to stand by and let people get their heads cracked open," I said. "If we trigger a bloodbath, I guarantee you not many unions will try to challenge scabs again. This way, if we buy some time, we can get back to bargaining – and the company still won't be able to operate the plant."

Some questioned our strategy, but I thought the risk worth taking. The next day we got a break. The CEO of PC World called and wanted to meet. My only goal was to get his signature on a collective agreement. I was willing to be the most flexible, agreeable, friendly guy in the world as long as violence could be avoided and we got our issues addressed. The risk paid off. He signed.

As I was leaving my office with my assistants and staff to go to the picket line and announce our tentative agreement, I received a call that the police were moving in. I got the sergeant in charge on the phone. He said we had fifteen minutes to clear the area or the police would move on the picketers. We were thirty minutes' drive away.

"Listen, sergeant," I said. "You're going to look some damn stupid tonight on the news if you use force to move our people when you've just been told we have an agreement. The responsibility for what may happen will be totally on your shoulders."

He paused. "You have twenty minutes."

We raced to the plant site. As we turned into the industrial plant where PC World is located, my jaw dropped. The cops were massed on a side street in numbers I had never seen before. They were ready to move in – to crack some heads, do some real damage – and our people wouldn't have stood a chance.

We arrived just in time. I announced that we'd reached an agreement, and the crowd went wild. I thanked those who had fought so hard and commended those who had occupied the plant for their courage and determination. "Your bravery forced this company back to the bargaining table," I told everyone. "And make no mistake, we've sent a strong political message to the Harris government that they can legislate away workers' rights, but workers, especially CAW members, will continue to resist and fight back."

As the strikers congratulated one another, a couple of questions kept recurring in my mind. How could the owner of a small Toronto production plant call upon that amount of police protection? Who would have authorized this astonishing police action – the premier? the mayor? To bring so many police officers to this site, with all their equipment, must have cost a fortune. I knew who would eventually pay for it: the Ontario taxpayers, including those who worked at PC World.

ONE OF THE REASONS the CAW is prepared to be militant is that, even when we have the law on our side, it seldom means anything. During the PC World strike, the Ontario Labour Relations Board investigated our complaints and ruled that PC World was guilty of unfair labour practices. The company had refused to bargain in good faith as required by the Labour Relations Act. But it was a paper victory because the board did not provide any remedy. There is no power on our side of the table to force employers to act in good faith. Unions can't call the police. A judge will not enforce our paper victory through other means. There was no pressure on PC World to comply with the law, so we took the only action left to us. We occupied the PC World plant to stop production in an effort to get our members' jobs back and get negotiations on track.

In the neoconservative Canada of the late 1990s, the labour movement needs to become more militant, less accommodating to the demands of corporations and governments. If this sounds like a return to the days of the 1930s or the 1950s, so be it. It's either that or watch decades of hard-won gains disappear. This resistance will mean arrests, charges, maybe even jail terms for some of our leaders and members. But if we are to check this massive wave of unfairness, we simply have no alternative.

4

A FORK IN THE ROAD

At their best, unions are in the
vanguard of challenging the status quo
and driving social change.
— *Sam Gindin*

When I joined the union staff in 1975, the Canadian UAW was a decade into its long march from militant union to militant social movement. Dennis McDermott had watched what was happening in the 1960s – the hippie movement, the revolt of the youth culture, and the rebellious demands of militants on the shop floor – and recognized that this energy could be a stimulus for real social change. He gave the young and impatient in the union their heads and challenged them – then stood back and watched the sparks fly.

McDermott belonged to a generation of activists inspired by the UAW's Walter Reuther. During the 1950s and 1960s, no name was more identified with social unionism than Reuther's. A whole generation of labour was moved by his oratory, his vision, and his social conscience. He was a true social democrat. He marched with Martin Luther King Jr. and Cesar Chavez. But he was also a friend of presidents – John F. Kennedy and Theodore Roosevelt – as well as Roosevelt's wife, Eleanor. He discussed world affairs with European heads of state and argued with Stalin on the merits of capitalism versus communism.

Reuther was a first-generation American, born in 1907, the son of German immigrants. He was elected president of the UAW in 1946. His determination to see improvements in working conditions resulted in higher workplace standards and in benefit packages that were the envy of the rest of the North American labour movement. Under Reuther's guidance, UAW members doubled their wages in the fifteen years after the Second World War. He made the UAW the largest, wealthiest, and most powerful union on earth. Under his leadership, the UAW became a major force in the demand for a national health care plan and the expansion of public pensions.

Despite Reuther's success in battling the Big Three, his leadership was also a time of organizational tension. Rifts were beginning to grow between the U.S. and Canadian factions, with their different cultures and histories and somewhat differing social and political attitudes. Dennis McDermott worked to inspire our branch of the UAW with the gospel according to Walter Reuther. He intended to put our union at the centre of social change and progressive politics in Canada. He had a strong streak of Canadian nationalism, and came to resent the control the international office in Detroit had over the Canadian section of the UAW. He moved the Canadian headquarters from Windsor to Toronto to establish a physical distance between Detroit and the Canadian UAW operations.

Throughout, McDermott retained Reuther's support. With Reuther's backing, he persuaded the UAW to recognize that Canada was not just another "region" within the UAW, that it deserved special status. The Canadian region director – McDermott's position at the time – would automatically become a vice-president of the UAW.

The roots of the UAW – and, therefore, of the CAW – reach deep into bitter and disaffected soil. When Henry Ford introduced the assembly line to industrial manufacturing in 1913, he also introduced one of the world's most dehumanizing and degrading systems of manufacture. Through the years to 1929, when auto manufacturing on both sides of the border was booming and the auto makers were raking in massive profits, the assembly line in non-union auto plants represented one of the worst exploitations of human beings on the planet. The work was not only tedious but filthy and dangerous as well.

Unions organizing to fight these conditions and bargain for better wages during the 1920s fought an arduous battle. To join a union in those days, or to try to organize one, was to put your life on the line. Auto makers hired thugs, spies, and enforcers to keep union organizers out of the workplace. GM even had a "department" for spies, with as many as 3,000 working the plants and beating up anyone courageous enough to discuss the idea of unionizing.

In Canada, as in the United States, company goons were backed by the police and even the militia. Both governments and employers effectively declared war on workers. If you didn't get your head cracked open, there was always the chance of going to jail – just because you supported the concept of a union. The pressure put on workers by the companies triggered a rash of strikes in 1928–29: at General Motors in Oshawa, Chrysler in Windsor, Willys-Overland in Toronto, and Ford and Studebaker in Windsor. Most strikes lasted only a few hours, but they were a signal that dissatisfaction over wages, work conditions, and layoffs was mounting. By 1933, one-third of the workers in Windsor – most of them dependent on auto manufacturing jobs – were unemployed. Destitute workers began to challenge governments and employers openly with militant action.

The test for unions in the Canadian auto industry came from south of the border in December 1936. The United Automobile Workers of America had been formed in South Bend, Indiana, the previous April. Led by Roy Reuther, Walter's younger brother, the UAW set its organizing sights on General Motors's massive production facilities at Flint, Michigan. GM had refused to recognize the UAW. Rather than try to force a strike, the UAW decided on a tactic that would render GM, its goons, and even the Michigan state police powerless. It organized a sit-down in GM's Flint production plant.

There was no prearranged date for action. The event was triggered when GM tried to transfer manufacturing dies to plants with a weaker union base so it could continue churning out vehicles – and profits – while the workers were left without jobs. (It was roughly the same tactic that GM tried on the CAW in 1996, a move that led to our occupation of the Oshawa fabrication plant. That twenty-one-day strike cost the company $1.4 billion in lost auto and truck production. And in June 1998 GM again removed stamping dies from the Flint plant, sparking one of the largest and costliest strikes in North American history.)

In late December 1936, the UAW workers took over Fisher Plants One and Two at the Flint complex. Two weeks after the occupation began, the police launched an attack on the workers. The sit-in, led by Walter's older brother, Victor, rallied the workers. They stopped the police with a barrage of auto parts and water from fire hoses, an effective weapon in mid-winter. The National Guard was called in, this time to keep the peace and prevent further attacks by the police or GM's goon squads. On February 11, 1937, GM relented and recognized the UAW. The company agreed to enter into discussions on a collective agreement. Flint was the effective birthplace of the UAW.

The breakthrough in Canada also came at a General Motors plant. The first Canadian UAW local – Local 195 – was organized at Kelsey Wheel in Windsor in 1936. But on Monday, February 15, 1937, the same day the Flint workers returned to work, sheet metal workers in Oshawa put down their tools as GM Canada demanded an increase in assembly line speed from twenty-seven to thirty-two cars an hour. The speedup order prompted another in a series of grievances filed by the Oshawa workers. Other issues included demands for higher wages, shorter hours, overtime pay, seniority, and recognition of the UAW. The workers also objected to harassment and abuse from supervisors and bosses, unsafe conditions, and the insecurity of working for a company always demanding concessions. By April 8, 1937, no agreement had been reached. The Oshawa strike was on.

A settlement came two weeks later. Although it included some wage gains, Canadian wages would remain 10 to 15 percent below those paid at GM's U.S. plants until wage parity was achieved thirty years later at Chrysler Canada. Seniority would now determine layoffs and rehiring, and a grievance procedure was put in place. The work week was shortened to forty-four hours, with provision for overtime. But the union settled in Oshawa without achieving its original goal: recognition of the UAW.

When war broke out in 1939, members of the Canadian industrial union movement were loath to give their government a no-strike pledge, as their American counterparts would do two years later. The war raised two pertinent and perpetually nagging questions. First, why were workers subject to government-imposed wage and price controls while corporations were enjoying record profits from wartime production of planes, ships, tanks, armaments, and munitions? And second, if governments could plan so effectively for the production and full employment needed to win a war, why could they not perform the same function during times of peace? Many of us are still asking those questions.

The wartime peace between labour and management was broken on September 12, 1945, with one of the most dramatic events in Canadian labour history – the strike at Ford in Windsor. The Ford workers were quickly joined by UAW Local 195, which included GM and Chrysler workers. Many stayed off the job for a month, at a time when the union provided no strike pay. The Ford workers frustrated the Royal Canadian Mounted Police and company goons by surrounding the plant with a massive car blockade of as many as 1,500 vehicles. The workers were supported by the Windsor community, including small business, church groups, even the mayor – who promised to pay welfare benefits to any worker's family in need.

The strike was significant for the entire Canadian union movement, not just the UAW. It was settled with the appointment of Justice Ivan Rand as arbitrator. Rand's decision – which we still rely heavily upon today – endorsed the issue of full union checkoff for dues, even for employees who chose not to join the union. His reasoning was simple but enlightened: since all employees benefited from the gains realized from union representation, it was only reasonable that all should pay their fair share of dues.

The Canadian section of the UAW entered the war lagging behind its American counterpart in numbers, strength, supportive legislation, and social programs; it emerged as the largest union in Canada. It was born on the shop floor, in the daily conflicts between workers and management, but it was also instilled with a robust sense of social unionism, thanks in large part to the influence of Reuther and his family and their effect on people like Dennis McDermott.

Reuther and his wife, May, were killed in the crash of a UAW-chartered Lear jet in northern Michigan. It was May 9, 1970. I was at the local union hall getting ready for my first UAW Canadian Council meeting in Windsor when word came. People were devastated by the news. They stood there, stunned, and cried. People wondered if Walter's passing meant that the UAW was in trouble, but the UAW was a strong union, and over the years Reuther's vision had worked its way into the core. Even though the CAW separated from the UAW in 1985, we still remember our roots with the UAW and pay tribute to the Reuther family. The main assembly hall at our Family Education Centre in Port Elgin, Ontario, is named the Reuther Family Building. Victor and Sophie Reuther attended our founding convention and every subsequent convention until Sophie's death in 1996, and in 1997 we invited Victor to speak to our constitutional convention in Vancouver.

THE 1960S WERE a marvellously energizing decade. The Canadian section of the UAW went into the period hurt, bleeding, and distracted by in-fighting and fierce confrontations with the Big Three, and came out the other end tough, well heeled, and ready to play a role in Canadian society. It was also a decade that propelled us towards independence from the international UAW.

It was a time of generational revolt and widespread unrest. In 1966 Canadian companies lost more time to strikes than in any year since 1946. Most of the stoppages were wildcat strikes. Young union members were more impatient and less likely to put up with employer obstruction than their predecessors had been. An internal UAW poll revealed that, angry as these young people were at working conditions, they were just as angry at their union leaders. They held their own leaders as responsible as management for the lousy working conditions they faced.

That was the era in which I started working at Chrysler in Windsor. I was as young and unruly as anyone. In the 1960s atmosphere of revolt, we were prepared to take on anybody over anything. Walter Reuther admitted that the 1960s introduced a new breed of worker in the auto plants, one "less willing to accept corporate decisions that preempt his own decisions." Thinking back on our dissatisfaction in the workplace, I think of the scene from Marlon Brando's film *The Wild Ones* in which the girl asks the Brando character what he's rebelling against. Brando smirks, cocks his eye under his motorcycle cap, and says: "Whaddya got?"

For Canadian UAW members, the Auto Pact with the United States, signed in 1965, was one of the most important trade initiatives ever undertaken. Coupled with rapid economic growth, the Auto Pact sparked the construction of ninety new plants on this side of the border and provided thousands of jobs. Suddenly jobs were easy to get. If you did not like your work at one plant, by the end of the day you could be working in another. Those who stayed were not about to put up with sass from management – or from the union, for that matter. When Chrysler tried to impose compulsory overtime, Local 444 reacted immediately. After a number of suspensions, discharges, and wildcat strikes, overtime became voluntary after eight hours each day and forty-eight hours each week.

At de Havilland Aircraft, Local 112 followed suit and forced the employer to put a limit on overtime when other workers were being laid off. Even wives and girlfriends got into the act. In St. Thomas, women picketed Ford operations to challenge the loss of their partners on Saturdays. The workers then turned around and threatened management with job action if they did not let them off early to cheer fellow workers in a local hockey tournament.

Those in-your-face days became a spawning ground for the future leadership of the UAW. The members honed their militancy on the shop floor with demands for better working conditions. In 1971 aerospace workers of the UAW struck the aircraft manufacturer McDonnell-Douglas for two months. Wage controls had been implemented in the United States, and a settlement appeared to have been reached within the guidelines. But Canadian members refused to accept an American-imposed solution and continued the strike. They no longer looked at the U.S. experience in bargaining as a model and wanted to set their own terms and conditions. The UAW's international office ordered the Canadians to vote on the offer anyway. It turned out to be another nudge towards independence.

Without question, the 1960s permanently changed our union. Part of it was the successes we achieved on the shop floor and at the negotiating table, but mostly it was the times: the protests against the Vietnam War; the spillover of civil rights issues from the United States; the demands for equality and a proper social welfare system for Canadians; the expansion of collective bargaining rights to a large part of the public sector; the advent of feminism and its impact on women in the labour movement; and, in Canada, the birth of the independence movement in Quebec. This exciting period of change was captured in Pierre Trudeau's challenge to create a just society. It was our responsibility, individually and collectively, to make it happen. Trudeau's summons to social action helped stimulate the Canadian labour movement in general, and the UAW in particular, to become more involved with the political system.

UAW members began moving aggressively into a new role as political activists within the New Democratic Party, filling the political vacuum on the left side of the party created by the expulsion of the strongly nationalist Waffle group. Dennis McDermott had always been active in party politics and had been an early member of the CCF. Now he wanted the UAW to become more involved with the NDP. He believed there was a natural alliance between trade unionism and democratic socialism. But by insisting that the UAW draw closer to the NDP, he touched a nerve. Not all union members are comfortable voting for the NDP, or being involved in politics. Some thought Dennis was trying to tell them how to vote. Others felt the NDP was too far to the left for their thinking; still others thought the NDP was not far enough left.

Even today, one of the CAW's toughest challenges is getting large numbers of our members to vote NDP. This is particularly true in the aftermath of Bob Rae's disastrous NDP government in Ontario. A surprising number of union members vote Reform. One Reform Party poll puts union member support for the party, outside Quebec, at more than 40 percent. It's a sad fact of labour life, sad because, if there is anything Preston Manning would like to do, it's break the unions and take away our hard-fought gains. Given how blatantly anti-union the Reform Party is, voting for it is like playing Russian roulette. Still, McDermott recognized the natural alliance between trade unionism and democratic socialism. He hoped, as many of us do now, that if members witnessed the NDP supporting working people and the underprivileged, they would naturally be drawn to support the party.

THE ECONOMIC ACTIVITY of the 1950s and early 1960s lulled people into thinking that capitalism could provide a constantly rising standard of living. Even with short periods of recession in the late 1960s, and rising inflation in the early 1970s, there seemed to be a universal sense that, finally, we might have got our economics right. All that changed for good with the OPEC oil price increases beginning in the fall of 1973.

The quadrupling of the price of oil brought rising consumer prices, employee demands for higher wages, shareholder demands for higher returns on investments, and a new phenomenon called "stagflation." Job losses escalated until unemployment figures began matching the high rate of inflation. Out of this turmoil eventually came the government's notion that by reducing inflation to zero, it could make all other economic problems go away. The first response by an uncertain Trudeau government was the wage and price controls of 1975. This remedy was based on the assumption that workers might have to put up with some short-term unemployment to ensure long-term economic stability for the nation. Instead, it simply introduced chronic, systemic unemployment into our lives.

In the 1970s there were twice as many strikes in Canada as in the United States. In that decade, Canada lost more work days to strikes than any other developed country. One-third of those strikes were wildcat strikes. Again, the UAW led the way. General Motors Canada faced fifty-nine wildcat strikes in the ten years after the famous 1970 Long Strike at GM operations. In the 1970s de Havilland workers struck for a total of 468 days to get three barely satisfactory agreements. On October 14, 1976, the Canadian Labour Congress organized the Day of Protest over the Liberal government's wage and price controls.

If the Trudeau government's wage controls did anything for labour, they crystallized our resolve to fight back and helped focus our energies on the enemy – a federal government backed by big business and the policies of the Bank of Canada. While the Liberals saddled workers with the burden of trying to fix the shaky economy, it left the banks free to earn what they could. The Liberals did not slap a lid on the profit expectations of employers. There was no inclination to introduce even a modest progressive tax reform to help offset wage controls. No effort was made to improve social programs to soften the blow of layoffs on workers and their families.

Many unions took the easy way out, telling their members there was little they could do. They might not like what the Trudeau government was doing, but what power did they have? Our union did not see things that way. Selling the government's wage controls policy as too tough to fight only ate away at the confidence of a union's members.

Oddly enough, the UAW's refusal to recognize wage controls in collective bargaining did many companies a favour. It forced them to be more creative, to work doubly hard to find the money our union demanded. They usually found it through better management practices, which told us something about how economically hard-pressed many of them really were. It was an important lesson we carried to the table when we took on Chrysler over concession demands in late 1979 and early 1980. Although the labour movement was not successful in defeating wage controls, the Trudeau government was forced to end controls a year earlier than planned. Again, the experience helped underline what we in the UAW already knew – concessions made by employees are always an irretrievable step backwards. What employees concede, they lose forever. Trudeau told us that if workers made this three-year sacrifice in wages, we would all enjoy lower inflation, decreased prices, higher wages, and more jobs. We're still waiting.

In the three years after this Liberal experiment, inflation was higher than in any preceding period in this century. Unemployment had risen by 1974 to 6.4 percent, which was called then, even by the Liberals, an "extremely high" number. Of course, we have not been lucky enough to see 6.4 percent unemployment since. The unemployment rate has never come within even 1 percent of that figure since the Liberal government tried to fix our economy with wage controls. Wages did go down, of course, and, quite predictably, profits soared, moving up even faster than the double-digit annual inflation of the 1980s.

The wage control fight should have been another wakeup call for labour. Within a year of its phaseout, employers across Canada began demanding wage concessions from workers. Those demands were incessant, and by the end of the 1970s the labour movement was back on the ropes. The reeling economy was supposedly the fault of unions, with their members' fat salaries and comfortable benefits. In the United States, unions had been battered by a succession of increasingly reactionary federal governments – the administrations of Richard Nixon and Gerald Ford. By the early 1980s even the UAW – the big boy of American labour – was agreeing to wage concessions. American labour had become a paper tiger.

In Canada, the legislative influence of the federal NDP, led by David Lewis, and the election of NDP governments in Manitoba, British Columbia, and Saskatchewan, provided political support for more equitable labour legislation and social reforms. At the same time, though, unions like the Canadian section of the UAW were fighting tough battles with employers. International Harvester and Rockwell International were struck by the UAW, and a renewed militancy began to boil throughout Canada.

Canadians were told constantly that the recession, coupled with "high worker wages," was destroying business. But by then, the Canadian section of the UAW had learned that giving in to demands for concessions was a form of death by a hundred nicks – a lesson learned in spades at Chrysler between 1979 and 1982. By 1979 the Chrysler Corporation was in serious financial difficulty. The company estimated it needed $8 billion to redesign and retool for lighter, smaller cars, having refused for years to produce smaller, more energy-efficient cars as oil prices rose and the market swung away from gas guzzlers. Customers were walking away from Chrysler in droves. Chrysler's chairman, Lee Iacocca, was pleading poverty. He claimed the company would be dead by the spring of 1980 if major employee concessions were not made and government loans not forthcoming.

The UAW international leaders, led by Doug Fraser in Detroit, agreed to delay the March 1980 implementation of a recently signed contract. It was the first time in the history of the UAW and the Big Three that a negotiated and ratified pay increase had been deferred. It cost Chrysler workers US$203 million and it applied to Canadian as well as American UAW members. Our members were furious. They felt that the UAW had sold them out, and an angry strike followed.

The Canadian section of the UAW was then headed by Bob White, with Bob Nickerson and me as his assistants. Bob was a master bargainer, with a keen sense of what the local leaders and members would take.

He loved to bargain at the local level with the members' committee. Our people were openly hostile about the wage deferral deal, but we did not have the independence to say "No way!" Our members could at least vote on that international agreement, which was narrowly ratified in Canada.

The Chrysler experience again says a lot about who runs unions. Our system places power in the hands of the members. They tell us what they want out of the bargaining process. They tell us their priorities. After we negotiate, we must go back to the council – representatives of the locals – and explain the details of the negotiated settlement. As well, we're required to attend all-member meetings and explain ourselves. The members then vote to accept, or reject, the proposed agreement. And if they're unhappy about what we've negotiated for them, they can throw the contract back in our faces. If they're really angry, chances are we'll be out on our behinds at the next election.

CHRYSLER CONTINUED TO CLAIM it was headed for bankruptcy unless the U.S. Congress bailed it out to the tune of about $2 billion. Congress passed a law that made any federal bailout conditional on employee wage concessions. Those concessions would eventually total US$662 million. For Canadian members of the UAW – who were opposed to concessions in principle and insulted to be forced to give up hard-fought wages to a foreign legislature – this was the beginning of the end of our international UAW.

Once again, it was the workers who were forced to make major concessions. No one put pressure on the banks – the sources of capital – to help Chrysler out of its hole. There are only two basic inputs to operating a business: capital and labour. If both are required, why is it that labour always has to be flexible – giving in to demands, reducing jobs – in the interests of economic survival? Why are the sources of capital rarely, if ever, requested – or forced – to show the same flexibility?

When Iacocca returned the second time for concessions, in January 1981, the argument was made that it was not the company asking for concessions but rather the Loan Guarantee Board, set up by Congress. The Canadian bargaining team rejected the demand that we reopen our contract for further concessions. The Canadian government had granted loan guarantees to Chrysler without demanding employee wage concessions. Who were the Americans to tell us we had to open the contract now? Needless to say, the U.S. leaders of the UAW were angry over our stand. Later that year the company was back for still more concessions. This time Iacocca said that unless we gave up a $1.15-an-hour cost-of-living allowance clause, future wage increases, and some paid time off, the Loan Guarantee Board would not approve any more money for Chrysler. The solidarity between American and Canadian members was growing thin.

We had known that the concession-demand ball would not stop rolling if we caved in to Congress's order to help bail out Chrysler a second time. Other companies would be at the UAW's door immediately, demanding similar concessions. And they were. Behind the Big Three were all the auto parts manufacturers, demanding the same preferential concession treatment Chrysler had received.

Concessions were a disastrous spiral. Companies began "whipsawing" unions: arguing and winning concessions, then demanding similar concessions from other unions. They would then go back to the first unit and argue for additional concessions because the other unions had given up even more. Angry workers looked at their shrinking wage packets and asked what the hell they needed a union for. The concessions diverted attention from the fundamental causes of the industry's problems – high interest rate policies, the banks' inflexibility, and, in Chrysler's case, the failure to design and build the kind of vehicles consumers wanted.

Precedent was involved here as well. In the first round of Chrysler's financial problems, the Canadian government had approved a $200 million support package for the company without demanding employee wage concessions. The federal government knew that if it had demanded concessions, it would have had to pay a huge political price to an angry labour movement. Similarly, all it would have taken in the United States was an unyielding stance on the UAW's part. Instead, it melted. Rather than fight, Doug Fraser put his best efforts into selling Chrysler workers on the idea that there were no alternatives.

I recall being in Washington with Fraser and the bargaining team at Chrysler. I kept thinking that what I was seeing was not really happening.

Doug had been a friend, especially to those of us at Chrysler, where he had been director of the UAW's Chrysler department. I believed he had a plan to avoid cutting workers' wages and I kept expecting it would eventually unfold. To my way of thinking, he'd never be part of a scheme to take money out of the pockets of the workers.

Well, I was wrong. He was torn between his responsibilities to his members and his belief that Chrysler was really going under. I watched him work the bargaining team, including the three Canadian representatives. He convinced everyone there was no alternative but to agree to Iacocca's concessions. I watched him work the media, using their reporting of events to condition the members to support wage cuts. I listened as he instructed Chrysler's vice-president of labour relations on when to leak a story about a major parts supplier that would refuse to deliver parts to Chrysler plants because the supplier was not being paid. It was designed to drive home to our members just how bad Chrysler's financial situation was. Whether it was true was another matter, but it had the desired chilling effect on union members.

I watched in amazement as Doug deliberately went without shaving to make himself look as though he was working night and day to get his members an agreement they could live with. As he prepared for a meeting or an interview, he'd ruffle his hair and draw his face into a weary, worried look that would have put some of Hollywood's best actors to shame. I phoned Ken Gerard to brief him on the discussions. Having watched Doug's performance on television, Ken said, "Poor Doug, he looks like they're putting him through hell. It must be tough."

I watched as we headed into the final hours of negotiations. A farewell dinner for friends of President Jimmy Carter was being held at the White House, and Doug had been invited. I was in his suite as he put on his tuxedo to attend the White House dinner. As he dressed, he talked about strategy – not strategy at the bargaining table, but strategy to get in and out of the dinner unseen by the television reporters with their cameras. Here we were, at the eleventh hour of one of the most significant labour–management events in the United States in many years, and Doug's people were on the phone talking about how to stage his entrance and exit at the White House.

THE CANADIAN SECTION OF THE UAW was not about to follow our U.S. leaders. We had, as an international union, reached a fork in the road. The Americans seemed resigned to the route they had taken. It seemed the prudent thing to do. But our Canadian leaders chose a different, more contentious path – so contentious, in fact, that it would, within three years, lead us right out of the UAW.

The key moment came in early 1982 when the Canadian UAW, led by Bob White, broke ranks with the Americans and rejected any early opening of agreements with General Motors and Ford. We had learned our lesson, and had taken a series of strikes over the years – nine and a half months at Kenworth, a heavy-duty truck manufacturer in Quebec; eight months at North American Plastics in Wallaceburg, Ontario; and eight months at Rockwell's auto component plants in Milton and Chatham, Ontario – on the issue of concessions.

Not all our strikes in that period were about concession demands. Some were over a fundamental issue we thought we had left years behind – simple recognition of the union as the bargaining agent for employees. The infamous Fleck strike was an example of the regression we faced as employers and governments began turning the screws on organized labour. Located in London, Ontario, Fleck Manufacturing made electrical wire harnesses for automobiles and trucks. Our union local was mostly made up of poorly paid young women. In 1977 the workers voted 80 percent in favour of joining the UAW. In early 1978 Fleck refused to recognize the union, setting off a strike. Even though the workers had every legal right to strike, Fleck called in the cops. It was another lesson in power.

The Ontario Provincial Police immediately came to the rescue of Fleck. They hectored, threatened, and lectured the women on what the Criminal Code said about mass gatherings – but did not talk to them about their right to picket. Five hundred OPP showed up to police eighty striking employees. The bill for the OPP duties on behalf of Fleck was the largest ever run up by the OPP in any large-scale police operation – all to bully a bunch of legally picketing women.

Another tactic employers were beginning to use more frequently was the threat of plant closures as a means of achieving wage rollbacks.

We took strikes and occupied plants at Houdaille in Oshawa, Beach Appliances in Ottawa, and Bendix and Windsor Bumper, both in Windsor, in response to this escalating threat of plant closures. South of the border, the UAW was doing the opposite. It was agreeing to wage concessions in return for something called "profit sharing," a euphemism for making less money this contract than you had in past contracts. All the American UAW workers got for their concessions were lower wage packages, fewer benefits, and increased belligerence from the employers who, now that they had the union on the ropes, proceeded to punch the hell out of them.

Bob White kept pointing out to our American counterparts that if you agreed to concessions, you did not just lose in the pocketbook. You immediately triggered dissension and conflict within the union. A dispirited and divided union could not expect to win big gains at any bargaining table. Just as important to the Canadian section of the UAW, a union without the strength to bargain successfully for its members would be in no position to act as a mechanism for social change.

The real test of the two differing philosophies came in 1982 at General Motors. We had rejected early opening of the contracts. The American UAW had not. GM went on a foul rampage. GM Canada president Don Hackworth threatened to pull all GM operations out of Canada if we did not accept the U.S. pattern agreement. GM made sure whole communities would feel unsettled. The message was clear: the local economy would collapse, throwing thousands out of work. This was tough stuff. (Hackworth would again be a key player for GM in the 1998 strike at two plants in Flint, Michigan.)

In the end, we settled with gains – modest gains, to be sure, but gains nevertheless. We rejected profit-sharing. We got company movement on wages, pensions, and benefits. We managed to keep the number of paid personal vacation days as negotiated in the old agreement. And we settled without a strike, which, given the charged atmosphere of the times, was an accomplishment.

We Canadians had a final chance to prove our point in November 1982 when we struck Chrysler Canada, demanding the reinstatement of the $1.15-an-hour cost-of-living allowance clause we had given up in

1981. Our members were not about to accept anything less, even though we appeared to be losing the public relations battle. It seemed that every editorial writer in the country was sounding alarm bells about how the Canadian UAW would ruin the country's economy by demanding, of all things, that Chrysler give us back our money. Doug Fraser even prophesied that a gain of 25 cents an hour by our Canadian union would bankrupt Chrysler, throwing hundreds of thousands of North American auto workers into the streets.

It took five weeks on the picket line, but Canadian UAW workers got the $1.15 back, plus future cost-of-living benefits. Did Chrysler go broke as a result? By the second quarter of 1983, with this "dangerous" contract in place, Chrysler was reporting its highest profits in sixty years.

Things were unravelling quickly in the international brotherhood. By the start of bargaining with the Big Three in 1984, we seemed headed for a breakup. The UAW in Detroit agreed to settle with GM for no real wage increase, accepting lump sums instead of wage increases. Doug Fraser had retired and been replaced by Owen Bieber. Bieber and his bargaining committee agreed to not only the lump sum but to continue the profit-sharing plan of 1982. However, this latest concession contract was ratified by only 57 percent of the American section's members. There was a lot of unhappiness among rank-and-file UAW members at GM. Worse yet, its concession-riddled contract had been negotiated while GM was reporting record profits.

THE 1980S MAY WELL GO DOWN in labour history as the Decade of Gimmick Bargaining. Consultants churned out hundreds of cute new ideas to benefit employers by extracting more and more compromises from workers. One of the gimmicks was the offer of one-time, lump-sum cash payments instead of wage increases. This was a way for the employer to avoid higher labour costs in the long term. Regardless of how large the sum was – and they were never large enough to compete with a standard annual wage increase – after three years, workers were toiling for the same money they had had four years previously. But with the times as tight and fearful as they were, lump-sum payments began to catch on.

Then came "two-tiered" wage structures. Unions began bargaining for their current members at the expense of future members. Two-tiered wages kept the senior workers' wages at current levels, but penalized new employees by offering them lower entry-level wages. Of course, this was a huge cost saving for corporations, but at the expense of newer union members and worker solidarity.

Two other gimmicks were "profit sharing" and "employee ownership," schemes that offered stock in place of wage increases. Why would workers, who already had so much of their lives invested in these companies, give up wages they needed to survive in order to help an employer's bottom line? Consultants argued that it made the workers more committed to the success of the company. Workers are already heavily committed to the company's survival because it involves their survival, too. Workers feed, clothe, shelter, and educate their families based on the income from their jobs. They pay for their cars and trucks, go to the occasional movie or dinner, enjoy a summer vacation, and plan for their future financial security based almost solely on those jobs. How could they become more committed to their jobs?

Auto workers in the United States have not generally been opposed to profit-sharing, but the scheme has not made them any more efficient. In head-to-head comparison of plant operations in the United States and Canada, the Canadian auto plants are, on average, more productive. They put out a higher-quality product at lower cost, and make more profit, per capita, for the Big Three than the American plants do with their profit-sharing incentives.

In 1984 Owen Bieber and the UAW executive were nervous over the backlash they were facing from their members, largely over gimmicks and concessions. No matter what happened in Canada, it was inevitable that they would feel even more heat. If an agreement could not be reached here and we struck GM Canada, as many as 50,000 UAW members in the United States would be laid off. If we achieved another contract that saw our wages and benefits package improve in comparison with the American's, there would be an ugly outcry from American UAW members who had been forced, contract after contract, to make concessions to the Big Three.

Our master bargaining committee with General Motors was made up of Bob White, Bob Nickerson, Sam Gindin (our chief economist), Phil Bennett (chairman of the master bargaining committee), and me, plus twenty-five local union leaders. Although all we really wanted was to negotiate a contract our Canadian members would be prepared to ratify, we knew there were two bigger questions to be settled: Did we have the right, as a section of an international union, to negotiate a contract – even conduct a strike action – that was solely in the interests of Canadian UAW members? And could we continue to operate as a section of an international union if all the major decisions had to be made in Detroit?

With Bieber's concessions in its pocket, GM was coming to the Canadian table determined to get the same deal in Canada. If the company was adamant, we were headed for a strike. But Bieber and the UAW executive had control of the union strike funds. If they did not like what they saw happening in Canada, our members could be hitting the street without strike pay. That would play right back into GM's hands because it would make it easier for the company to wait us out.

Bob White made it clear to GM that there would be no American deal in Canada. In fact, GM's director of industrial relations, Rod Andrew, claimed he was willing to bargain a made-in-Canada agreement, so long as we eventually arrived at something close to what GM had achieved in the United States. Andrew claimed that the industry was getting extremely competitive and that workers, as he put it, "had to accept competitive conditions."

General Motors Canada workers already enjoyed a $7-to-$8-an-hour labour cost saving over GM in the United States. There was room to negotiate. But when Andrew tabled GM's first offer, it was essentially the same as the American agreement – worse in some cases. It was easy for GM to toss that threat on the table and maintain that a U.S. deal was the only one the company would agree to. GM was sitting on some of the largest piles of cash it had ever accumulated. It could afford to play hardball.

But our members also knew about that pile of cash and the fact that GM had just reported record profits. We were not talking about trying to run GM into bankruptcy. We were talking about a company that had just made its shareholders wealthier, thanks, in large part, to the contributions made by the workers. This same company was now demanding that our members agree to lump-sum payments instead of wage increases, while its shareholders made out like bandits.

A strike deadline had been set for October 17, 1984. A few days into negotiations, it was clear that a strike was inevitable. Our members wanted nothing to do with gimmicks. The bargaining committee was obviously willing to take a strike rather than back off. At the same time, we were getting more signals that Detroit might not authorize strike pay for the Canadians.

With twenty-four hours to go before the strike, GM made a second proposal that looked almost exactly like the first one. It still called for lump-sum payments, no wage increases, and take-aways in some benefit areas. As one of our bargaining committee put it, that offer was "a bag of s——t." GM clearly did not want to settle. We turned the offer down.

Bieber was in a frenzy over the possibility that the Canadians would strike over issues he had already agreed on in the United States. He threatened Bob that he was prepared to revoke the authorization for a strike – in effect, let the Canadian members twist in the wind without strike pay. When Bieber heard we had rejected GM's second offer, he was furious. He claimed we were trying to destroy the UAW by refusing to accept terms that had been acceptable to American members. Bob put it to him bluntly: "We have one union, but we have two countries. We're going in two different directions. If that means we take a strike at GM, we take a strike."

On October 16, barely sixteen hours before the strike deadline, an angry wildcat strike broke out at the Oshawa plant. Three thousand night-shift workers jumped the gun and went out. Word circulated that workers in Ste-Thérèse were ready to go as well. As energizing as a wildcat strike might be for workers, it is the kiss of death at the negotiating table. It might look great on supper-hour TV – all those placards and raised fists – but it takes away any leverage the bargaining committee has. The employer has nothing more to lose by standing by its last offer. Worse still, Bieber could use the illegal wildcat strike action as his excuse to deny strike pay. Phil Bennett was able to get on the phone and cool things with our members in Oshawa, but the damage had been done.

White was meeting privately during the strike with Rod Andrew, but GM refused to alter its position even though, six days into the strike, GM losses were estimated at $200 million a week. By this time, 36,000 workers were on strike in Canada, and another 40,000 were laid off in the United States. We were having a hard time figuring out why GM was being so hard-headed. Bob was of the mind – and I shared his suspicion – that GM was getting a message from Bieber that it did not have to yield on wages; that if it sweetened the lump-sum payments, the Canadians would jump at the offer. The word came back from Detroit and confirmed our fears. It was disappointing news for all of us because it marked the end of our union as an international brotherhood.

The bargaining committee also realized it would be impossible to continue to fight on two fronts. We had to make peace with one of our adversaries – GM or our own union executive – or we would surely lose. We were also responsible for the well-being of 36,000 workers out on strike and their families. We had to find a middle ground somewhere. By the time Bob met with the company one more time, they had ironed out a draft agreement that would get us an increase of 25 cents an hour in year one, 25 cents more in year two, and another 24 cents in year three. We had defeated the lump-sum payment idea. Instead, we got wage increases in every year of the contract – not as much as we would have liked, but increases.

In addition, the agreement gave Canadian members some innovative new benefits, including child care, an affirmative action program for female workers, and a pre-paid legal service program that was the talk of the Canadian labour movement. In an unprecedented clause, GM workers, retirees, and their families now had free access to lawyers for wills, real estate transactions, and traffic court defences. In the end, our made-in-Canada agreement, with a few last-minute sweeteners, was ratified by 87 percent of production workers and 83 percent of skilled workers. The assembly lines began to move again on October 29, 1984.

But the disassembly line of our international union had been set in motion. In early December we went to the staff and later to the UAW's Canadian Council to get support for a change in the way we worked with our American leaders. We were determined never again to have to fight them over our right to develop our own collective bargaining program, or to pursue it without interference. We felt, at the time, that we could achieve these goals through the UAW.

Bob and I, together with Bob Nickerson and Wendy Cuthbertson, our communications director, headed to Detroit knowing we had support for a demand for the Canadian section to be free to bargain on purely Canadian goals and criteria – and to strike if necessary. The UAW international summarily rejected our proposal for autonomy. At a Canadian Council meeting on December 11, 1984, the members in attendance voted 350 to 4 to establish a new Canadian union. A ratification vote of the Canadian local unions resulted in only one local – the 1,500 members of Local 251 in Wallaceburg, Ontario – voting, by a narrow margin, to stay with the UAW.

After some tough and acrimonious negotiations, Detroit agreed to transfer $36 million to our new union. We considered this much less than our fair share of union assets. Our tallying revealed that the Canadian section was entitled to something more like $60 million. But the $36 million did fine, and we were free.

At our founding convention in Toronto in September 1985, we designed a constitution for our new Canadian union. The convention established the United Auto Workers Union of Canada, with some 123,000 members. In the summer of 1986 that name would be officially changed to the Canadian Auto Workers union. We were no longer a house divided, and we were free to run our union as we saw fit.

5

TRIAL BY FIRE

The rich get richer, the poor get poorer,
and the middle class gets confused.
— Dave Barrett

The years just before and after the split in the Canadian UAW were among the most exciting in the union's history. The decade following the split brought two recessions, the widespread introduction of a startling array of new technologies, and a rash of corporate restructuring. All this resulted in workplace closures and the loss of tens of thousands of jobs. Between 1985 and 1995, the CAW suffered through 250 workplace closures, which affected 28,000 of our workers.

Rather than lose ground, however, the CAW embarked on an aggressive campaign to organize members and merge with other unions. Bringing new members into the union was hard work for our staff and local leaders. The hours were long, the travel exhausting, and many of our staff paid a steep price in terms of family life and personal relationships. Most of the time you're living out of a suitcase in a strange city or town. You don't have ready access to workers in the plant, so you chase them down at home, usually late at night, and make your pitch while babies are crying and spouses are eyeing you warily across the kitchen table. Many workers are hesitant to join unions, wary of challenging the bosses' power. It usually takes a long time – sometimes months – to convince workers to sign on.

Despite the tough economic times, the CAW's membership in the decade after the split increased through organizing and mergers by about two-thirds to almost 200,000 members. (In contrast, membership in the UAW over the same period fell by one-third. In 1995 the UAW had only half the members it had had in 1979, the year before concession bargaining began.) Given the economic battering workers were taking in the late 1980s and early 1990s, other unions liked our stance against concessions and our willingness to fight the corporate agenda. Almost 80,000 members joined us through mergers, changing the union dramatically.

Once we were a male-dominated union in an industry preoccupied with auto manufacturing. The majority of our members made auto parts, cars, and trucks. Today, our 215,000 members represent fourteen different industry sectors ranging from vehicle production to auto parts, from airlines to aerospace, from ship building to electronics, from manufacturing to railways, and from fisheries to mining and general services. We added 40,000 women, as well as many new immigrants and people of colour. For every member ten years earlier, when the Canadian union was formed, there were now two members who had not lived through the split from the UAW. The number of members outside the automobile industry tripled. Members who worked in auto plants used to outnumber other members three to one; now they were a minority. Previously, fewer than 10 percent of the union's members were outside Ontario; now, more than one-third came from outside that province. When the union celebrated its tenth anniversary, it was remarkably different from the one that had nervously left the UAW in 1985.

Not that everyone agreed with the direction we were taking. There was heated internal debate about whether we should be pursuing this multisectored path. Some of our leaders argued that we should go slow, that as an industrial union our strength had always been in the auto manufacturing sector, and that admitting smaller and more diverse sectoral units – which often cost us more to serve than they paid in union dues – would weaken the CAW. To me, diversifying our membership by moving into the service sector was a way of keeping in step with changes in the economy. I felt we had no choice.

To my way of thinking, we organized new members not because it made us a larger union but because we had a responsibility to welcome any workers we could help. Mergers are not about collecting more dues; they're about gathering like-minded people to fight for social justice for all. We had simple criteria: Can we assist these workers? Will being in our union make things better for them? Can we help them through our education program, our health and safety program, the financial assistance we can provide? To me, expansion based on these criteria was a vital aspect of social unionism. Diversification gave our union a national base of compatible groups and allowed us to keep playing a leading role in the formation of a militant left in Canada.

IN APRIL 1992, when Bob White stepped down as president of the union to take over as head of the Canadian Labour Congress, I was elected to succeed him. It was an exhilarating moment for a poor kid from backwater New Brunswick, with little education, who'd been taken in and nourished by the union. I was being given the opportunity to lead an organization of more than 200,000 workers and help chart a better future for them, their families, and their communities. To this day, I often wonder at my good fortune.

In my inaugural address to a special convention on June 27, 1992, I tried to set a tone for my leadership by stressing the importance of solidarity while we entertained new, more contemporary issues. We had, in recent years, said no to business unionism. We had said no to wage controls, to concessions to employers, to the opening of negotiated agreements, to the new direction of American unionism, and, in Canada, to free trade. I told the convention that the future called for more than fighting back by saying no. The CAW had to show the way in fighting racism and sexism. We could help our country become more tolerant by becoming more tolerant ourselves. We had to begin with our own attitudes toward women, people of colour, gays and lesbians. The social and cultural environment was changing and we had to change with it. The demographics of our union had changed. We were becoming more diverse, and our attitudes had to change as well. People with different lifestyles and from different cultures had to be given equal rights to progress, real opportunities to be part of the next generation of union leaders.

We had to adjust our attitudes on other social issues – gun control, for instance – while moving our bargaining focus to take into account changes in the larger society. We needed human rights education for our members, greater awareness of the needs of Canada's regions, vastly improved child care facilities. We had to help our women members when their duties called them away from home. In the three years after that convention, nine of twenty-one new staff we hired were either women or workers of colour. It was a start.

My speech was one of only three items on the agenda at that convention, the others being speeches by Bob White and Dennis McDermott. My own speech ran on a bit longer than theirs. Sam Gindin had assured me that the pages would add up to about thirty-five minutes; in fact, I ran an hour and thirty-five minutes and earned the nickname "Fidel" – for the speech's length and haranguing nature. When I passed McDermott in the hallway later, he whistled, rolled his eyes, and laughed, "Damn, you're a long-winded fella!"

The years of aggressive mergers and organizing had been a blessing to our union, increasing morale and boosting the confidence of our leaders. I was taking over a union with a momentum that other unions could only dream of. By the early 1990s, much of the Canadian labour movement felt weak and uncertain. Wage increases were at their lowest levels ever recorded. Unemployment was at 11.6 percent, meaning 1.6 million workers or more were out of jobs. For those aged fifteen to twenty-four, it was closer to 23 percent. The cod fishery in Newfoundland, Labrador, and parts of the Maritimes was closed; thousands of Maritimers were out of work. The nation's airline industry was in tatters, thanks to deregulation and the privatization of Air Canada. Both major air carriers were teetering on the edge of bankruptcy, dumping employees, and begging for handouts to stay alive. A leaked memorandum written by a top executive at Canadian National Railways revealed a corporate plan to lay off 10,000 workers, with possibly more to come. Yet interest rates were at their lowest in twenty years and inflation was falling. All the ingredients the Mulroney government and the corporations assured us would bring us better times were in place. As I wrote in my first president's report, in August 1992, "The only thing missing is prosperity for ordinary Canadians."

In 1993, as the CAW geared up to negotiate with the Big Three auto manufacturers, most workers felt trapped by this depressing economic atmosphere. The NDP government in Ontario had introduced its dreaded Social Contract, and public sector employees were fighting to hold the line on their wages. A zero increase was considered a major win. In the private sector, unions were celebrating if they got agreement for a 1 percent increase. Here was my baptism by fire: the first Big Three negotiations with Buzz Hargrove as president. More than a few people, both inside and outside the union, were watching to see if I'd fall on my face.

In this dark time, the only industry that did not seem in decline was the auto industry. I took the position that we had a great opportunity with the Big Three, a chance to improve the whole labour environment by challenging them and shifting the trend from concessions to making real progress for our members. We had an opportunity to do something radical, though it would require the CAW leaders to go out on a limb.

There used to be a secretary-treasurer in the UAW international who always wore a small wooden turtle on a leather lace around his neck. When asked the significance, he smiled: "It's there to remind me that even a turtle sticks his neck out once in a while." That thought has stayed with me. I knew that our members did not elect me to the presidency so I could chair meetings. They elected me to lead, to challenge myself and the people around me. When the leaders challenge a company with aggressive demands, we build support for our bargaining agenda with heightened worker expectations. Heightened expectations let companies know that, during bargaining, the pressure will be on us – and, therefore, on them – to meet that expectation. If we raise expectations too high, of course, and fail to meet them, we're on the spot with the members. I've always felt it's better to be aggressive, to go into negotiations strong and confident.

The other thing we knew the Big Three wanted was longer agreements. A number of unions were signing such agreements, often covering five or six years. Again, the CAW wanted no part of that one. Instead, we made sure our members were cranked up about improving their contracts and not accepting rollbacks or concessions in any form. We went into the Big Three negotiations looking to make major gains. Our bargaining committee expected to win cost-of-living adjustments, additional wage increases, more paid time off, larger pension hikes (including increases for the 23,000 Big Three workers in retirement), improvements in income security, and significant advances on social issues. It was a gamble, but one that could pay off handsomely.

COLLECTIVE BARGAINING IS about long-term relationships. It's about knowing the union can't take advantage of the good economic times, and the company can't take advantage of the bad times. We can't walk in to GM and say, "Okay, you're making money hand over fist, open up the vault." Nor can companies expect the workforce to give up previous gains when times are tough. Such a short-term outlook would create constant turmoil in labour–management relations. A union has every right to seek better wages and benefits for its members. Collective bargaining was entrenched in law for the benefit of working people; it recognizes the imbalance of power between employers and workers. Workers need this protection because companies, no matter what the circumstances, will always tell them: "This is not a good time to demand increases." Costs are rising, or about to rise; money needs to be spent on expanding capacity; consumer demand might fall; the cost of borrowing money is going to go up. Good times or bad, there's always a reason.

The best employers accept that workers' wages are simply a cost of doing business, that increases in workers' benefits are no different from increases in the price of steel or the cost of money. Banks don't drop their lending rates in bad times out of compassion for the company. Why should workers not be allowed to play by those rules? A constant challenge for the union is to establish recognition among employers that workers are entitled to seek gains and make progress in any set of negotiations. Just as there is never a good time for a company to give workers better wages and benefits, there is never a good time for a union not to seek them.

At the CAW, our approach to collective bargaining allows for the widest possible consultation on contract demands among our members and, at the same time, opens up lines of communication with employers so there are few surprises. Well in advance of bargaining, we bring in staff and local union leaders to go through the issues the members consider important. At a convention of as many as twelve hundred delegates –

which includes bargaining committees from all locations, plus chair-persons and presidents of local unions – we debate issues, prioritize them, and design strategy.

In the auto sector, our bargaining committee will meet with man-agement bargaining groups from all three companies in off-the-record sessions. At the same time, I'll meet with the top management person to see where the company stands on key issues. This is an important stage because we get to know each other personally. It's crucial that each per-son understands what makes the other tick. Believe it or not, as many strikes have been caused by personality clashes as by seemingly insol-uble issues.

After the bargaining committees meet in these off-the-record sessions and I've had my one-on-ones with the head negotiator, we meet again in a small group, which in our case usually means Jim O'Neil, our national secretary-treasurer; Sam Gindin; and my assistant responsible for that company. This is a pencil-and-paper session where we test our ideas on each other, trading observations on demands and how they fit with our agenda. Nothing is carved in stone here; nothing can be used outside the meeting room. As we head into the Labour Day weekend we decide which of the Big Three companies we're likely to make the most progress with on the union's priority demands. We'll typically spend two or three days in heavy debate, deciding which company to take on first.

A major consideration is which way the UAW in Detroit is set to go. If the CAW and the UAW are bargaining with the same company at the same time, we know we're not going to get much attention. Chrysler has 15,000 workers in Canada, 100,000 in the United States. At General Motors, the numbers are 21,000 hourly workers in Canada and 224,000 in the States. Ford has 15,000 hourly workers in Canada and 140,000 in the United States. A strike in Canada could be long and costly if the company's decision-makers south of the border are busy with the UAW and not paying much attention to us. All these factors are taken into account before we decide which company to deal with first.

In formal negotiations, I have one rule: never stop talking. Even if all progress stops, keep talking. Communication is the cheapest and most effective weapon in our arsenal. Some union leaders insist that when talks break down, it's up to the company to come up with a counter-offer to get things back on track, that if you contact the company first, it will be interpreted as weakness. That macho approach can be costly during a strike. If you're not talking, the company is losing money on stopped production and our members are losing money in wages. It's dumb to sit back and let things deteriorate. During Chrysler bargaining in 1996, I called the negotiating head five or six times a day, just to keep in touch. During the strike at GM in 1996, I talked several times a day to the labour relations vice-president, making sure their people understood exactly where we were coming from.

If you're not talking with management, it's almost axiomatic that you'll misunderstand each other, and misunderstandings lead to break-downs. I tell our committees to remember that management lives on a different planet. They will not automatically pick up on something you say. They speak a different language, have different priorities. Their vocabulary is all about dollars and production and how the plant runs. They don't think about the employees in the same way we do. You can't assume that, just because you say something to them that you feel gets your point across, they actually understand how important that issue is, or see what it would take to settle.

These principles of open communication are built into our education programs for negotiators. The idea is, if we have a strike or a lockout, it had better be on the issues, not on an inability to get along with some-one from the company or to understand where that person is coming from. There's no shame in picking up the phone during a stalemate and asking your counterpart: "You got any ideas how we can settle this thing?" That's not weakness, it's smart negotiating. I can't think of any-thing dumber than letting a strike drag on out of ignorance – because you don't understand the other's position – or, worse, out of spite – because you don't like someone personally.

In the 1993 Big Three negotiations, my first as president of the union, we won more paid time off from the job. A new program, called a "special paid absence allowance program," gives workers more time off from the plant and compels the company to hire more workers to keep the pro-duction lines running. That was a major victory on the job creation side.

At Chrysler we demanded an end to overtime in Windsor and the establishment of the third shift at the assembly plant. We got agreement on a third shift. (The industry had always maintained you could not run an assembly line on three shifts, because of the need for maintenance.) We had the plant up and running on three shifts by December 1993 – two months ahead of schedule – and they never missed a click. Quality was up, productivity was up, absenteeism was down. And we created 1,000 new direct jobs and several thousand indirect jobs. It was great progress at a difficult time.

We'd fought for years with our members about overtime. When our members were young and had young families to support, they worked as much overtime as they could. The leaders had wanted an end to overtime, partly so we could create more jobs at the plant, but also to keep our members healthy and able to enjoy the families they worked to support. Now, as hair started to turn grey along the production line, fewer of our members were willing to work those extra hours. The third shift was a real accomplishment.

We also won improvements in wages and benefits. We negotiated an excellent pension agreement that encouraged workers to retire early when they felt they could afford it. We put together a restructuring agreement – knowing layoffs would be coming – that gave older workers $37,000 in an up-front payment to retire, so younger workers would not be laid off. We came out of the 1993 negotiations with progress on every major demand we made going in, including a number of equity issues. We bargained for the first time for the right of women workers to be able to refuse work if they were being sexually harassed; for workers of colour to refuse work if they were being harassed; and for anyone to refuse work if facing harassment on the basis of religious beliefs.

We took on the social issues so that everyone understood that the CAW is a social movement as well as a union. We did it without a strike. And we did it while an entire nation of union members – and critics of the labour movement – watched. The message for Canadian labour was clear: if the CAW can win in dismal economic times, other unions should be able to do the same thing. The message for right-wing columnists and union critics who said that higher wages and benefits would make the

Big Three less competitive and less profitable soon became equally clear: after 1993, the Big Three began a run of five straight years of profits so high they were embarrassed, at times, to report the numbers.

ONE OF THE MOST PERPLEXING CHALLENGES I've faced as CAW president was the 1994 decision by our staff – members of the staff union – to strike the CAW. "Staff" are local union leaders appointed to act as liaison with the union's locals, and to do bargaining, grievance arbitration, community liaison work, and problem-solving in the local unions. I was not caught completely off guard by the strike. Some staff felt our union was moving away from its roots. Others were upset that, when we formed the CAW, much of the political power the staff once held had been shifted to a new, more broadly based, elected executive board. Still others had not wanted me to succeed Bob White and had tried to find an alternative candidate, though no one came forward. For most staff, though, dissatisfaction stemmed from a sense of exhaustion after a decade of banging their heads against the government and corporate wall. As Sam Gindin put it, "After swimming so hard against the tide, the swimmer gets tired."

Even so, I could not fathom why senior union leaders would take such drastic action. Our staff have privileges most workers can only dream of. Everything we bargain for with the Big Three, for instance, we pass along to staff – pension improvements, wage increases, health care benefits. In fact, they get more. Their wages are higher than the top-paid skilled trades workers. Their pensions are richer. I don't quarrel with any of that because they work long and hard and deserve what they get. But they definitely are privileged, and I could not understand how they could perceive the CAW leadership as "management" or the "employer."

Within the first two days of negotiations, we gave the staff all the normal increases in wages and benefits, and then some. They countered with demands for higher pensions and larger disability benefits, which angered me, since both programs are excellent. More significantly, they wanted to change the seniority structure of our union. The CAW is a political organization. It cannot afford a rigid seniority system because we need the flexibility to match our principles. We're not a plant that puts fenders on cars, a place where, because the fenders always fit, it doesn't matter who does the work. We're a political organization that has to respond to the changing environment in the union. When I joined the staff, in 1975, we had three women and maybe one person of colour out of sixty-five staff members. A rigid seniority structure would have made it impossible for us to address this inequity. In my final meeting with staff union president Bruce Davidson, he informed me the strike was on. "Nothing personal," he added.

"Nothing personal? You're shutting down the best union in the country in the middle of the worst attack by governments on the rights of working people. You're shutting down our ability to fight on behalf of our members, their families, and their communities. You treat me like I'm the head of some big corporation. You treat this organization like it was a profit machine instead of a social movement. You're goddamn right this is personal!"

The staff strike had the potential to get nasty. There was more than a little testosterone on the picket line. After all, hitting the bricks in a labour dispute was like the good old days for some of these people. But the staff were, and are, incredibly important to the relationship between the regional leaders and the local unions. If we acted hastily, we could do serious damage to the union's organizational structure. Undermine the staff and you undermine the union in the long term. This was a short-term problem, and my wish was to deal with it by keeping our heads.

There were two schools of thought among my advisers about how to respond. Some were inclined to circulate leaflets to the local union leaders and members, explaining our position and pointing out how privileged life was for staff and how the strike might be taking things a bit far. But I belonged to the other camp. We supported the right to strike for every other worker, after all, and I was damned if I was going to change that support just because this strike involved our own people. We decided to do nothing to aggravate the situation. We would not attack the staff leaders or try to win our local leaders to our point of view. We would simply follow our own advice: keep talking, as we would when any negotiation broke down. We stayed out of our offices, so as not to cross the picket lines, and we kept talking, trying to find common ground. After two weeks, we did.

Some people are dumbfounded that the CAW had an internal strike. "How does it happen?" they ask. "How does a union have a strike with its own union?" The answer is simple: we're an organization of human beings, subject to all the human strengths, weaknesses, and frailties. A better question might be: How in an organization that builds strong leadership, encourages its people to think independently, and urges them to challenge corporations, governments, and themselves – how did we last sixty years without a strike?

Many staff people now talk as if the strike never happened. Some can't even remember what the issues were. But it had a traumatic effect on a lot of people – especially me. I found it a real challenge to maintain my broader beliefs and principles in a labour dispute so close to home.

THE STRIKE MADE ME RECALL my own days as a staff rep. I held the job for three years, after eleven years as a shop representative, and I loved every minute of it. When we moved to Georgetown, I was nervous. I'd been involved on the Chrysler shop floor in Windsor, mostly doing grievance work, but had done very little bargaining. It was intimidating to walk in and head up bargaining committees, though I soon found that workers' problems everywhere are generally the same.

My introduction as service representative to Local 1285 was strange. Dennis McDermott asked Gord Parker, then Toronto area director, to take me to Brampton and introduce me to the local executive. Parker was reluctant because he didn't want to lose credibility with his friends if I turned out to be a dud. He argued that he didn't have time to "babysit," but McDermott persuaded him.

The local's president was Terry Gorman, a stubborn little Englishman who was suspicious of this new guy being foisted on them. Gorman called the meeting to order and Parker stood up. "We got a new staff member," he said, nodding in my direction. "I've been asked by McDermott to come and introduce him – his name's Buzz Hargrove. I don't know him from Adam. All I can tell you is that he comes out of Charlie Brooks's local – a good, progressive local union – but I don't know a goddamn thing about him. I guess you'll get to know him, same as I will." He shrugged and sat down.

Staff did all kinds of things in those days. I immediately got a delegates' badge from Local 1285 so I could be involved with the labour council and help stir up some action. I especially loved the community politics. We set up an unemployed workers' help centre, where we offered advice and guidance to unemployed people who had no support groups to turn to. We hounded the provincial government into putting up funding. We offered assistance on a range of issues – how to file for unemployment insurance, where to go to place job applications, how to fight a former employer if you thought you'd been ripped off on severance or back wages.

We organized a survey – designed by York University and conducted by the UAW – that showed that unemployment in Brampton was much higher than Statscan was reporting. Brampton was a conservative community. It was, after all, former premier Bill Davis's home town. It was your typically affluent Ontario town where people say hello, tip their hats, and everyone seems to have a job and three square meals a day. People had the impression that everything was wonderful. Most denied there was an unemployment problem.

We trained some of our people to carry out the survey. People would work their shifts and then volunteer their time. Most of the work was done in the evenings, and it took three or four months to complete. We'd knock on doors and find out how many people in the family were unemployed. When the survey was finished and the university had analyzed the data, we called a meeting of unemployed people in the Legion Hall and released the results to them and to the media. Our findings were a shock. The *Brampton Times* carried its first editorial on unemployment in thirty years. It concluded that Brampton did indeed have a problem. The survey helped draw public attention to just how many people in the community needed help or a job.

It was a fascinating time. As a staff member, there was nothing we weren't allowed to do. We never had to ask permission of anyone. If we had an idea about attracting public attention to a labour issue or wanted to set up an educational activity, no one stopped us. Our labour council was looking for people to challenge it and show leadership. I'd go weeks, even months, without hearing from anybody in the UAW head office. Every now and then I'd get a personal note of congratulations from Dennis McDermott, usually because he'd seen a media release about something we were doing in the Brampton area. I remember being told a couple of times that if you didn't hear from Dennis McDermott or Bob White, you must have been doing a good job.

It was around this time that I learned a valuable lesson about power. Our union struck a Brampton outfit called Butcher Engineering, a tough-minded company. We struck over a first contract that included union security. The company was run by the son of the owner, Chris Butcher, and he was determined he would have no union in the plant.

Our UAW Toronto area director, Larry Sheffe, had signed an agreement to end the three-week strike without ensuring that we had the Rand Formula in place. The agreement merely stated that over its two-year course, employees would be free to sign up for the union or not. Employees who chose not to join paid no union dues, even though they enjoyed the higher wages and better conditions the union had negotiated. My job was to figure out a way to get the majority of employees to sign membership cards. The company had a large group of Portuguese workers who were frightened of their employer and nervous about the union's ability to protect them. If they refused to join they'd put a quick end to our plans of keeping the union at Butcher Engineering.

The sign-up was to be held in an office at the local Legion Hall. The agreement allowed Butcher to have a company witness in the signing office to make sure the union did not intimidate or bully the workers. All the witness could do was watch – he could not say anything. Butcher was nobody's fool. He called to say he himself would be the company's witness. Now I really had my hands full.

I looked around the Legion the day before the vote. The place displayed the usual signs of "authority": the office had a big wooden desk and a big black leather armchair for "the boss." A picture of a military officer with a chest full of metals adorned one wall. The room also contained standard wooden chairs for visitors and a small, three-legged stool in the corner with a potted plant on top.

The sign-up process called for employees to be escorted into the office one at a time. I'd explain the rules and that they were entitled by law to sign a union dues check-off. The first thing I did was remove all but one of the chairs for visitors. I took the plant off the stool and placed the stool beside the desk. The next morning, before the vote, when Butcher strolled in, I pointed at the stool. "Have a seat."

"Like hell I'm going to sit there," he shouted. "That stool is for the workers. I'm sitting in the chair."

"Like hell you are," I shouted back. "I'm in charge of this vote. According to the agreement, if you want to observe union business you sit where I say and you keep your mouth shut. And you're not allowed to stand up, either, because that could be interpreted as trying to intimidate the employee."

I sat in the boss's chair and the process began – 170 workers coming in one at a time to vote for or against the union. To Butcher's dismay, the first eighty or so signed up without a fuss, including many of the Portuguese workers. Butcher, perched on the stool, was seething. When he'd start to say something, I'd tell him to keep quiet.

Finally, the eighty-first employee – a woman of Portuguese descent – entered. I repeated what I'd said to the others: this is what we're doing here and why. Mr. Butcher has nothing to do with this process and is only here to observe that you're not signing under threats or intimidation. "It's your decision," I said, "and I'm requesting that you sign."

She turned to Butcher and asked, "I don't have to sign, do I, Mr. Butcher?"

Butcher could not keep his mouth shut. "No, you don't," he told her.

"Excuse me," I jumped in. "The rules you agreed to are that you keep quiet."

The woman said, "Then I don't sign."

"Fine, thank you very much," I said, and watched her slip out the door. The first thing she did was whisper in the ear of another worker. I worried that Butcher's comment might have tipped the scales, but by the time the vote was over, only fourteen workers had refused to sign union cards. It was a great victory for us.

My years as a staff member were memorable for all kinds of reasons. My two girls were born then and it was grand watching them grow. In terms of income, I couldn't have asked for better wages and working conditions. I was self-assigning. I was working for one of the most progressive social democratic organizations in North America. I was having fun doing things I loved, and told people the biggest challenge I faced was learning how to tie a tie. I'd never worn one before going on staff.

When I joined the staff, there were only sixty of us (today there are 132 staff). We had a lot of ground to cover and a lot of members to serve. But we were active in everything. A UAW staff job was not just a matter of doing union work – bargaining, processing grievances, helping the locals and the people on the shop floor. We were point men for a social activist movement.

Social activism meant you could spend as much time as you wanted pursuing issues important to your community, whether collecting for the United Way or fundraising for a community beautification project. That was all union staff work, all a part of the UAW's community action culture. The idea was to share – your time, your ideas, your labour, and your money – with the community.

Another part of the job was getting into politics. I did organizing and funding work for the NDP. I helped out at election time, striving to get the voters out. I did canvassing. At the drop of a hat I'd agree to debate Liberals and Conservatives, on radio and cable television. We had some wild debates, especially with the local Liberal MPP, Ross Milne. It was no-holds-barred stuff. It was invigorating, and personally rewarding, to find myself becoming an outspoken member of the left – calling for help for the disabled, the elderly, and the indigent; demanding equitable pay for women; urging the introduction of affordable daycare. All in all, it's hard to imagine a job more challenging – and satisfying – than that. I loved the work and couldn't understand how staff members could find so much to gripe about, let alone the time to complain. As I say, I found the staff strike in 1994 a real challenge.

BESIDES BEING THE LARGEST PRIVATE SECTOR UNION in Canada, the CAW is also, without doubt, the most politicized. The urge to be an agent for social change is as strong as the desire to do well at the bargaining table. We strive to be a mechanism for working people to make progress, but our mission is about community as much as it is about collective bargaining. We want to see our communities prosper. We want them to develop values that are inclusive, not exclusive. We want to see the less fortunate cared for. We want all to share in the country's wealth.

Members of the labour movement do not live in isolation from their society; wealth spreads quickly from the bargaining table to the community. Gains made by unions – gains in health care, drug plans, pension plans, paid vacations, support for the disabled, care for the elderly, and the right to work free of harassment or health risks – help raise standards for everyone. The fight for safer workplaces easily becomes a fight for better environmental controls. The fight for cleaner air in the factory evolves into the fight for a cleaner environment. The fight for incentives for early retirement or shorter work time transforms itself into job creation in the community.

The CAW has always backed up its demands that governments and corporations do more for the less fortunate by asking our members to support charitable organizations. In many communities, our union sets national records for United Way contributions. The CAW has also worked to help our cities and towns become more liveable, supporting initiatives for co-op and not-for-profit housing and improved community services. In Windsor, for example, our local union leaders are always involved in community projects. If they're not pressuring city council for new parks and recreation facilities, they're advocating a clean-up and beautification program for the old rail yards along the waterfront. Some of our local unions have sports clubs that raise money for youth sports activities.

The CAW provides financial support for shelters for battered women and for food banks – help that has become more urgent, thanks to the economic policies of two Mulroney and two Chrétien governments, and the Harris government in Ontario. At a recent CAW Council meeting, I tallied up the total of non-union–related donations our leadership approved – including money for strike support for non-CAW strikers – and it came to more than a quarter of a million dollars.

People stumbling on an agenda for a CAW convention are often surprised at the range of public issues we debate. We focus on how well our locals are doing with employers, of course, but our members also debate

CAW policies on gender sensitivity training, anti-harassment programs in the workplace, and continuing education programs for our members. We have an active women's caucus that leads our union – perhaps the labour movement – in modernizing attitudes toward women. Our conventions include a gay and lesbian caucus and a caucus for workers of colour. Their discussions have helped cause a massive shift in attitudes among our leaders and members. One of our current goals is to stamp out stereotyping and sexist attitudes. We know we won't change everyone's attitude, but this kind of thinking leads to debate among our members, and spills over into the community at large. Challenge triggers debate. Debate strengthens an organization. Strong organizations with progressive ideas make a stronger society.

Two of the CAW's most progressive undertakings in the last two decades have been our membership education program, known as Paid Education Leave (PEL), and our Social Justice Fund. If our Toronto office is the "head" of our union, our $35 million Family Education Centre, at Port Elgin on Lake Huron, is the "heart." We put more of our members through education courses at our Port Elgin facility in a month than the rest of the Canadian labour movement does in a year. Dennis McDermott taught us that a successful union is a smart union, with members well versed in union history. The way to maintain enthusiasm and solidarity among members, he argued, was to provide opportunities for them to learn about the political process, labour and social issues, human rights, and collective bargaining. When strikes were in progress, he required workers who were not on picket duty to attend classes as a condition for receiving strike pay.

The credit for the original PEL curriculum goes to Daniel Benedict, a great trade unionist and friend. As a labour economist and member of the UAW's education department, he developed the curriculum for the PEL program twenty-one years ago. The program is run out of the Family Education Centre. Its purpose is to educate our members on a broad range of topics: collective bargaining, labour economics, the role of unions in the community and society, and the history of unionism in Canada and around the world. PEL is funded by a corporate "tax" the CAW negotiates from companies. We bargain for a certain number of cents per compensated hour. The money is assigned solely for education purposes.

Some management types are offended that they're paying their employees to be better informed bargainers. We point out that the education employers and managers received was largely paid for, or subsidized by, the Canadian taxpayer. There's little taxpayer-funded education for people who want to learn about unions, or about trade union leadership. It seems only fair that those who benefit most from their public education should foot the bill for our members' continuing education. The CAW would be happy to look at whether to continue the PEL program if, in some enlightened future, provincial governments introduced more courses on labour history, labour economics, and trade unionism. Imagine teaching kids not about the triumph of building a railway to open up markets in the west, or about the commercial successes of legendary entrepreneurs, but about the struggles and small victories of their own working-class parents.

If I'm any good on my feet, I owe it to the union's commitment to continuing education. I took a union course in public speaking many years ago and found it invaluable, a tremendous confidence builder. I can also thank my local union leaders who never allowed us to forget the value of education – people like Charlie Brooks, Ken Gerard, and Ed Baillargeon.

Charlie Brooks was instrumental in helping Local 444 establish its progressive outlook, and a firm believer in union education. When I was elected to the executive council of Local 444, one of the first debates I got into was about a leadership course in Port Elgin in the early 1970s. Some of the old guard argued that we should only send the top leaders of the union – executive board members or a chairperson – because the shop stewards or committeemen on the shop floor were not bright enough. I thought that was preposterous, and got into a heated fight over this issue. Charlie and Ed both sided with me. Perhaps I seemed self-serving, for having won the debate I was selected to attend. In any case, the CAW gave me my first real educational opportunity.

The ultimate purpose of the PEL is to build leadership skills. In the mid-1970s, as employers began adopting more aggressive bargaining techniques, workers were hard pressed to argue in a sophisticated way against the contention that we had no recourse but to accept the "new realities" of wage and benefit concessions. A better informed worker, we knew, would be an invaluable part of our "fight back" strategy. New members seldom have a broad understanding of the principles of unionism. This is especially true as we organize young people in non-traditional sectors of the economy.

The Mulroney and Chrétien governments have practised the politics of permanent recession, and young Canadians pay a disproportionate share of the human cost. Between 1989 and 1996, about 500,000 jobs for young people disappeared. Although their official rate of unemployment is said to be around 17 percent, the real youth unemployment rate is significantly higher. When discouraged young workers are taken into account, the real rate of youth unemployment probably ranges between 20 and 30 percent. The labour force participation rate for young Canadians has fallen from over 70 percent before the latest recession to barely 60 percent today.

Despite all the hype about Canada's "improved economic fundamentals," our "great success" in export markets, and the "dynamic growth" of the private sector, a young Canadian between seventeen and twenty-four might as well be living through a depression. Among major industrialized countries, Canada ranks second to Great Britain for the worst record in providing jobs for its young people. Many of today's jobless young have university degrees, college certificates, or technical school diplomas, yet they are forced to accept dead-end, minimum-wage, or part-time jobs to pay the rent, if they can find jobs at all.

No wonder there's a groundswell of young people joining the labour movement. These kids are not dumb: they can read the statistics as well as anyone. In 1997 wages and weekly earnings for union members were 31 percent higher than for non-union workers. In the full-time category, according to Statscan, union members took home an average of $18.84 an hour, compared with $15.18 for non-union workers. In the part-time category, unionized employees pocketed $16.74 an hour while non-unionized workers made $9.76 an hour – a 71 percent difference. Add in the fact that members of a union are twice as likely to enjoy a wide range of benefits – from pensions to health and safety protection, from extra holiday time to dental care and sick leave – and it's not unusual to find young people walking around workplaces handing out CAW leaflets and membership cards.

The future strength of any movement, like the future strength of a nation, depends on its young people. Their generation provides the next leaders. The CAW has the strength it enjoys today largely because, at a critical moment in our history, we turned to our younger members to set a pace that distanced the CAW – industrially, socially, and politically – from most of the Canadian labour movement.

We teach our young people that unions introduce a measure of democracy into the workplace and offer people some control over their lives. And we stress that unions are not just "there" – more than ever they have to be built, sustained, and constantly strengthened.

AS FOR OUR SOCIAL JUSTICE FUND, it was established in 1991 to provide humanitarian relief and development assistance internationally as well as in Canada. It donates about $1 million a year to worthy causes. Support for the fund's activities is possible because of the awareness our members develop through the PEL program.

Most of the money to support the Social Justice Fund also comes from a designated clause in our contracts with the Big Three. It calls for the employer to pay at least one cent for each compensated employee hour. The funds go into a registered charity administered by six union officers and three prominent Canadians representing our social partners. The most notable recent donation was the announcement in 1997 that, over three years, the CAW would contribute $1.25 million to removing land mines in Mozambique. After three civil wars, that country is littered with land mines. Thousands of citizens, especially children, were being killed and maimed. The *Globe and Mail*'s Michael Valpy pointed out that the CAW was the only Canadian organization to donate money to global de-mining: "None of the Big Three Automakers has put up money. None of the Big Six chartered banks in Canada has put up the money. One by one these days, like bloated ducks in a row, they are busy announcing record profits. None of the members of the Business Council on National Issues has put up any money. So, applause for the CAW."

In conjunction with Care Canada, the Social Justice Fund donated $1.5 million for refugee assistance in Rwanda. We've also used the fund to help people affected by attacks from militia and police in Chiapas, Mexico, and we've donated money for education in post-apartheid South Africa. We've developed projects in many other Third World countries as well.

In Canada the fund provides sustaining support of $160,000 for food banks and for women's shelters. We donated $250,000 to the Canadian Red Cross to help the victims of the devastating ice storm in Quebec, New Brunswick, and eastern Ontario. Our union also contributed $250,000 to victims of the 1996 flooding in the Saguenay– Lac St.-Jean region of Quebec, and $191,000 to victims of the Manitoba flood in 1997.

I've been asked how the CAW manages to donate such large sums without facing a backlash from members. First, our members know that the union was forged with that strong sense of social responsibility the Reuthers and the McDermotts taught us. And second, if we're doing a good job bargaining on the issues that most affect them – wages, benefits, pensions, job security, and so forth – they have no trouble seeing the Social Justice Fund as the right thing to do. Only if we fail at our primary task will they question our broader social initiatives.

We went into the 1996 GM negotiations with same-sex spousal benefits on our bargaining list. You could almost hear some members' heads turn in disbelief. "What are we messing with that stuff for?" they asked. We went into negotiations prepared to strike over outsourcing – a critical issue to the members – and stopped it. Same-sex spousal benefits were an add-on. If our negotiating committee had walked into the contract ratification meeting and said, "Gee, folks, we couldn't get GM to back off on outsourcing, but we got this great package on same-sex spousal benefits," we would have been lucky to escape with our lives.

So long as we're fighting and winning on the issues most important to the members, they'll accept our bargaining for social justice issues. That principle applies as well to the CAW's efforts to play an important part in the political debate of the country. If the members understand that you're working on political issues that impact their lives – fighting for policies that lead to more jobs, preservation of their health care system, protection for programs like unemployment insurance and public pensions – they'll support your political pursuits. It's all part and parcel of the fight to create a more humane Canada.

IN JANUARY 1997 one of our local unions held a Super Bowl party in its union hall. A few days later I received faxes and e-mails from some members complaining that the party included exotic dancers. We could have argued that the entertainment was just a bunch of the boys blowing off steam. That sort of stuff was commonplace in the old days. But those days are gone in the CAW, as far as I'm concerned.

When contacted by the local newspapers for a response, I told them the behaviour was a violation of the CAW constitution. It was unacceptable, period. I recommended that the members of the local demand the resignations of the elected officers participating in the party or those responsible for organizing the performance. When members phoned to complain about my going public, I asked them, "Does this sort of conduct show respect for human rights, human dignity?"

Hell, I'm no saint. Twenty-five years ago I would been at that party myself. But I've come a long way since then – in lifestyle, in attitude, in my goals. I only wish that in my early days our union had had the same commitment to gender issues and human rights that it has today. I don't pretend there aren't still members who think we should stick to collective bargaining on bread-and-butter issues, as many unions do. Our challenge is to get these members to understand that we can't sit out these moral, ethical, and political debates in our society. Doing that would make our movement irrelevant.

One way we help our members accept changing attitudes is by focusing on the importance of family. Doing so tends to highlight how social change affects us personally. Look at what "family" means today compared with forty years ago. Less than a quarter of Canadian families now conform to the traditional model of a male breadwinner as the main source of income. Two-thirds of single mothers with children under sixteen are in the workforce, 85 percent of them working full time.

Almost three-quarters of two-parent families with children under five are dual-income families. They have to be.

A recent study showed that the average two-income family must work a total of seventy-seven hours a week just to cover basic expenses. Almost one-quarter of those families would fall below the poverty line if the head of the household lost a job. Even then, almost 20 percent of children under sixteen in Canada live in families below the poverty line. Union members who refuse to support anti-poverty groups, or who consider politics somebody else's job, miss the connection.

The question I'd ask them – and the way I explain our union's active role in these broader issues – is this: With that sort of economic pressure imposed on Canadian families, who else is going to step up and try to improve their lot? Who if not the labour movement and the NDP? Chrétien's Liberals? Mike Harris in Ontario? Preston Manning and his herd of Reformers? Ralph Klein in Alberta? The Fraser Institute? The Business Council on National Issues? The Chamber of Commerce? The CAW is a social movement because you can't leave the remedy for social damage to those who caused it.

6

SCORCHED AND SALTED

The Social Contract was a good idea, but it was a political failure,
and I have to take my share of the blame.
— Bob Rae

If you don't know where you're going, you'll end up somewhere else.
— Yogi Berra

Like most people in the labour movement, I was ecstatic in September 1990 when the New Democratic Party was elected to govern Ontario. At long last the halls of power at Queen's Park would be open to working people. Those who had steadfastly supported the party over the years realized our time had come. The left was in power in a province of more than ten million people. Some of us could hardly believe our good fortune, giddy with excitement at the thought of what an NDP government could do to make Ontario a more decent place to live.

The cabinet's swearing-in ceremony at the University of Toronto's Convocation Hall was a festive event. While a small coterie of business and social elites gathered quietly in the corners, the room echoed with hoots and applause as cabinet member after cabinet member was sworn in. It seemed the opportunity of a lifetime, a chance to show people there was a different way of doing politics.

In 1990 Ontarians had clearly been looking for a change in political leadership. Brian Mulroney's Free Trade Agreement had decimated the province's economy. We were entering the worst recession since the Great Depression. Between 1990 and 1991 unemployment in Ontario would sky-rocket 50 percent, from 6.3 percent of the working population to 9.6 percent – a post-Depression high. Real wages were falling. People were struggling. The housing market had collapsed. Downtown Toronto was a sea of For Sale and For Lease signs. There was incredible insecurity.

The Ontario electorate had bounced from a Tory majority government, to a Liberal minority government, to a Liberal majority government, and then to "those other guys." The NDP received only 38 percent of the vote – hardly a ringing endorsement of social democratic principles, but we'd take it. Some voters casting their ballots for the NDP, and for Bob Rae in particular, had never voted NDP in their lives.

Many NDP candidates were as shocked as anyone at being elected. Politically, they were a pretty inexperienced group. Only fourteen of the seventy-four elected NDPers had served previously as politicians. Only five were lawyers with experience in how laws are made. One new NDP member had apparently been selling hot dogs at baseball games before the election. Half the cabinet seats went to political neophytes. Some cabinet members seemed chosen at random. As Thomas Walkom remarked in *Rae Days: The Rise and Follies of the NDP*, this administration was going to be "an exercise in making the best from pretty thin gruel."

Personally, I was elated. After the many decades of frustration labour had experienced under Tory and Liberal administrations, we felt we could rely on this government to open exciting avenues on social policy, fair taxation, labour legislation, economic development, and equitable treatment for all citizens. Instead, we got a government going in the opposite direction. In less than eighteen months it had turned off many of its supporters. The excited smiles turned to frowns, the euphoria to bafflement, the giddiness to silence, until, finally, confusion turned to dread and more frustration than we had ever felt under any Liberal or Tory administration.

In retrospect, the NDP government that suddenly appeared in office, then disappeared in 1995, now seems like a terrible accident. Blinded by the glare of a major political victory, too many NDPers – both in caucus and in the party organization – lost sight of traditional NDP principles. The Rae government not only reneged on many of its election promises but did everything it could to keep the province's corporate sector satisfied. It refused to honour major pledges, such as public auto insurance. It chose to fight the deficit by slashing programs rather than engaging seriously in job creation. It made deals with doctors, and cut nurses' wages. It made concessions to multinational drug manufacturing firms, raising the cost of drugs and medicine for the elderly, the poor, and the

infirm. It slapped heavy taxes on the few perks a working person has –
cigarettes, beer, wine, and gasoline – and let corporations and the
wealthy off light. It legislated out of existence legal collective agreements covering almost one million public service employees. It violated
provincial employees' basic right to bargain collectively and offered
their unions the worst choice possible: accept wage rollbacks or expect
compulsory wage cuts. These policies may sound like something devised
by Mike Harris or Ralph Klein, yet this was a government supposedly
of the left.

In my estimation, nothing has done more damage to the cause of
social democracy in Canada than the Rae government. The election of
the NDP turned out to be the worst of all worlds. By 1995 a good number
of members of the labour movement, and many on the left of the NDP,
were rooting for the Liberals or Conservatives to wrest power away
from this sad assembly of presumed socialists. The controversy, bitterness, and soiled policies left behind by the Rae government opened the
gates and made it easy for the Harris-led Tories to implement one of the
cruellest right-wing legislative agendas this nation has ever seen.

For those of us who've spent our lives promoting the politics of the
NDP, the experience was a shock that still haunts us. Those five years of
ideological bewilderment, broken promises, and political ineptitude
were exceeded only by the government's lack of dedication to NDP principles. Some pundits believe that the lack of political experience in cabinet allowed Rae to concentrate decision-making power in the Premier's
Office. With the help of his chosen advisers, he was free to chart the policy
voyage for his new government himself. But that analysis lets too many
cabinet ministers off the hook. Many might have been short on electoral
experience, but many were nonetheless well-educated, mature profes-
sionals. This is certainly true of a number of cabinet ministers who
claimed extensive experience in labour affairs.

In the first couple of months after the election, everyone stood back
to see what would happen. Enthusiastic at having new options in
Queen's Park, the public showed support for the government that
reached close to 60 percent in the first year. The honeymoon did not last.
For some of us, the first disturbing clues appeared in Rae's acceptance

speech. There was little mention of the Agenda for People – the election promises that helped get him into office. Nor was there any indication of how his government would address Ontarians' massive insecurity in the wake of deregulation, privatization, and the Free Trade Agreement. Ontarians were crying out for change, for new ideas and new ways of governing. What they got was a 1990s version of Bill Davis, but without the savvy.

It's interesting to compare Rae's acceptance speech to that of Mike Harris five years later. Harris's speech was a marvel of transparent commitment. He acknowledged that the voters had elected him to change things. Rae did not. Harris thanked those who voted for him and assured his supporters – his political constituency – that they would get what they had elected him for. He invited the rest of Ontario, if they were so inclined, to get on board his movement for change. The direction the Tories were heading was the direction his supporters wanted to go. He was not about to change his government's course for anyone but his political constituency.

Rae, in contrast, declared he was elected to govern by all the people of the province, even though the voting percentages hardly indicated his government had the confidence of all those people. He would repeat that refrain, along with the assurance that the corporate community had nothing to fear from an NDP government.

The difference in the two approaches is revealing. One said, in effect, I know who got me elected. I owe it to them to see that we change government to suit their interests. The rest of you can either climb aboard or fume from the sidelines. The other said, I'm here to try to broker deals that will satisfy everyone. I do not intend to favour one group of interests over another, even if some of those groups were responsible for my party's success at the polls. We are all in this together. Our friends and supporters will just have to bear with us. If they do not like the direction we're heading, we'll make new friends as we go along.

Bob White and I both cautioned Rae that it would be a mistake for the NDP government to do too much too soon. We suggested it might polarize the province. It would allow the right-wing ideologues in the business community to mount a concerted attack on the "socialists" who had taken over Queen's Park. In the longer term, moving too quickly and without proper consultation could actually be detrimental to labour's cause.

Because we had always been up against Tory or Liberal governments, labour's progress in Ontario had been slow but steady. We had always had to engage in lobbying, rallies, strikes, sit-ins, and demonstrations to make our points and gain legislative advances. It had been decades of tough fighting, but at least we had never suffered serious setbacks in labour legislation.

White suggested to Rae that he ask the provincial labour movement to submit six or seven key concerns and let the government move as quickly as possible to legislate those changes. A few changes, presented after requests for public input, and after proper public hearings – plus a decent interval for debate in the legislature – would show the business community that the NDP respected formal democratic processes. The NDP government could not then be accused of ramming through pro-labour laws.

Rae rejected the advice. He set up separate working groups from labour and business to advise him on labour legislation reform. It was not even a joint council. Rae loved to talk about his passion for broad consultation on policy matters, but to some of us the talk looked like a way to avoid having to make a decision. It was a way of trying to please everyone – which was impossible. The "consultation" ended with neither business nor labour satisfied, or else with demands so extreme that both groups were polarized. The process was doomed to failure.

As expected, the labour advisory group came up with suggested reforms that amounted to nothing more than an outlandish wish list. The business group tabled an equally appalling set of demands that would have set Ontario labour back decades. The process, as White had predicted, gave the business community the excuse and the time to mobilize. The extreme demands trotted out by the labour advisory group only helped trigger a campaign in the business community to defeat any serious proposal for labour reform.

In the end, the NDP brought in some modest changes to labour legislation. Ironically, the changes were consistent with what White and I had suggested at the outset, but Rae wasted more than two years getting there. The labour law amendments were not passed until January 1993. Only the anti-scab law, Bill 40, was of real significance, and it was one of the few times the Rae government didn't cave in to business demands. Yet to the Ontario business lobby group, the anti-scab legislation heralded the beginning of the end of the world.

SOON AFTER RAE'S ELECTION, many outspoken lefties began to get the feeling we were being frozen out of serious deliberation on government policy. We in the CAW, with our strong social policy interests, hoped to influence the government on social as well as economic policy and labour reform. There was a lot of work to do, a lot of social welfare legislation to repair. Changes were needed to the taxation system, to make it more fair for young families, for the elderly, and for those struggling with poverty. As the months wore on, less and less consultation took place. Not once did the Rae government seek the CAW's views on these issues.

What we did pass up the chain of command was not listened to. In fact, a siege mentality seemed to build around the Premier's Office. The walls went up particularly quickly if we had the temerity to criticize publicly the direction the Rae government was going in. Any loud critic, especially from the left, was seen, as Thomas Walkom put it, as "a dangerous and ignorant fool."

I remember making one submission to Finance Minister Floyd Laughren before he brought in his second budget. I was politely listened to; then he and his advisers, with no warning, slapped Ontarians with the "gas guzzler" tax. This followed an NDP budget that had raised taxes on cigarettes, beer, wine, and gasoline, but did not increase corporate or bank taxes, did not tax windfall corporate profits, and did not introduce a new wealth tax. Instead, Rae stuck it to working people. To slap a guzzler tax on a province that thrives on the manufacture of automobiles was astoundingly shortsighted. The Ontario automobile industry is an $80 billion-a-year industry and the engine of Ontario's economy. One in five jobs in the greater Toronto area is tied to automobile manufacturing.

I was devastated when I got the call from a staff member who was in the lockup to get details of the budget. This was an important legislative move, but there had been no advance consultation with the CAW – the union most involved. We had angry people to answer to. The tax affected almost every plant we had in Canada. Our members were furious. "Here's *our* government," they said, "and it's imposing a tax that might cost us our jobs. Not even the Tories would have threatened our jobs!"

The Rae government had an amazing capacity to forget its friends. By chance, I sat next to Frances Lankin, a long-time labour activist and one of the stronger ministers in cabinet, at a Premier's Council conference in late 1993, when we received the news that, exasperated with NDP policies, our Local 222 had voted by more than 80 percent to disaffiliate from the party. When I told Lankin, she replied: "Well, we'll see how they like it when we refuse to support General Motors' request for government funding for training." Rae and company just did not get it.

The Big Three, sensing the angry mood in their plants over the gas guzzler tax, wrote letters to our members and their families expressing outrage that the NDP was threatening their jobs. It was a shrewd move on their part. It stimulated more outrage. Our local leaders received call after call from irate members accusing us of having been part of the decision to introduce the tax. They could not believe that "our party," "our government," would act on this issue without consulting our union.

I fired off a protest to Rae and Finance Minister Laughren. Meetings were held and, with the efforts of my assistant, Sam Gindin, who brokered the deal, the government eventually backed off on the most damaging parts of the tax. But the political damage was done. There would be no erasing the bitterness.

IF THE GAS GUZZLER TAX gave a picture of what life might be like under the Rae government, there were more surprises ahead. We sensed this was a strange bunch of "lefties" when they began appointing Liberals and Tories to patronage positions (along with some NDPers) because, so we were told, they wanted to be seen as non-partisan. Politics is about being partisan. The skill with which you exercise that partisanship indicates how adept you are. To be in politics and want to be non-partisan is naive.

A year after taking office, the Rae government reneged on its promise to introduce public auto insurance. It said that this long-held NDP platform promise was now "impractical," even though public auto insurance had been a valued public service in Manitoba, British Columbia, and Saskatchewan for years. When the Rae government gave in to pressure from the insurance lobby, it threw away the one high-profile promise that said the NDP stood for something – saving money for the average Joe. The insurance industry was making – is still making – immense profits. Most of it is shipped outside this country. The decision to cave in on auto insurance also gave the corporate community the confidence that it could influence the policy direction of the NDP government. It exposed the Rae government as one without the courage of its convictions.

In April 1992 the government's budget raised taxes for senior citizens and individuals but cut taxes for business. It trimmed welfare spending but gave subsidies to business for training employees. In July 1992 the government tabled an industrial strategy paper that read like a manifesto drafted by the Business Council on National Issues. The document called for industry to be more "competitive" to meet "new challenges" in a global economy. It decreed that business and labour should work together in a "partnership" as the provincial economy grew through this difficult period of "adjustment." It suggested that unions begin making compromises, buying into concessions and wage cuts to help get the economy out of the ditch.

This was fiscal conservatism of the worse kind. Yes, the government had a deficit problem. At the time, it was thought to be about $10 billion, or three times what had been expected when the Liberal government of David Peterson was kicked out of office. But why the panic? In relative terms, the Ontario NDP government faced a deficit that ate up 12 cents of every tax dollar. At the time, the Mulroney government's deficit was eating up 34 cents of every tax dollar.

In December 1992 I wrote my quarterly report for presentation to the CAW Council. I was critical of the government, and I fired off a copy to Rae so he could prepare himself for media questions. He was furious and phoned to say so. More than a few four-letter words passed between us. But that was the idea: I was looking to get a reaction. It was time somebody started pushing from the left wing of the party. It was clear that the Rae government had ample capacity for doing even more damage to itself and, by association, to the rest of us on the left. Someone had to get the message across.

Under the title NDP *Governments and Worker Frustration*, my council document warned that criticism of the Rae government was building among working people. More than two years into the administration's mandate, we were clearly in deep and dangerous waters. The biggest problem we faced was the government's refusal to challenge the power of capital. In fact, it wanted to be the friend of capital.

Rae was not using the tools that government provides to offset the failure of right-wing policies. Canada was digesting deregulation and privatization, a shift in taxation away from the corporations and onto individuals, an expansion of regressive sales taxes such as the GST, elimination of the Family Allowance, continuing attacks on our national medicare program, cutbacks to unemployment insurance and government services, job loss due to the Free Trade Agreement, and now we were facing NAFTA. We had done everything the right had persuaded us would make the country economically successful, yet Canada's unemployment rate was the highest among major developed countries.

After all this right-wing mumbo-jumbo, Ontario was experiencing a virtual repeat of the Great Depression. The bottom had fallen out of our economy. To walk down Yonge Street was to be shocked at the number of dispossessed young people. Yorkville was a succession of vacant storefronts. We were entering an era of food banks, soup kitchens, and street beggars. And here we had a "left-wing" provincial government wanting to implement more of this right-wing agenda. "Why is the NDP government not aggressively exposing the failure of this agenda?" I asked in my council report.

What we needed was a commitment to stop further cutbacks in social services. We wanted to eliminate tuition increases for university students and reinstate student grants and interest-free loans to previous levels. We wanted the government to mobilize support against federal cutbacks to transfer payments. The CAW was not merely critical of the Rae government; we had ideas for turning the economy around. We just could not seem to get through that cone of silence around the Premier's Office.

I thought we had an impressive list of practical reforms. To create jobs, we suggested that both the provincial government and the municipalities pressure the federal government to embark on an expanded infrastructure program. We proposed an incentive program for small businesses to reward them for creating new jobs. We encouraged the provincial government to use its immense purchasing power in health care, education, and transportation to develop a "Buy Canadian" strategy, one that would boost sales and increase jobs in the province. Finally, we recommended that an Ontario Development Bond be issued to raise the money to rebuild the provincial economy. The bond could be advertised as a "war bond," since we were engaged in a battle to maintain living standards for working people. It would be a war to eliminate food banks, end homelessness. Working people would be asked to invest in improving their own and their children's future. As they saw their money at work across the province, they would gain strength and confidence that all was not lost in Ontario.

Our pleas fell on deaf ears. Instead of the social democratic agenda we championed, the Rae government merely parroted the theology of the right: the Bank of Canada's high interest rate policies seemed reasonable; free trade was inevitable; global competition made sense; cuts to public spending were necessary; lower corporate taxes would result in more jobs. As Walkom wrote: "Other NDP governments had tried to make peace with business. But none had done so with such a combination of enthusiasm and naivety as Rae's." We had elected these guys because they said they had alternatives. Now they were telling us there were none – that the neoconservatives had been right all along.

These economic policies had already thrown hundreds of thousands of Ontarians out of work. They cut dramatically into provincial tax revenue while simultaneously creating an explosion in demand for welfare and other social services. The times called for radical solutions, not old bromides. But Rae and his colleagues took the easy way out and never addressed the underlying factors that had caused the crisis. Power went to their heads. They thought they knew what they were doing, and they tried to redefine social democracy in the image of their actions. They began to see themselves as "technocrats" – problem solvers, fixers, manipulators – occupying a high ground we did not understand, coming up with "a better idea" of how to govern the province.

BECAUSE OF OUR UNION'S TRADITIONAL TIES to the New Democratic Party, the CAW was slow to react. We kept hoping the government would recognize the dead-end street it was taking us down. The government, in turn, kept thinking that we would fall in line.

By mimicking the Bay Street mantra about the need to appear "reasonable" and "responsible" in performing its fiscal duties, the Rae government bought into the anti-union ideology of the right. It helped strengthen the anti-union business coalition that was building in the province. Rae said his government's strategy looked for "compromises" with labour. We saw it as an open attack on everything we had fought for over the years. What was fundamental to the future strength of the labour movement, the NDP government saw as a broad area for compromise and concessions.

Rae was intent on selling public sector wage cuts. He kept repeating that notion until it was impossible to distinguish the NDP's economic thinking from that of Brian Mulroney. The NDP kept delivering the message, "We are all in this together." Yet this collaboration was patently untrue, for the government never asked corporations or their CEOs to cut back to the same degree. It was working people who were pressed to contribute to the right-wing cause.

The Rae cabinet aligned itself with corporate Canada's agenda as the only way to deal with economic crisis. I remember a dinner meeting with Labour Minister Bob Mackenzie at the Senator Restaurant in Toronto. Bob was a veteran unionist with the Steelworkers, and our CAW group was trying to convince him not to impose a legislated wage cut on public service workers. I argued it would destroy the party. Better to deal with the deficit by increasing revenue through more equitable taxation. Mackenzie told us he had bought into Mulroney's deficit-debt argument. "I never believed in anything Mulroney did," he explained, "but I sympathize with him now, given that we face the same problem with a deficit in Ontario."

I could not believe what I was hearing. Mackenzie ignored the fact that Mulroney was primarily to blame for the debts that both the federal government and the Rae government were saddled with. It was the Mulroney government that had turned in the highest deficits in the nation's history and created the massive debt load Canadians had to carry. The Mulroney government had cut corporate taxes and income taxes for the wealthy, driven unemployment into double figures, and given us free trade with the Americans that cost Ontario close to 500,000 jobs – and Mackenzie sympathized with him! I left that meeting disillusioned. "These guys are in self-destruct mode," I muttered to my colleagues.

The Rae government did not have a competing philosophy to challenge the economic logic of business. It certainly did not pursue the one most social democrats were following, nor did it appear to have a theory of government. Rae accepted the notion that all classes have common interests – though, of course, they don't. He hoped to broker accommodations between business and labour, and liked to call these accommodations "partnerships." He was quoted as saying that, in his effort to be fair, he represented the interests of bank presidents as well as working people. Banks do not need anyone representing their interests. They already have power and wealth. They do not need more friends in government, except to expand that power and wealth.

A COUPLE OF MONTHS after bowing to the auto insurance industry, the Rae government shifted its pro-business stance into second gear by easing the pension responsibilities of large corporations. General Motors – one of the world's biggest and richest manufacturing companies – had, for two years, been in contravention of a provincial pension law that required companies to pre-fund their pension contributions. The law was meant to ensure the solvency of the pension plan should the employer go out of business or leave the province. General Motors had refused to put up more than $500 million required under the Pension Benefits Guarantee Fund.

Negotiations between GM and the Rae government had gone on for months. GM wanted the law changed so it could fund its pension liability on an operating basis. It could then take that half-billion dollars and invest it to make more money. GM Canada president George Peapples lobbied Rae on the issue. Late in December 1991 I was in a meeting with Peapples in Bob White's boardroom, when White was still president of the CAW. At one point Bob's secretary, Helen Kramzyk, came in and said: "Excuse me, Bob, but the premier's on the phone." White rose from his chair to take the call, but Helen interrupted: "No, it's not you he wants. He wants to talk to Mr. Peapples." The GM president took the call in the outer office and returned with a big smile. "There is some good news today," he said. "The premier just notified me that his government is going to amend the Pension Benefit Act and we will not have to meet the solvency funding requirement."

GM was getting permission to use that half billion without anything else being bargained in return. In effect, GM got a freebie. We knew what hard negotiators GM management were, but they could be bargained with. Instead, GM got exactly what it asked for without having to make a single concession.

The incident reveals two things. First, it showed the poor state of communications between the Premier's Office and a large segment of the labour movement in Ontario. One would think that with so much at stake, someone in the Premier's Office might pick up the phone to call Bob White and get his advice or to at least inform him of their decision on an issue of no small importance to our union.

Second, when it came to dealing with large corporations, this government was clearly out of its depth. The CAW bargained with GM every three years. We knew their strengths and their weaknesses. We could have told the government that there were serious rumours, which turned out to be true, that GM intended to close a couple of plants in Ontario. With that information, and knowing how much GM wanted to get its hands on that pension money, we could have, together, bargained for a new investment commitment from GM and hopefully saved the province a lot of jobs.

The Rae government desperately wanted the endorsement of the corporate community. It wanted business to see that here was a government that could finally deal with unions – that could get them to join in partnerships with business. No Tory or Liberal government could ever do that. "Business needs the New Democrats" was the message, but it clearly missed its mark.

In 1992 GM decided to close its foundry in St. Catharines and to close or sell off its axle plant there. Roughly 2,200 jobs were at stake in the foundry, another 700 in the axle plant. While the CAW was bargaining with GM over the closures, Tim Armstrong, the deputy minister of industry, asked me where the CAW would stand if a management group took over operation of the foundry. If these investors could swing a deal, they might save 800 of the jobs. But they demanded major wage and benefit concessions, on the order of 30 to 35 percent, before they would take over the plant.

"No way," I replied. "We're not going to agree to anything like that. These plants are part of GM and come under our master agreement. If we agree to open up the contract in St. Catharines, GM will tell us every other plant in the company deserves the same concessions. We're not buying into this. It makes no sense." Armstrong was not surprised at my stance. He was one of the more knowledgeable people in the government bureaucracy and a friend. I knew he was fishing around on behalf of his ministry and the Premier's Office.

A couple of weeks later I was attending CLC meetings in Ottawa when I got a call from Rae. He wanted me to attend a meeting in his office later that afternoon. He said he had some new ideas that could possibly save the St. Catharines foundry. He would not go further than that. I headed for his office along with Jim O'Neil, our national secretary-treasurer, who was also responsible for our dealings with GM. We could smell a rat the minute we walked in the door. The room was crowded, but among the faces we recognized the minister of industry, the minister of labour, a team of bureaucrats, and a collection of GM executives, including Peapples.

Rae opened the meeting. He said the GM managers were willing to run the foundry as a new company so long as a few key allowances were made. First, the NDP government would need to put up some financial help, which he said he would do. Second, GM would have to hand over the plant and equipment to the new company for a dollar. It would also

have to guarantee at least three years of orders, which would give
"Newco," as the company was called, time to get competitive. Finally,
the union would have to agree to wage and benefit cuts amounting to
30 percent.

I could not believe the insensitivity of the premier. In effect, he was
attempting to orchestrate a major setback for our union and our members, not just in St. Catharines but across the province's auto industry.
He turned to Peapples and asked, "George, what about it?"

Peapples said he was not in the least offended by his managers trying to make a go of the St. Catharines plant. He appreciated the effort
the premier was making to see if 800 jobs could be saved. But there was
no business plan, as far as GM could see, that held any interest for the
company. "There's no saving to us to pay for auto parts from the
Newco plant," he said, "because our foundries in the United States are
presently running at sixty to sixty-five percent capacity. We'll get our
parts by increasing productivity at the U.S. plants. That way we won't
have to hire one worker or spend one dollar. We don't need the parts
that would be produced at Newco."

"Well, I can tell you, George," Rae snapped, "if you close the plant,
you'd better not rely on the province to pick up the tab for environmental
clean-up. Don't come to us to clean up the mess you leave behind." It
was not much of a retort, but Rae had little room to move.

"GM hasn't asked for any help on environmental clean-up, Mr.
Premier. We know what our obligations are. We're not asking for government help."

Rae turned to me. "Buzz, what have you got to say?"

"Well, I'm with George Peapples up to a point," I said. "I don't see
any business plan here on the table. How can these managers have the
gall to come in, cap in hand, asking for millions in taxpayer support and
employee concessions, and not put a detailed business plan on the
table?" I was getting angrier by the minute.

"There are always people out there who'll come in at the eleventh
hour with an idea to save a company – so long as labour makes life comfortable for them and fills their pockets. And you, George, you and your
company have made a lot of money out of your St. Catharines operations.

You made a lot of money off this province, off our workers, off this community. You should be ordered by the province to keep the plant open. You have an obligation to St. Catharines here, not just an obligation to GM's bottom line. There are people's lives at stake here, damn it."

I turned to Rae: "How can you sit there and think this discussion might lead to any suitable agreement? George is the guy you should be talking to about keeping the plant open. I'm not getting involved in any silly hypothetical discussion about a thirty percent cut in wages and 'donations' to our 'entrepreneurs' sitting over there. George is right. There's no business plan here. GM's not buying in. Don't waste my time trying to talk about what the CAW might be prepared to do."

Rae didn't bite. He just sat there. Towards the end of the meeting, he turned to Peapples and said, "Well, George?"

Peapples replied, "Well, Mr. Premier, General Motors has made its decision."

Rae, along with most corporate executives, was convinced that the union would agree to the logic of wage cuts as a way to save companies. He did a similar thing during negotiations over the possible closing of de Havilland Aircraft in Downsview. As early as 1990, Boeing of Canada announced it would bail out of its ownership of de Havilland. The company was either up for sale or due for closure. If it closed, roughly 2,000 high-technology jobs would disappear. A French-led European consortium – Aérospatiale – was first in line to buy, but it was de Havilland's competitor. Anyone could see that the consortium's intention was to buy de Havilland, run it for a while, then close it down.

We were able to convince Rae to help keep de Havilland out of Aérospatiale's clutches, though initially he was sceptical about a government-supported bailout. It was early in his administration and it would have looked bad if the NDP had ignored an opportunity to save thousands of high-value-added jobs. Rae brought in Laurent Beaudoin, chairman of Bombardier, and Raymond Royer, the company's president, to be the operating partners. Sure as hell, one of the first items on the government's agenda was the possibility of wage cuts.

Early in January 1992 I got a call from one of the deputy ministers telling me the rescue package for de Havilland would have to include pay cuts of about $2.50 an hour. I said, "Not on your life! You tell Rae, or whoever is pushing this, he'll have a public relations war on his hands. This deal has nothing to do with wages. Labour costs at de Havilland are in line with industry norms.

"Yes, there's a slowdown in the STOL market, but that will change. When it does, de Havilland has the best product in the DASH 7s and, if we do the right thing here, we'll soon have the DASH 8 as well. We have the skilled workers. All we need is for the market to improve and some new technology to make the plant more efficient. No one's going to get a penny of the workers' wages. You try and there'll be out-and-out warfare."

Although we emphatically rejected wage cuts, we were prepared to propose a one-year extension of our collective agreement – but with our annual cost-of-living protection in place. Both Ottawa and the NDP government were now prepared to come on board. Ontario became a minority shareholder, at 49 percent, and Ottawa joined the Rae government, putting up $250 million for research and development.

The next day, January 22, 1992, the government announced the new ownership consortium for de Havilland. There was no mention of wage cuts or concessions. More important, this episode showed again that chopping workers' wages has nothing to do with making a company "competitive." By 1996 de Havilland was one of the strongest and most competitive STOL manufacturers in the world. Employment at the plant was up to more than 4,000. The DASH 8-400, which seats seventy-seven passengers, is one of the hottest aircraft on the market. Employee wages went up, not down. The company was making money, and Ontario got its investment back.

WAS BOB RAE a New Democrat? He carried an NDP membership card, but I don't think he saw himself as a true social democrat. He writes in his book *From Protest to Power* about being intrigued by the Trudeau-era Liberals. Rae worked for Trudeau at the 1968 Liberal leadership convention. He also worked as a canvass organizer on Liberal Charles Caccia's successful run for a parliamentary seat in Toronto's Davenport riding the same year.

Rae's political stripes have been questioned before. In his early days he seemed to be, as Walkom describes him, a "Liberal with doubts." Later he came across as a "sceptical social democrat." As a young articling law student with the Steelworkers Union, Rae claimed he "was aware of the shallowness of his NDP roots." Many of us knew when he ran for the party leadership that he was a questionable choice. But we thought the strong labour movement in Ontario, and its presumed influence on the party, would keep things under control. We felt we could put pressure on him to keep eyes left, if you will.

I'd joined with Bob White in encouraging Rae to leave federal politics and run for the leadership of the provincial party. We felt the only way the party could ever become a serious national force was to win in Ontario and work from there. Rae was a bright young politician. We needed that kind of leadership image and we needed a win in Ontario. Rae looked like the guy to do it. I don't think anyone guessed he'd try to make the NDP the darling of the business community, jettisoning traditional NDP economic thinking and plugging into the same train of thought as the Mulroney government and the Bank of Canada.

In January 1993, at the Howard Johnson Hotel in Toronto, the CLC executive council met with the national NDP leader, Audrey McLaughlin, and the three NDP premiers at the time – Rae, Mike Harcourt from British Columbia, and Roy Romanow from Saskatchewan. In Rae's account, labour got together to gang up on the politicians. That was not our motivation in calling the meeting. People were frustrated with the lack of communication between NDP governments and labour. Harcourt and Ken Georgetti, president of the B.C. Federation of Labour, had a close working relationship. There was no problem there. But there were problems in Saskatchewan. Romanow had decided to fight the debt he inherited from the corrupt Conservative government of Grant Devine by making sizeable cuts in social services and by laying off public service workers. Labour had asked Romanow to look at alternatives to slash-and-burn fiscal tactics, but felt its case was not being heard.

By the fall of 1992 in Ontario, the NDP's deputy premier and finance minister, Floyd Laughren, shocked voters with the announcement that, although the provincial deficit was sitting at about $10 billion, it could go as high as $17 billion in the months to come. Despite this looming crisis, no one was asking labour's advice – certainly not in Ontario or Saskatchewan. We wanted to talk about alternatives to wage rollbacks and cuts to social programs. So Bob White, as head of the CLC, requested a meeting. It would be an opportunity to talk about the concerns of the labour movement and to see if we could open up lines of communication.

Rae let it be known he did not want to be there. He showed little respect for other ideas and generally conducted himself with an air of indifference. Much of the time he turned his chair around and sat with his back partially to the table. At one point, as I was making my way to the washroom, I had to pass by Gord Wilson, head of the Ontario Federation of Labour, who was seated close to Rae. We both heard Rae mutter that this was "the dumbest f—g meeting" he had ever attended.

Romanow, in contrast, who was initially sceptical about the meeting, made a convincing case for the way his government was fighting its debt and deficit problems. Although I have never accepted the argument that a province should sacrifice its social safety net because of debt, Romanow made a strong case that Saskatchewan had a far greater fiscal problem than either British Columbia or Ontario. Despite this burden, he never got into union-bashing or talks about forcing workers to accept wage cuts.

Rae seemed unable to understand that it did not always have to be the workers who had to accept less. He wrote in his book that "collective bargaining had shown its strength in dealing with the world of more; the issue was, for both the private and the public sectors, how well could collective bargaining respond to a world of less." He missed the point that while we grew as a society, the power of capital grew in step. So why shouldn't capital – investors, financiers, and shareholders – have to deal with receiving less during times of economic trouble? Why should capital get to hold on to its relatively steady growth while working people inevitably had to accept less?

This rigid kind of thinking was at the heart of a heated argument during the meeting at the hotel. According to Rae, Bob White asked why Ontario could not "do like the Reichmanns and declare bankruptcy, maybe pay fifty or sixty cents on the dollar." The response from

Romanow, according to Rae, was that no "self-respecting social demo-crat would ever take that attitude." Romanow and Rae, one assumes, were in the camp that says we have to accept what the banks and for-eign investors tell us and pay our bills on time, or the Gnomes of Zurich will not love us any more.

Rae's quote of White's question was fairly accurate: "Why the hell should working people see all their benefits and everything we've been fighting for all these years go down the drain because you guys bought into all this neoconservative economics? You're elected to fight for our people, not to stick your nose up Mulroney's ass." But White was not suggesting that bankruptcy was a reasonable option. He was posing a question for debate. Companies and corporations declare bankruptcy all the time. They refuse to pay their bills and end up with their personal fortunes intact. If they come back a year or two later with another busi-ness plan, the financial community has no trouble shovelling more cash into their pockets to help them make a go of it again. Why did govern-ment have to attend to its debt obligations while business did not?

If there is sacrifice to be made, White asked, why should it not include bankers and bondholders, the people who profit most from the system? Could we not come up with a concept that induced bankers and bondholders to share in the downside? Whatever happened to taxing wealth? Rae depicted this approach as White urging the province to declare bankruptcy. That was not the way it happened.

The meeting in Toronto of the NDP "family" did nothing for the labour movement except widen the divide between us and our NDP col-leagues. Rae remained fixed on trying to solve his government's debt woes on the backs of workers. Neoconservative solutions were still front and centre. But we were making headway in one area. There was so much confusion about what to do next in Ontario that parts of the labour movement soon found themselves with more invitations to engage in dialogue with the Rae government than they once thought possible.

In mid-February 1993 Rae called a meeting of his top cabinet mem-bers and various labour leaders, including me. At the meeting, Judy Darcy, national president of the Canadian Union of Public Employees, brought up the idea of a modest "social contract" that would allow for wage restraints in exchange for real job protection for public service workers. Her idea was apparently modelled on what the Harcourt government had put in place with hospital workers in British Columbia.

On March 11 we met again with Rae, Floyd Laughren, and other cabinet ministers at the Park Plaza Hotel in Toronto. They again sought to impress us with the severity of the province's economic problems. Ontario was in real trouble, according to Rae. We were about to hit that infamous "debt wall," where no matter what we did we could not pay down the debt unless we took drastic action, such as sweeping cuts to services and public sector wages. To reinforce his point, Rae trotted out a video done for CTV's *w5* by Eric Malling. The segment was about New Zealand and what had happened when that country hit its debt wall.

Malling's report had aired in February. It was shoddy television journalism, full of flaws and inaccurate conclusions, but it had a huge impact. Malling made it sound as if New Zealand had narrowly escaped going broke and that Canada could well be next. New Zealand had saved itself by privatizing public services, slashing social spending, cutting salaries, and opening up the country to a full-scale market economy. What Malling neglected to report was that under this neoconservative onslaught, unemployment rose from 4 percent in 1984 to 12 percent, poverty and homelessness increased overnight, and suicide rates jumped to the highest levels in the world. And here was the NDP premier of Ontario, presumably a social democrat, trying to peddle Malling's right-wing economic propaganda.

"I don't want to watch your damn videotape," I burst out. "I've talked to people in the New Zealand labour movement, and our economists have studied the situation closely. I think we know something about what's going on there. Eric Malling sure as hell does not." I was furious, Rae was furious, but there was no way I was going to sit through that video. Members of the NDP cabinet had no doubt already viewed it and had their ideas confirmed about which economic path to follow.

RAE'S PLEA FOR HELP in dealing with the deficit played nicely on divisions within the province's labour movement. Many members of private sector unions thought public sector unions led cosy, sheltered lives. Public service workers were seen by some private sector leaders as fat cats who had been able to avoid major layoffs and wage concessions already forced on private sector unions. At the time, there was also rivalry between the CAW and the other major private sector unions in the Ontario Federation of Labour. We competed for members, but we also had different philosophies about collective bargaining and political action. The other unions saw merit in partnerships and worker-owner-ship plans. We did not.

In making his case at our February meeting, arguing that we all had to sacrifice, Rae pointed at me and said, for the benefit of Judy Darcy and Sid Ryan of the Canadian Union of Public Employees: "Buzz Hargrove over there, his people are paying the penalty. His people have lost their jobs through workplace closures." Then he gestured at Leo Gerard of the Steelworkers and said: "There are people in the Steelworkers Union losing jobs and being forced to take pay cuts. Everybody in the private sector is feeling the pinch. The public sector cannot sit and ignore reality."

He was right in one sense. Workplace closures were indeed going on. Some workers were taking pay cuts. But to a large extent these were normal adjustments during recessionary points in the economic cycle. To me, there was no logic to the argument that because the private sector might be facing cutbacks and layoffs, the public sector had to as well. Yet Rae and his people kept trying to make that argument. You could see the divide-and-seduce strategy play itself out. The more we talked, the wider the divisions became.

I remember a discussion with Ruth Grier, minister of the environment, and Harry Hynd, Ontario director of the Steelworkers, who was also arguing that it was time for public sector workers to share some of the economic pain. I pointed to the closure of the GM truck plant in Scarborough. As many as 3,000 CAW members might be out of work. "Don't tell me our people are going to feel any better if public sector workers in Scarborough take a pay cut as well, or a bunch of them lose their jobs," I said. "That just makes the economic problem worse, not better. Purchasing power in a community like Scarborough would fall further."

A social contract based on public-sector wage concessions was a risky proposition. We did not agree with it. But if the government had as serious a fiscal problem as it thought, and it wanted the public service unions to cut it some slack, then we recommended that the two parties sit down at the bargaining table. We opposed any unilateral action by government that would tear up the rights that unions had fought for over the decades.

In early June I was in my car on my way to Port Elgin when the premier called. He wanted to bring me up to date on discussions with public sector unions on the Social Contract. There were a few snags, he said, but he was confident they'd get a settlement before the deadline. "I wanted to give you a head's-up," he said. Good, I thought. They're bargaining, and that will mean no arbitrary wage cuts. I had also read in the morning paper that Laughren had made a promise to attack the unemployment problem in the province. Things seemed to be looking up.

"If you can find a way to bargain a settlement with the public sector workers, great," I said. "We don't care what's in it, so long as it's bargained. That'll allow the public sector leaders to go back to their members and say: 'Look, we bargained hard with the Rae government, and we're recommending this settlement because it's in your best interests.' Then you let the members vote on it and ratify it. That's a system we in the CAW can always live with."

I told Rae I saw a bargained agreement as a major step forward for his government. "The NDP's in a pile of trouble right now, but it's not too late. There's a sour mood in our plants about the government. If you let bargaining take its course, maybe we can turn this thing around and get people onside again. But if you arbitrarily bring in legislation, you'll destroy our ability to say to our members that the NDP is our party. Do that, and you'll be just another right-wing, anti-union party to them."

The last thing Rae wanted, apparently, was my advice on how to proceed with the Social Contract. The night before he introduced it in the legislature, he called a meeting of the major private-sector union heads to advise them how the NDP would proceed. Everybody who was anybody was there – except Buzz Hargrove. Rae knew that if he stood in front of me and said his government was going to force public sector workers to take a wage rollback, I'd jump all over him. On the other hand, he knew he'd take little criticism from the rest of them. And that's what he got.

On June 3, one day before the government's self-imposed deadline for negotiations, a frustrated group of public-sector labour leaders walked out of the talks with the government, leaving Rae with two options: legislate the Social Contract and trigger a labour backlash, or back down. Later that month, Bob White of the CLC, Gordon Wilson of the OFL, Leo Gerard of the Steelworkers, and I held a press conference to warn that there would be trouble if the NDP overrode existing collective agreements with a legislated settlement.

We were aiming our message at NDP backbench MPPs. We knew public sentiment was not on the side of public sector employees – MPPs were being encouraged to roll back their wages. At this point, most of our NDP government colleagues began jettisoning their principles. The Agenda for People was long forgotten. Many of these MPPs owed their seats to the organizing work done for them by labour, but, like water seeking the path of least resistance, they legislated the wage rollback. They seemed unaware of the damage it would do to the party, to the labour movement, and to their own chances of re-election.

On July 7 the Social Contract legislation – Bill 48 – passed in the legislature with only three New Democrats opposed to it. I have never been so ashamed of being an NDPer as I was when they passed that bill. I knew there was little chance of seeing an NDP government come to power again in Ontario in my lifetime. Bill 48 superseded existing labour acts and stripped public sector unions of their bargaining rights. Wage rollbacks took the form of twelve compulsory unpaid days off for each worker for three years. Appropriately they were branded "Rae Days."

To the CAW, Bill 48 was so odious that we felt we had no recourse but to withdraw our support of the NDP. It was generally accepted in our union that we could not expend our energy and resources to endorse a government that had turned its back on the most basic principles of our movement.

Although the CAW was criticized by the more conservative and compliant unions in Ontario, our council decided to deny all support in the next election to any member of the NDP caucus who voted for Bill 48. Ontario CAW locals would restrict their contributions to the Ontario NDP to the level required for membership. We committed to work with other social movements to mobilize political pressure on any government that tried to take away our rights. We were not about to leave the NDP, but the CAW was not going to pay to have its butt kicked again.

Our decision to refuse financial support to the NDP did not mean we had abandoned the social democratic movement. But our commitment to the party could only have credibility with our members if it was mutual, a commitment that respected the principles working people have fought so long to achieve: the right to organize, the right to collective bargaining, and the right to strike. What the Rae government did was violate the trust of members of the labour movement. It took labour's money and support – without which many of its MPPs would never have been elected – and then slapped a virtual tax on public sector workers.

We learned a valuable lesson. From here on, the CAW will not support NDP candidates unless they declare their personal commitment to protect the rights of unions and workers, preserve social programs, and support programs such as public housing, child care, public education, and care for the less fortunate. Henceforth, the CAW will check the philosophical teeth of every NDP candidate.

Oddly enough, some members of the Rae government saw the Social Contract as a major accomplishment. They finally had a majority of the Ontario population on their side on an issue. They basked in praise from editorial writers for putting labour "in its place." But those instant allies were nowhere to be seen when it counted. Their support was, of course, a mile wide and an inch deep. By the time the 1995 election rolled around, these one-issue converts were as scarce as principles at an Ontario NDP caucus meeting.

Many former NDPers did not wait for 1995 to express their outrage. During the debate over the Social Contract, federal NDP leader Audrey McLaughlin was preparing for the federal election that fall. Union members and political activists who would normally have thrown their support behind the federal NDP were so disgusted by the Social Contract that they refused to work for the federal party. Hundreds tore up their membership cards. Thousands voted for other candidates. The 1993 defeat was the worst ever suffered by the CCF or the NDP in a federal election. NDP seats in the Commons went from forty-three to nine. The NDP received the lowest level of support from the Canadian people since the birth of the CCF in the Dirty Thirties. The NDP lost official party status. All nine NDP members in Ontario lost their seats. Oshawa, once a hot-bed of NDP support and a union stronghold, home of former NDP leader Ed Broadbent, went Liberal for the first time since 1968.

In other provinces, the simple mention of the NDP sent shivers up the spines of NDP supporters and premiers. As Walkom wrote, quoting NDP premier Roy Romanow, "Every time Bob Rae appeared on national television, the NDP's popularity in the west dropped."

By the time the Rae government called an election for June 8, 1995, public support for the Ontario NDP had bottomed out in the mid-teens. Consequently, the NDP had delayed calling the election until almost the last month possible. The NDP's 1995 campaign had to be the most lack-lustre in the history of the party. There were no promises, there was no real platform. Perhaps, as some pundits put it, the NDP did not need a platform because it had no new ideas, no new policies, and no programs. The Ontario NDP was bankrupt. Rae admitted in his book that he knew well before June 8 that the party "didn't have a chance." When, months before the election, he tried to prepare his daughters for the possibility that he would be defeated, one of them replied: "Dad, you're toast. You had better get ready for it."

Rae's "no promises" campaign reconfirmed for many voters that the NDP had nothing more to offer. But with Ontario's political earth scorched and salted by one of the saddest displays of political ineptitude ever seen in Canada, the Harris government had ample room in which to plant the seeds of its so-called Common Sense Revolution.

Some critics, including some in our union, blame the CAW for the defeat of the Rae government. They claim we should have stood behind the NDP, thick or thin. They credit us with the election of Mike Harris. It was the politics of the Rae government that brought it down. The CAW did not tell hundreds of thousands of voters to switch from the

NDP. The NDP did it on their own. Our biggest mistake was that we waited too long before we started pushing from the left. Had we begun to mobilize sooner and demonstrate for more progressive action from the NDP, we might have been able to mitigate the disaster of the 1995 election.

The wounds remain deep enough that the NDP in Ontario will languish in a distant third place in the polls for some time to come. To repair the damage, we must go back to our roots. Some people refer to the NDP as a "federation." Others see it as a clearing house of left and centre-left ideals, still others as an increasingly old-fashioned protest party, dominated too long by the labour movement and working-class ideas. Maybe so, but until 1993 we were a party – federally and provincially – that survived because we knew who the enemy was. After each internecine spat, we found a way of settling our differences. In the end, we knew what we were fighting for. We never lost sight of the collective goals that inspired and encouraged us. We were allies – not necessarily bosom buddies – in a battle for what we knew was right. But after the experience in Ontario between 1990 and 1995, I'm no longer convinced we know who we are, or what the NDP represents.

7

UNCOMMON SENSE

The goal of government should be to improve the life chances of the citizen.
— *German sociologist Ralf Dahrendorf*

There is always a certain meanness in the argument of
conservatism, joined with a certain superiority in its fact.
— *Ralph Waldo Emerson*

I was in my office the Thursday before the Easter weekend in 1998 when my secretary, Rita Lori, came in and said the premier was on the phone.

"Glen Clark?" I asked, wondering what he might have on his mind.

"No," Rita replied. "Mike Harris."

"You've got to be kidding!" He was the last person I expected to hear from. "Hi, Mike, how're you doing?"

"Fine, fine. I was just calling to wish you a Happy Easter."

I almost fainted. He was on his way to his home in North Bay for the weekend, he explained, where he had only one formal engagement scheduled – a pancake breakfast. Other than that, he was going to put his feet up and enjoy a short holiday. "I'll spend some time reading and relaxing," he said, "and maybe go over the details of my new constituency boundaries with my executive assistant."

"If you need any help with that, give us a call," I joked.

He laughed, and we chatted, but I still could not figure out why he was calling. It had been ages since we'd talked. He certainly must have been aware of my frequent attacks on his government's policies. There was no mistaking how much the CAW detested the Tories. I remembered that earlier in the week I'd asked the Ontario industry and trade minister for a meeting with Harris to discuss auto industry and safety matters.

"Are you returning my call from Tuesday?"

"No," he said, "don't know anything about that. I was just getting my office cleaned up before I headed out, and I thought I'd wish you a Happy Easter."

I said my goodbyes, hung up, and wondered what the hell that had been all about. To this day, I still have no idea why he bothered to call. We are not friends by any stretch of the imagination. If the Rae government was a shocking disappointment, the Harris government is an unmitigated disaster – one of the worst things that has ever happened to working people in Ontario. He and I would soon be sharing space on the platform in Bramalea at the Chrysler assembly plant. Perhaps he was calling to remind me what a friendly guy he was, so I wouldn't hammer him too hard. The thought also crossed my mind that he might be trying to open up some avenues of communication before a possible election in 1999. Maybe it was time to patch up old wounds? Well, good luck, Mr. Premier.

I've been asked how, given my strong social democratic feelings, I can be comfortable spending long hours in the same room with reactionary, right-wing politicians like Mike Harris, or sitting across the bargaining table from hard-nosed corporate types who cannot see their employees as anything more than a cost of doing business. Generally speaking, I get along fine with such people. I don't care for their politics, of course, or their indifference to the damage their policies do to working people, but at least I know where they're coming from. That knowledge makes my job a little easier.

I first met Harris when he was elected to lead a rump of third-party Conservatives in Queen's Park. I believe in meeting with all the political leaders, regardless of their stripes, though I was probably the only labour leader in the province who asked for a meeting with him. It was not a friendly get-together. Harris made it clear that he did not support labour, that we were in basic disagreement, but at least we'd opened up a dialogue.

After he'd been elected premier, his office called a dinner meeting that included the Ontario Federation of Labour, various heads of unions, Labour Minister Elizabeth Witmer, Finance Minister Ernie Eves, and other key government people. You only have to read the guest list to sense what the atmosphere was like. The acrimony in the room was so obvious that we could not even agree on who called the meeting. The Ontario Federation of Labour's Gord Wilson insisted it had been the

Premier's Office. Harris shot back: "Oh no, it was your people who called us." We argued most of the evening. It was certainly no "dialogue" between government and labour.

In the fall of 1996, about a year into Harris's term, our union was bargaining with General Motors. The main issues were outsourcing, the sale of plants, and plant closures. GM wanted to outsource (get some of its parts and services from cheaper, non-union suppliers), and we were not about to agree to that. GM also informed the union that it intended to sell two plants. We were prepared to stop that from happening. The CAW had set a pattern at Chrysler that put a halt to outsourcing and we wanted the same from GM. We had also persuaded Chrysler to agree not to close or sell off any plant during the life of the agreement.

Outsourcing was a major issue. Like other auto manufacturers, GM saw it as a way to get around its collective agreements. By allowing the company to buy parts more cheaply from outside suppliers, we would undermine our own members. Many would eventually be laid off as a result.

A lot of people thought we were crazy to make heavy-duty demands at a time when Canada was near the peak of the downsizing craze and workers were on the defensive. Outsourcing was the plan, right across the economy. No large union had ever won in a dispute to stop all outsourcing, which was considered a management decision. But our success at Chrysler gave us heart and we told GM we intended to put a stop to it.

I also felt we could take a page from our wage-and-price battle from the 1970s. In 1996 the Harris government of Ontario was considering changes to health and safety legislation and to overtime legislation. Both issues had been put on the agenda by the lobbying of companies like General Motors and Ford, and would have eroded legislative gains of the past two decades. When the Big Three took the position that we should bargain with those legislative changes in mind, we countered that we would only settle with language that protected our members' right to work in safe conditions and to refuse overtime. What governments chose to do was neither here nor there.

In the early stages of negotiations we made it clear that the CAW had no wish to force GM to close down its U.S. plant operations. We did not want a strike, we wanted a settlement. But we also warned the company not to underestimate our determination to put a stop to outsourcing. From the start, GM negotiated as if it wanted a strike. Management knew a strike would show the world how tough the company could be with its unions (the same scenario that played out in the United States in the summer of 1998) and believed a confrontation would drive up the value of its stock. We were not surprised, then, that GM did not table its first proposal until a couple of hours before the strike deadline.

We went out on strike but kept negotiating. During the Thanksgiving weekend, Dean Munger, GM Canada's vice-president of labour relations, and I sent the bargaining committees home for the holiday while we went at it in the Royal York Hotel in Toronto – cajoling, arguing, yelling, screaming, threatening, laughing – to see if we could make some progress. The fundamental problem was one of communication. It appeared either that Munger was not passing along our message about not wanting to cripple GM or that Jack Smith, GM's chairman in Detroit, believed we were out to destroy the company. At least he said so publicly.

GM had followed pattern bargaining for sixty years. Because we were challenging their right to outsource parts, however, and in spite of the pattern set at Chrysler, they'd been willing to take a strike. I persuaded Munger that I had to meet with Smith: a meeting was set for the following Wednesday. That, we hoped, would be the start of serious negotiations to end the strike.

On the Tuesday, however, we were notified that GM had applied for an injunction to move their manufacturing dies from the Ottawa fabrication plant. We assumed that Smith was sending a tough message before the meeting that if we didn't settle, GM would operate in spite of the strike. Moving the dies could have kept GM in business while our members walked the picket line. The injunction threat upped the ante. An injunction could seriously have undermined the effectiveness of our strike.

"We have to take over GM's Oshawa fabrication plant," I told our bargaining committee.

The next day, while Sam Gindin, Peter Kennedy, and I were meeting with Smith; Munger; Maureen Kempston Darkes, GM Canada's president;

and Gerry Knechtel, the company's chief negotiator, Munger's cell phone rang. "Oh my God," he blurted out, "the workers have stormed the fabrication plant. They've taken it over!"

"I warned you our members would not sit by and allow you to destroy their jobs," I reminded him. "I asked you to withdraw the injunction, but you proceeded. Why the hell should you be surprised?"

Smith said he knew nothing about the injunction; Darkes and Knechtel had made the decision to seek it. To Smith's credit, he set aside the plant occupation and tried to find a solution to the contract impasse. He'd got the message: the CAW wanted a settlement, but we were not about to let GM take its work elsewhere and see our members lose their jobs.

"Buzz, you know we have a problem with Wall Street," Smith said. "They're saying we're not tough enough on unions. It's an optics problem. Wall Street is on our backs because it costs more to build a car at GM than it does at Ford or Chrysler. You have to help me out with this."

Here was the head of one of the world's richest companies telling me he had a problem and needed the CAW's help? "I'm prepared to say publicly that GM is a special case, a different company from Ford and Chrysler," I said. "If you agree to put an end to outsourcing, we're prepared to let you sell those two plants of yours, in exchange for protection for our members' jobs."

It was enough for Smith. GM agreed to introduce provisions in the contract that recognized the pattern set with Chrysler on outsourcing. On that basis, a settlement was ratified by our members. It was a major victory, unprecedented in the history of our relationship with GM. For the first time since the 1930s we had challenged management's right to manage, and won. It came at a time when the labour movement was reeling from government pressure and from incessant demands by corporations for concessions. It showed what you could achieve if you were prepared to fight.

I was a bit leery when, shortly afterwards, I got a call from Mike Harris, congratulating the CAW on reaching the settlement with GM. "As premier of the province," he said, "it's really good to see that people can still sit around the table and find solutions."

"Mr. Premier," I replied, "in case you missed it, our union just had a bitter three-week strike that kind of focused people's minds over at General Motors. It included a lot of the company's people in the United States, where GM plants had to shut down."

"That's probably so, but it was good to see that you could find some middle ground for compromise – that you worked out a solution."

"The CAW's good at that. When we do strike, it's usually because the other side refuses to communicate. Just like your government."

"Is that so."

"The reason there's so much anger and resentment throughout the province," I said, "is because you think you don't have to listen to any opinions but your own. You refuse to accept input."

"Fine, you have your demonstration," he said frostily. He and I would both be in Hamilton on the weekend, he to attend a Conservative convention, me to support the Day of Action protest. We'd be marching right past the centre where the Tories would be holding their meeting. I wondered if this was the real reason for the call – to stroke Hargrove, hoping he might ease up on the public demonstrations. Not bloody likely.

"I know you'll be there," he said, "and you'll have your chance to speak out publicly. I'm going to my convention." End of conversation.

The point of relating these encounters with Harris has to do with a fundamental belief in our union: you can't achieve anything in politics (or in collective bargaining) unless you're talking. Dialogue – good, bad, even confrontational – is the mechanism that provides the opportunity for progress. Even in an acrimonious setting, dialogue puts your position on the table. It forces stubborn people to think. Unless we can encourage dialogue in the political arena, our hopes for social change are flimsy. You have to talk. Talk some more. Keep talking, even to people you might not like.

Politics, like collective bargaining, is about power. Power – the ebb and flow of influences among adversaries – is what allows us to achieve our goals. It allows us to improve our members' lives. Power is not about sharing. I listen to our more conservative colleagues talk about the need for labour to evolve, to be more "modern" and form part of some government-corporate-labour economic trinity – three separate entities intent on sharing and making this country a more equitable place – and I come close to laughing.

These are good, earnest people who honestly believe that labour can advance itself by forming "relationships" with employers and governments. Who knows, some might even believe we can form alliances in future with the Chamber of Commerce. They fail to understand that the main goal of employers – and of governments like Harris's – is to increase the companies' power by diminishing labour's. The first line of defence for labour is to enter into intelligent dialogue, supported by a well-informed membership that's ready to fight, and bargain for gains. The second is to influence political action on labour's behalf. If the labour movement does not start thinking again in those terms – demanding gains for workers while seeking to influence the political environment – we'll be marginalized entirely. The fight to create a more humane Canada is not going to be won by forming "tripartite partnerships."

One morning, when Harris was still in Opposition, I was having breakfast in the Sutton Place Hotel in Toronto. Harris was sitting with some people and, after they finished their discussion, he came over and we started chatting. He said the Conservatives were planning a retreat and wanted to hold it in farm country around Paisley, Ontario. Paisley is not far from the CAW's Family Education Centre in Port Elgin. "There's not much in the way of meeting facilities in that area," he said, "except for your centre. Our people looked at it and say it's a first-class facility. We'd like to rent it."

"Jeez," I said, "I don't know. "We've never rented it to a political party before. It serves as a labour education centre. But let me give it some thought – I'll run it past our people – and I'll get back to you."

I was already thinking: after all the money the CAW had put into the New Democratic Party over the years – with few questions asked – the NDP government never once offered to rent our centre for a government conference. The fact that the NDP had deliberately stayed away from the centre had always ticked me off. The site was built by union labour, paid for by union labour, supported by union labour – yet the party we align ourselves with held its meetings in non-union hotels and convention facilities because, I was told, it did not want to be seen as "too close" to labour. Now, the average taxpayer would not believe the number of meetings the NDP government – like any government – was involved in after it took power in 1990. Any day of the week, you could walk into any of several of those non-union hotels around Toronto and find a meeting of one ministry or another in progress. I suggested to Bob Rae when he was premier that the centre was a perfect place for a strategy meeting between his cabinet and the labour movement. He said he thought it was a great idea, but I never heard from him again on the matter. Yet here was Harris eager to pay a good dollar to use what he thought were first-class facilities.

When I went to our national executive board and recommended that we rent the centre to Harris and his friends, you should have seen the horrified looks! Everybody said I was nuts. What kind of game was I playing? "Why wouldn't we rent it to the Tories?" I asked. We sure as hell were not going to make trade unionists out of them, but where was the problem? One or two of them might even read some of our brochures. They might gain a better idea of what motivates us. I also pointed out that renting our centre to the Tories would make it tough for the Ontario NDP to refuse to make use of it. The publicity would make these empowered "socialists" think twice before they spent another night in a tony, non-union hotel. Opposition to the idea was intense, though, and I phoned Harris to say we could not comply. Still, I would have loved to see the photograph on the front page of the *Toronto Star* – Mike Harris checking in to the Trade Union Hotel.

IN MY VIEW, Harris is the most dangerous politician elected to public office in Canada in a long time. During the 1995 provincial election campaign, he promised that his government would put a check on labour's power. Bill 7, introduced almost immediately after the Tories entered Queen's Park, sent a clear message about what they were capable of doing. It stripped away decades of hard-won labour rights. There was no hesitation on the government's part, no dialogue with labour. Unlike the Rae government's periodic efforts to seek broad consultation, the Harris government simply did not care what labour thought. Under the guise of the so-called Common Sense Revolution, the Harris government followed the same path with a variety of legislative initiatives. Not until it discovered in late 1997 that more than two-thirds of the Ontario electorate thought the government had gone too far, too fast, and was doing too much damage to the fabric of Ontario society, did the Tories begin cooling their neoconservative jets.

Bill 7 was Harris's "get even" legislation, dismantling the NDP's Bill 40. It was introduced with the false statement that the NDP's labour legislation had "tipped the balance" in labour-management relations towards the unions. If Bill 40 had truly tipped the balance in labour's favour, why during the 1990–95 period – while the NDP was in power – were unions unable to bargain increases high enough to keep up with inflation? Public-sector union members were forced to take wage rollbacks, and several unions declared it a victory if they were able to hold on to past bargaining gains. Thousands of workers lost their jobs, health care benefits, and severance pay, and many had to go to court to have their rights and benefits protected.

Harris's people claimed that Bill 40 had been a "job killer," that it had a negative impact on investment and the province's economy. In fact, in the two years following the introduction of Bill 40, investment in Ontario was up 18 percent and growth was up 5.5 percent – the highest of any jurisdiction in the Group of Seven countries. Profits, executive salaries, bonuses, pensions, and perks for corporate managers rose to an all-time high. To say that Bill 40 killed jobs and retarded investment was simply dishonest.

On the labour front, Bill 7 meant that anti-scab legislation was gone. The right to join a union has been severely watered down. The Workplace Health and Safety Agency has been dismantled. Employment standards have been relaxed. The minimum wage has been frozen at a 1995 level. Workers' compensation has been cut and qualification made more difficult.

At the time Bill 7 was introduced, labour wasn't the only group to show concern. More than sixty major corporations, which respected collective bargaining and knew that legislative changes should not be imposed on the workplace parties without input from them, signed joint letters with our union asking for consultation with the premier before any changes were made to the legislation. He refused to meet.

The Common Sense Revolution is not common, in terms of what most Canadians consider the proper way for people to treat one another, nor does its policy agenda make sense, if fairness and decency are two of the tests. The Harris government acts as if democracy is a small strategic hurdle to be overcome on their way to implementing the right-wing revolution. These people are not "doing" politics; they are doing ideology – stripping away the rights of individual Ontarians under the pretence of "doing what the people of Ontario want."

If the Rae government was an example of the forfeiture of power, the Harris government is a clear example of power's abuse. Harris and his people do not care about principles, ethics, public debate, access to government by the citizen – about the integrity of democracy. They're only intent on furthering an ideological agenda. If there is public resistance, if people demonstrate, Harris shrugs and says he's not impressed by pickets. He does not stop to think that there might be a problem here, that a group of citizens – entitled by law to be heard – could use some dialogue, some access to and response from their government.

If something the Ontario government is contemplating proves too controversial, the ministers back off until things cool down. They move on to something else. They know that if they keep their agenda busy enough, people will tire of trying to keep up with the changes being introduced and the turmoil that surrounds them. If people were mad about what Harris did yesterday, he shifts gears and gives them something else to get mad about tomorrow, distracting them from the original grievance. The idea is to wear down the electorate, neutralize dissent, while moving ahead with the "revolution."

This is a dangerous strategy in a democracy: refuse to listen, refuse to discuss alternative points of view, refuse to take other opinions into account in formulating policy. It's dangerous because in any democracy people must have the right to talk to, and influence, their government and its direction. When that access is blocked, they turn to the only reasonable alternative they have to manifest their power – demonstrations in the streets.

The Harris government is a government of bullies. They pick on the poor and the less fortunate. Many of their policies have hurt, not helped, vast numbers of people – especially those who do not share their beliefs. In its April 1998 Speech from the Throne, the government, feigning penitence for its insensitive legislative record, only underscored that record by promising to get tough on criminals, unions, and people on welfare. The media referred to this continuation of the Conservatives' vindictive legislative program as a "change of pace." The irony was delicious. The implication was that by attacking the poor and the unions, the government was somehow moving onto a higher, more socially sensitive plan of action.

That promise of a kinder, gentler Harris government was bracketed, in March 1997, by the confirmation it was moving ahead on Bill 160, education legislation that would cost as many as 10,000 teachers their jobs, and the announcement of Harris's reversal of his government's treatment of the three surviving Dionne quintuplets. Originally, Harris had claimed that his government had no legal responsibility to provide financial support to the Dionne sisters, even though, over the years, the quintuplets had contributed more than half a billion dollars to the Ontario economy. Despite the fact that the Dionnes were in desperate financial circumstances – living on a combined income of $746 a month – Harris initially gave them a take-it-or-leave-it offer of $2,000 a month. With typical indifference, he said the government would send the cheques to the sisters whether they wanted them or not. A public outcry forced him to fly to Montreal to apologize to the Dionnes and offer them $4 million as a new settlement. The media made much of his contrition, but it was less a gesture of repentance, of course, than the realization that his support was falling in the polls and he had better do something to make himself look good.

In April 1997, Harris announced that his government was prepared to cut supplementary payments of $37 a month to pregnant women on welfare so the money would not "go to beer." The money was meant to help expectant mothers buy fresh fruit, vegetables, and dairy products, food that was often too expensive for them to afford. Harris was playing to his right-wing constituency: those dishonest, slovenly women were simply using taxpayers' money to buy booze. In fact, as welfare organizers pointed out in disgust, few expectant mothers had ever been known to use their small allowance on beer. Again Harris apologized – sort of – and the media made much of his contrition.

Like many reactionaries, Harris shoots from the lip. His choice of targets and his spiteful tone make you wonder whether we're dealing with latent misogyny. After all, who is more susceptible, less able to fight back than a pregnant woman, without a job, and with no other means of support? How much more vulnerable can you get than having to rely on $37 as the difference between subsistence and desperation? Would the $2,000-a-month take-it-or-leave-it offer have been put on the table if the Dionne sisters had been men? Is it accidental that the majority of people affected most seriously by the Tories' massive cuts to social spending, welfare, and care for the elderly are women?

Of course, that Speech from the Throne was meant to show that the government had been listening and was prepared to ease up in its legislative nastiness. Ease up? That speech actually revealed that the government was still prepared to beat the hell out of the less fortunate with an agenda that would expand "workfare" for welfare recipients. Harris would rather send young offenders to boot camps than address the social problems, including a shortage of jobs, that cause some young people to turn to crime.

The one thing the Harris government does understand is confrontation. If not for the street politics initiated by the labour movement and our social coalition partners, Harris would, I suspect, be governing by personal fiat. The labour-supported Days of Action were loud reminders for Harris and his caucus that hundreds of thousands of Ontarians will fight him every step of the way.

Within months of coming to power, the Tories also introduced their Omnibus Bill 26, which gave the premier and the cabinet the power to close hospitals, deregulate drug prices, merge municipalities over the wishes of the citizens living in them, impose drug user fees, chop public service workers' pensions, make confidential medical records public, and control public-sector arbitration awards. All this was rammed through a legislature that had sat for only thirty days. Again, there was no consultation, and little public input.

Next on the Tories' agenda was another round of union-bashing. On June 3, 1997, Labour Minister Elizabeth Witmer introduced Bill 136, a sweeping piece of legislation that suspended the right to strike for roughly 400,000 municipal, health care, and school board employees. The Public Sector Transition Stability Act – Orwell might have come up with the name – was the Harris government's effort to "restructure" the public service. In fact, the act went further than that. It allowed the government to strip away contract rights from its employees so jobs could be contracted out and the work "privatized" or eliminated. Public sector unions were vocal in their protest; they saw the legislation, quite rightly, as a powerful blueprint to dismantle collective agreements, eliminate job security, and remove the right to strike. Witmer denied it would take away the right to strike for public sector workers. She also denied that the act would allow employers, with the help of government-chosen arbitrators, to gut collective agreements. Again, not true.

Led by the Canadian Union of Public Employees, and supported by other public and private sector unions, including ours, the call went out for a general strike. The Ontario Federation of Labour held its first emergency convention in its thirty-year history to debate the issue. It was a major breakthrough for the Ontario labour movement. Government employees had, for the first time, won the support of major private sector unions. I spoke at the convention and offered the full support of the CAW, including help to mobilize a province-wide shutdown if necessary. Bob White was there as the head of the Canadian Labour Congress. He pointed out how unusual this atmosphere of brotherhood and sisterhood really was. This was not just a public sector dispute, he said, but a "fight for the whole labour movement."

If any good for the labour movement has come out of the Harris regime, if there was one moment when we began to heal wounds inflicted by the Rae government's Social Contract and exacerbated by the Tories' legislation, it happened that July day in downtown Toronto. The memory of the Social Contract was still a bitter one for many of us, and deep feelings divide members of the province's labour movement to this day. But some of those divisions began to disappear when we recognized how much more pernicious and implacable an enemy we faced in Harris.

That fall, in rural townships across the province, nervous Tories listened as their constituents raged against the government's damaging incursions into health care, education, welfare, and municipal politics. Many voters were appalled at the government's assault on hospital services and care centres – an attack on the ill and the helpless. Things were so bad that sick people were avoiding going to hospital. Even hospital administrators were on the government's case, weary of working short-staffed and without adequate nursing care. In little more than two years in office, the Harris Tories had antagonized an amazing cross-section of voters. An Angus Reid poll taken in late August 1997 revealed that Tory support had dropped to 35 percent of the electorate. The Liberals were in front with 42 percent, and the NDP came in at 16 percent.

The polls made the government pause, but there's no doubt the key element in slowing the Harris juggernaut was the willingness of members in the labour movement, along with our coalition partners, to fight back with the Days of Action. These street protests had begun in late 1995 with a demonstration in London, Ontario. We followed with a Day of Action in Hamilton in February 1996 where, to our delight, more than 100,000 people turned out. Then came a massive demonstration in the Cambridge-Kitchener-Waterloo area, followed by one of the largest demonstrations in the history of Peterborough. We hit Toronto on October 25 and 26.

The Toronto protest was one of the most successful political demonstrations in the history of this country. On Friday, October 25, 1996, more than one million workers stayed off the job, a number that exceeded the National Day of Protest over wage controls two decades earlier. Downtown Toronto looked like a ghost town. The only people around were picketers, cops, and the media. The next day more than 200,000 people from all walks of life, and all areas of the province, joined in a massive show of solidarity with underprivileged members of society.

The Days of Action helped rekindle labour solidarity. And they showed something that the CAW learned long ago: polite pleas for conciliation and fairness are useless. What employers and governments understand is public protest and pressure. It draws the attention of the media, a necessary ingredient in getting your message out. And it shows that the less privileged recognize the power they hold in a democracy and are prepared to exercise it.

During the confrontations and threats of early September 1997 – including a call for a general strike that would involve more than 600,000 public sector workers and teachers – the Harris government commissioned another Angus Reid poll. The pollsters discovered that more Ontarians were siding with the unions than with the government. A majority believed the unions were being more reasonable than the government and that all the government wanted to do was break the unions. A majority also felt that the new law rigged the arbitration system, making it unfair to workers. The poll helped force the Harris government to back down on Bill 136. It was a major victory for the public sector unions and the labour movement as a whole.

The sudden Tory change of direction on Bill 136 did not alter our plans for continued public protest. On October 18, 1997, thousands of demonstrators in Windsor filled the streets in a display of solidarity. The Windsor Day of Action was the ninth in our series and involved more than 40,000 demonstrators. It shut down more than 200 businesses and cost the city $100 million in lost production. The protest shut the Chrysler van plant (at a production loss estimated at $32 million), five Ford engine and casting works, and the General Motors transmission factory, which together employ about 12,000 workers. The day ended with 15,000 irate marchers making their way to Windsor's downtown section for a rally.

Just two years earlier, fresh from the betrayal of the Rae government and confronted with a newly elected, extremely aggressive Conservative government, the labour movement in Ontario had been nervous, adrift, and demoralized. After eleven Days of Action – the final two were staged in St. Catharines and Peterborough – it was the Harris Tories who appeared dazed and confused. Those protests, I believe, helped change the political climate in the province. When the premier talked of the "inconvenience" of protests and the Chamber of Commerce began lecturing labour about "threats to democracy," we knew we were having an impact. The Days of Action represent one of the most impressive displays of democracy in Ontario history – citizens making their voices heard, refusing to wait to cast a ballot against the government.

Even then, Harris did not get it. He claimed that this widespread example of civil unrest was being orchestrated by the well-paid members of the Canadian Auto Workers union. What Harris failed to see was that these protests were not about union wages or benefits. They were about communities. Many people from many disaffected groups, along with the labour movement, were saying: we fear the damage you Tories are inflicting on our communities. It must stop.

The Tory government in Ontario has a particularly nasty way of playing with the truth. Harris claimed that Bill 160 – the misleadingly named Education Quality Improvement Act – had nothing to do with cost-cutting and everything to do with "improving the quality of education" in Ontario. During the fierce battle with Ontario teachers, he grudgingly admitted that Bill 160 was about money – $667 million in cuts the government wanted to levy. Bill 160 also contradicted what the Common Sense Revolution election promised – "that our children should be overseen by citizens, not politicians."

Bill 160 allows a minister of education to issue regulations and fire teachers, principals, or trustees who fail to carry out orders. It says that when a regulation made by a cabinet minister conflicts with any other statute, or previously established law, the minister's regulation – an arbitrary set of procedures, not a law debated and passed in the legislature – shall prevail. It is an astounding piece of authoritarianism, referred to as the "Henry VIII clause" because it is similar to the kind of unilateral decrees that king often made to rid himself of wives, the Holy Roman Church, and annoying parliamentarians. Henry VIII set aside any law he did not like, just as the Harris government can now do in the field of education.

Ignoring the growing protests in the province, the government drew its authoritarian line in the sand on this issue. The Education Quality Improvement Act had nothing to do with improving the quality of education in the province, of course; quite the opposite. It was a right-wing effort to disassemble the current education system and open the door to the privatization of education in the province. It could easily lead to charter schools – schools that exist on public funds, but with a curriculum that's left to business interests and the political pressure group they belong to.

Harris had reached office with the votes of a good number of teachers, their friends, and relatives. By the fall of 1997, many of those same teachers were attending noisy rallies in the middle of the longest series of walkouts in Ontario since the Second World War, chanting "General strike! General strike!" for all they were worth. Their protest over Bill 160 was courageous; teachers, after all, are not usually radical people. Many tend to be conservative in their thinking and moderate in their politics. I know how hard it was for many of those 126,000 teachers to walk off the job. It takes a lot to make most teachers pick up protest signs and march in the streets in a civil protest.

Given the bullying tactics of the government, the teachers showed remarkable solidarity. Fewer than 2 percent of them even attempted to enter their schools. They also enjoyed incredible public support. No "illegal" walkout had ever achieved such widespread backing. The Harris government accused the teachers of causing "irreparable harm" to the province's education system but it was the government, not the teachers, that was the source of harm. The strike sensitized millions of Ontarians to what was happening in education and helped link the teachers to parents, to students, and to the communities in a deeper and explicitly political way.

What the teachers put up with was amazing. On November 18, a stormy winter night in Guelph, more than 1,000 teachers and their supporters demonstrated outside a Tory fundraising dinner and attempted to stop Education Minister Dave Johnson from entering. Of course, the Tories made sure the cops were there. A squad of one hundred city police and Ontario Provincial Police grabbed protesters, manhandled them, and arrested a few for "breaching the peace." Some female demonstrators were forced to remove their clothes in front of officers and were strip-searched. They had to bend over so the officers could check visually whether they had concealed drugs.

What did this sort of brutal harassment have to do with a peaceful protest against a government run amok? What right did the police have strip-searching people arrested during a legal and orderly political protest? What did any of it have to do with the provincial education system? These are the tactics of a police state. Clearly, the cops were under orders to intimidate and humiliate. The Harris government demonstrated the truth of an old adage: the uglier a government's tactics, the more ruthless its agencies.

I was proud of what those teachers did, grateful for their activism, and I wasn't alone. One of our members told me she now has more confidence in Ontario's education system. Knowing that her children are in the hands of people who are not afraid to stand on principle against authority, not afraid of walking a picket line to defend our education system, has given that mother, and many other Ontarians, renewed respect for teachers.

Still, the teachers – like all members of Ontario's labour movement – need to be vigilant about keeping the Harris government honest and accountable. They can't afford to rest on their laurels, taking comfort in having fought the good fight over Bill 160. If anything, they need to sharpen the wooden spike of militant action in case the monster rises from the table. There are already signs it is stirring.

After a pause in the implementation of its program, the Tories in the summer of 1998 were once again making noises about turning back labour's clock. In June 1998 they rammed Bill 31 through the legislature, again with no public debate. This bill will make it harder to organize retail and service employees, easier for employers to fend off union drives. It will weaken unions and cut wages in the construction industry. The latest "labour" minister, Jim Flaherty, claimed the government had to force this important legislation through because Ontario, with its "well-paying union jobs," was losing construction projects to Alberta and Texas. That, too, was simply not the case.

Talk also spread of future anti-union legislation in the next session to replace the defeated Bill 136. The Tories clearly intend to take another large step to curtail what remains of union rights in Ontario. Worse yet, an Angus Reid poll in June 1998 found that, among decided voters, the Tories were now tied with the Liberals for support at 41 percent. The NDP trailed badly, with 12 percent.

Last year – 1997 – marked an incredible time of labour protest. In Ontario we probably had more man-days of work lost than in the previous twenty years combined. Are the times changing? Is labour becoming more militant? How could labour not become more militant these days? Working people are toiling for lower real wages than they were twenty years ago. Their spending power has been eroded. They watch their social programs being systematically dismantled. Their rights are undermined. Self-assured corporations, backed by right-wing governments, demand wage and benefit rollbacks or, as they frequently threaten, they will take their work to Juarez or Juhore. They "negotiate" contracts by beginning with threats to lay off workers.

In Ontario, public housing programs for the needy have been eliminated. Environmental protection is no longer even an issue, let alone a priority. Child support offices have been closed, social assistance slashed, battered-women shelters closed, rent controls gutted, and the price of drugs for senior citizens increased. University and college students have organized and demonstrated against the government's raising of tuition fees.

If Harris is re-elected, at the top of his government's agenda will be the introduction of right-to-work laws intended to destroy trade unionism. "Right to work" means employees would not have to become members of a union as a condition of employment, and not have to pay union dues, even though they would enjoy benefits negotiated by the unions. The Tories want to strike a death blow to the unions. My hope is that at the next opportunity, Ontario voters – like Canadian voters in 1993, sick of the Mulroney government's corruption and right-wing legislation – will strike a death blow to the Tories.

8

WHAT'S LEFT?

It is no exaggeration to say that, over the
past decade, the real political leadership within the left
has shifted to the labour movement itself.
— *CAW publication, June 1996*

Caw members know that unions do not exist in a vacuum. Our leaders' ability to satisfy members' concerns is greatly affected by the political climate. That's why we fight actively for economic policies that lead to full employment, and against policies harmful to the working person, like Free Trade, NAFTA, and the impending Multilateral Agreement on Investment. This is not what neoconservative columnists would view as legitimate union business, but our leaders, activists, and many of our members know how deeply politics affects their lives and those of their loved ones.

Working people can never expect to achieve political influence unless a union, or a political party closely aligned with labour, goes to bat for them. The individual is simply not in any position to challenge or change the system. To have any political say, workers must act collectively. Canadian workers would not enjoy many of the things now taken for granted – vacations, long weekends, minimum wages, pensions, workers' compensation, medicare, unemployment insurance – had it not been for collective action through their unions, which in turn lent support to the parties that best represented them, the Co-operative Commonwealth Federation and, later, the NDP.

The left in Canada today is experiencing a crisis of direction and confidence. The unions look for a political champion and see a party that's hung out a Do Not Disturb sign. Many NDPers are asking whether the NDP is even a party of "the left" any more. What could be a more fundamental topic of debate than whether the NDP still serves the political needs and aspirations of working Canadians? Yet party policy-makers and administrators are hard at work ensuring that no debate takes place. They think they can win back public support by doing nothing and saying as little as possible. They ignore the historical reality that the NDP was at its most appealing when enthusiasm was generated by healthy debates over the party's structure, purpose, and direction.

It frustrates me to see how NDP organizers have marginalized labour's influence on policy matters. Their instinct for control can reach juvenile levels. They've moved the structure of party conventions away from open debates in plenary sessions and replaced that time-honoured method of political energizing with behind-the-scenes discussions in workshops. This removes the very reason for political conventions. It puts a damper on energy and enthusiasm in the name of making the party appear "businesslike" and "responsible." It takes the "politics" out of a political party.

Being in the NDP these days is like being asked to march in a parade without a band or a drum major. Everybody is expected to dress the same, look the same, keep in step – all without a recognizable beat or common rhythm to march to. If you take a misstep, look out of place, or cause a commotion, you're ignored or censured. Little wonder the NDP occupies a political never-never-land. It might have been successful in establishing a non-contentious, low-profile image, but to what end? If the profile gets any lower, the NDP will fall right out of the visual range of most Canadians.

THE POLITICAL MERGING of workers and other democratic socialists first came about in 1932, with the founding of the CCF during the Great Depression. An even stronger labour movement joined with the CCF to form the NDP in 1961, with Tommy Douglas as leader. The NDP has always been strongest when it worked closely with, and enjoyed the full support of, the labour movement. Ridings in cities like Windsor, Oshawa, St. Catharines, Hamilton, and London, where the UAW and United Steelworkers, for instance, were strongly represented, regularly sent NDP members to the House of Commons.

Collective political action began to lose its attraction for many union members in the early 1970s. Although NDP governments appeared in Manitoba in 1969, in Saskatchewan in 1971, and in British Columbia in 1972, they were, to many union members, governments running out of ideological steam. Although each NDP government introduced some progressive legislation, only that of Dave Barrett in British Columbia could be considered left wing in the traditional sense. Barrett's government did one thing that distinguished it from the others. When it reached office, it introduced a wide program of legislation meant to redress longstanding grievances for workers and others who had long been without a political voice. It did not leave its supporters – industrial workers, forestry workers, fishermen, educators, even small businessmen – to wait for redress. It did not waffle on pre-election promises. It never blinked, in spite of a massive anti-NDP lobby by the business community and the province's largely right-wing media.

Labour's shift away from unquestioned support of the NDP began in the late 1960s and early 1970s because many traditional unions were uncomfortable with blatant political action. Some resented the coalition nature of NDP membership, the fact that the party was made up of different groups all fighting for their own particular versions of social democracy within the NDP. Many could not see that these single issues were often really social democratic issues in the broader sense. They did not understand that by working with these groups, and recognizing the importance of their issues, they strengthened both the labour movement and the NDP.

A number of the unions affiliated with the Canadian Labour Congress thought that an NDP that entertained a number of single issues in a broad coalition made for a weak political party. But the history of the NDP, and of the CCF, is a history of diverse and often competing interests. The CCF and the NDP were formed by single-issue groups recognizing that they had a greater opportunity to bring about change if they came together in one political party. Farmers, church groups, women's groups, labour academics, peace activists, and social activists all joined forces to form the CCF. Did they agree on every issue? Of course not. Did they debate one another over those issues? Of course. Different factions took different positions on nearly every important issue. This kind of open debate over fundamental issues was seldom seen in the political parties of the right and centre; it's one of the reasons the socialist party attracted a broad range of progressive people.

Today, in the NDP, that kind of constructive debate is often seen as unnecessary, messy, and divisive. Debate over differing political ideas and strategies is perceived as destructive to the party's interests. Because the modern NDP – and, to a large extent, our country's labour movement – has become conservative and cautious in its political aspirations and methods, open discussion is seen as a challenge to the party's hierarchy. Someone outspoken, with a different set of ideas, values, or organizing techniques, is often viewed as "the enemy within."

At times these days, the NDP, the supposedly progressive socialist party, represents the very antithesis of progressive political thinking. The cautious, go-slow, centrist ideologues in the party, working with large, conservative elements of labour, are more intent on cloaking the party in moderation than in opening it to healthy debate. Those seeking urgent debate on the party's direction, or lack of velocity, are ignored. This refusal to entertain open discussion not only runs against the history of the NDP, but is, to my mind, the clearest threat to its continuing health.

For many years, through thick and thin, the CAW had supported the NDP as labour's logical choice for political action. We'd invested millions of dollars and countless hours in organizing and getting the voters out. Today, however, many of our members are no longer sure that the NDP – certainly the NDP in Ontario – is our party. Many of our activists and leaders – perhaps a majority – no longer see it as the party of the traditional left.

A debate is going on in the CAW over this very issue. A sizeable proportion of our members have taken a liking to the Reform Party or even the Conservatives federally, or the Liberal Party provincially, as their political alternative. The failure of the Ontario NDP government under Bob Rae was the start of this disaffection. And since its defeat by the Harris Conservatives, the Ontario NDP has continued to advocate policy positions at odds with the views of most CAW members and leaders. As a consequence, a debate rages in our union over political alternatives. Do we let our displeasure with the NDP be known by switching support to another party? Or do we stay and fight to rebuild a party truer to traditional democratic socialist principles?

In response to the Rae government's Social Contract, the CAW not only reduced its financial support of the Ontario NDP dramatically, it also supported the Ontario Federation of Labour's convention resolution to cut off *all* support to the provincial party. Our feeling was basically this: If you can't trust your friends, who can you trust? Given the attack by corporations on collective bargaining gains, and by governments on social programs, surely we should not have to waste time battling right-wing tendencies in our own party. The divisions in the left consume energy at a time when we should be fighting the Harris government, with its reactionary agenda, and the Chrétien government, with its neo-conservative policies.

Given our union's dissatisfaction over the direction of the Ontario NDP, it's hardly surprising that some of our members have raised the idea of starting a new party. The history of political movements, world-wide, is one of new parties rising out of the ashes of disillusionment and frustration. In May 1998 a number of Saskatchewan voters began gathering signatures in the hope of founding the New Green Alliance – this in a province already governed by the NDP, led by Roy Romanow. "There is no representation on the left right now in Saskatchewan," a spokesperson claimed. The new Alliance party would be committed to social justice, protection of the environment, human rights, pay equity, and promotion of fairer trade rather than "free trade" – all characteristics of a traditional left-wing party that, some say, despite the current government, does not exist in Saskatchewan at the moment.

Others in our union argue that the CAW should adopt a neutral position – forgoing formal alliances and opting instead to broker political influence with whichever party is prepared to support our agenda. I've been a member of the NDP for more than thirty years, and this is a tough issue for me. Personally, leaving the party is not an alternative. Still, some NDPers would dearly love to throw both me and our union out of the party. After the 1995 election loss in Ontario, the NDP executive debated whether to have me expelled.

We in the CAW do not see ourselves supporting any party that has swallowed the debt-and-deficit mantra of the neoconservatives or the competitive globalization theology of the neoliberals – both of which mean cutting jobs, lowering wages, and laying off Canadian workers. Some of my critics have taken my attacks on deficit-cutting and preoccupation with debt as proof that I'm a Keynesian throwback, someone who thinks deficits don't matter because they are a way to stimulate the economy. The question I pose is not whether deficits are good or bad, but who pays for them? Like Tommy Douglas, I believe that you can't allow governments to be shackled by bank debt. We must deal with deficits and the debt, through job creation and through an increase in government revenue, achieved partly by taxing wealthy individuals and profitable corporations, not by slashing social programs.

Through the mid-1990s, we witnessed an amazing period of wealth creation. Many corporations and a relatively small number of citizens enjoyed unbelievable prosperity. Instead of increasing revenue through an increase in corporate taxes, or through the implementation of a wealth or inheritance tax (which the CAW encouraged the Rae government to impose), governments cut taxes for those who could most afford to pay them and increased taxes for those least able to pay. They then cut the social services the latter group depended upon.

Another issue complicating the debate about the CAW's relationship with the NDP is that much of our frustration had been with the Ontario wing of the party. If we cut our ties with the party in general, what impact might that have on the federal NDP? Alexa McDonough is doing a good job as leader. After the party's years in the opposition wilderness, we're finally hearing an alternative voice in the House of Commons (though the media do their best to muffle it). Issues such as high unemployment, outrageous youth unemployment, the profits of our banks, and the question of who decides the future relationship of Quebec and Canada – the people or the courts – are now receiving scrutiny, thanks partly to the parliamentary performance of the federal NDP. Given a fair shake by the media, the national NDP could well be a force in opening up broader debate on these important issues.

(I might add that our union, and I personally, did not support McDonough for the leadership. Svend Robinson was our choice. We

felt he had the most activist track record on issues important to us. He's
joined us on the picket lines, he's a loud supporter of human rights, and
he fights for the little guy. He supports people on social welfare, the
unemployed, the less fortunate. He would also have stirred the controversy the NDP needs to attract the media attention that would give
Canadians a clear picture of what the NDP stands for. That said, it's my
view that McDonough has been doing a good job in Ottawa.)

Just after Alexa was elected leader of the party, I proposed that, in
an effort to give the NDP a higher public profile, she contest Sheila
Copps's seat in Hamilton. Copps had resigned over her commitment to
the GST and was running for re-election. To me, it was a terrific opportunity for a newly elected NDP leader who did not yet have a seat in the
House of Commons. It was only a by-election. The party's big worry
was, "What if she loses?"

Well, what if she did? She had a fall-back opportunity to run in
Nova Scotia in the next federal election. She might even have had the
edge on Copps. Despite Copps's popularity, Hamilton has historically
been a strong labour-NDP town. Voters were mad as hell at the Liberals
for breaking so many promises. Even if the NDP didn't win the Hamilton
riding with a fresh political face, I argued, a loss would have generated
great interest in Alexa and the NDP. All the party apparatchiks could
think about, however, was the negative outcome if Alexa lost. Their
strategy was somehow to get the NDP back in the public eye by saying
nothing and doing nothing.

In the CAW's quandary over a continuing relationship with the NDP,
the deciding factor may be just how far and fast the Ontario party keeps
inching away from the policies, thinking, and responsibilities of the traditional left. Trying to curry favour with the business community, as the
Rae government did, is a sheer waste of time and effort. If Rae thinks his
efforts at appeasement caused a single bank manager or Chrysler vice-
president to vote for him in 1995, he's mistaken. The CAW learned
through many decades of hard bargaining that employers do not make
concessions, even obvious ones, unless forced to. Any pacts, agreements,
or partnerships they make are temporary, existing only until they can
swing the advantage their way again. For labour, for any well-meaning

democratic socialist, collaboration with corporate Canada is a kiss of death. The workers always end up paying the freight.

I can't see the CAW supporting an NDP that is prepared to tear out its roots every time the Chamber of Commerce or the Business Council on National Issues comes calling. The history of the CCF and NDP is a history of looking after workers and the less fortunate. The right looks after its friends well enough when it's in power. As democratic socialists, we need to do likewise, as Barrett did in British Columbia.

HOW'S THE PARTY PERFORMING outside Ontario? In Saskatchewan, Romanow and the NDP have provided honest and balanced government. Despite the criticism from the left demanding more attention to traditional left-wing issues, it's hard to blame that government too harshly, given that it was saddled with enormous debt by the Conservatives of Grant Devine. At least Romanow did not force wage cuts on Saskatchewan's public sector workers.

Still, tallying up Romanow's performance, it's hard to distinguish his government from a Liberal or Conservative one. From the day it took office, the Saskatchewan government's central focus was to balance the budget. To do that it increased the sales tax and slapped a 10 percent tax on net income, but put a relatively smaller capital tax on corporations. It cut grants to hospitals (and closed fifty-two rural hospitals), schools, and universities. It cut the health budget, lowered royalties on the oil industry, completed the privatization of Crown corporations in the resource sector, and promoted gambling casinos and video lottery terminals. These policies have led to a major shift in government revenues from corporations to individuals. As Saskatchewan political economist John Warnock wrote in *Canadian Forum*: "The budget had been balanced, but the cost has been very high to low-income earners."

In British Columbia, the NDP, led by Premier Glen Clark, is, I believe, as good a model for the future of the NDP in Canada as one can point to. Clark has a vision. He's cool under pressure and, despite criticism from some quarters, he's true to the basic principles of democratic socialism. Like Barrett, he knows who his constituency is and the degree of support it requires. He also knows that an NDP government must govern on behalf of all citizens and that the test of good leadership is how to balance your convictions with reality. Any party that believes in fairness and equity can govern in good times. For a democratic socialist government, the test is how you represent the less powerful in tough times. And it looks as if B.C. is in for some tough economic times.

The performance of the Clark government should also be assessed in the context of what its predecessor – the NDP government of Mike Harcourt – was able to do during two terms in office. Harcourt, in my view, was one of the most honourable and effective provincial premiers Canada has seen in the last twenty years. Unfortunately, the greed of a few former NDP executives, coupled with a primitive display of cheapshot journalism by the province's right-wing media, led to his resignation.

Harcourt faced that test of political leadership with courage and integrity. He knew the party was headed for defeat. He chose to put his party, his province, and the principles of social democracy ahead of personal ambition. His resignation opened the NDP leadership door to allow Clark to succeed him. Clark brought a new face, but similar principles, to the NDP, and he was able to defeat the overconfident Liberals in the next election. One can only wonder what would have happened in Ontario in 1995 if Bob Rae – knowing his government was headed for certain defeat – had taken a page from Harcourt's book and resigned before the provincial election was called.

The NDP is beginning to make strides in Atlantic Canada. Under McDonough's leadership, and riding a wave of voter protest against the Liberals, the NDP elected twenty-one members to the House of Commons in 1997, regaining party status. Eight of these members came from Atlantic Canada. In 1998 the Nova Scotia NDP, led by Robert Chisholm, elected nineteen members to the legislature, tying with the Liberals and establishing the NDP as a major force in provincial politics. It was a historic breakthrough in that province. In New Brunswick, Elizabeth Weir is the lone NDP voice in a legislature overrun with Liberals. She's widely recognized as the "official opposition" with her persistent questioning and hounding of the Liberals. As my elderly mother said, "Just think what Elizabeth could do if she had some help in the legislature."

What of Quebec? At the end of the day, as Preston Manning well knows, you can't lay claim to being a national party without a base of support in Quebec and a strong position on sovereignty association. To take a position that would build support in Quebec might be controversial in the rest of the country. But if you have no position on Quebec, you're simply a non-entity in that province. That's where the NDP – with its no-debate, no-dissension, low-profile policy – finds itself today. The NDP basically has a non-policy on sovereignty association that suggests the issue is entirely up to Quebeckers. This policy keeps the party out of the line of political fire, but it also ensures that the NDP scarcely exists in the minds of most Quebeckers.

Why do NDP policy-makers want to keep a low profile on one of the most important issues facing this nation? They're concerned that the party might lose the few seats it has outside Quebec if it's perceived as cosy with the Parti Québécois or the Bloc. I'd argue that if you're serious about being a national party, with some hope of forming a government or at least being part of a coalition that has some influence on legislation, you have no choice but to address the issue.

Personally, I fear the NDP has already missed the boat where Quebec is concerned. The opportunity came while the Liberal government was slashing our social programs and the Bloc Québécois became their unlikely protector. The NDP and the Bloc share a social democratic philosophy. Here was a way for the NDP to align itself in defence of our social fabric and, at the same time, strengthen its support in Quebec. Forming an alliance with the Bloc would have been a courageous and imaginative move, however, and courage is in short supply in a party intent on protecting its single-digit popularity in the polls.

What's most frustrating about the NDP's attitude is that a deal to keep Quebec in Canada is clearly possible. Regardless of what people think of Lucien Bouchard, he is a strong leader who enjoys the support of a majority of Quebeckers. He knows the value of dialogue and public debate. Unlike Jean Charest, whose principles depend on who he last spoke with, Bouchard, as *Le Devoir* columnist Mario Cloutier wrote in the summer of 1998, "believes in the role of the state, and in taking a firm, principled position and thrashing it out with your opponents before achieving some form of consensus."

I'm convinced that with Bouchard in power in Quebec, a deal with the rest of Canada is possible. He's the best chance we have of keeping the country whole. I've watched him for years – in the Mulroney cabinet, then in the Bloc, and now as premier of Quebec – and I'm certain he's not a separatist, not in the way that most people think. While he was leader of the Bloc Québécois, he and I sat together at a dinner in Quebec City at the party's convention. We talked at length about Quebec's aspirations and the mood of the rest of the country. Granted, this discussion took place more than a year before the referendum on October 30, 1995, but he said, "You know, Buzz, one hundred and twenty-seven years and the debate over Quebec's place in Confederation is still going on. You'd think that in that time, intelligent people would have been able to sit down and work out a relationship that was acceptable to Quebec and English Canada."

Bouchard made clear that Quebec did not hold to an intractable position. He talked about finding alternatives and identifying options. He was looking for meaningful dialogue, searching for solutions. He was not saying that the only way was Quebec's way. This was a guy looking for a deal.

I think Bouchard has a vision of a new relationship between Quebec and the rest of Canada, one that preserves national institutions but accepts that Quebec is unique and that its cultural differences need to be respected and preserved. A deal requires strong leaders on both sides of the table. Bouchard is certainly a strong leader, and Chrétien is in a position to move boldly on the issue, if he's so inclined. I believe the opportunity is there. In light of the recent Supreme Court's decision respecting Quebec's right to self-determination, why wait for the next referendum? Let's begin to negotiate a new relationship with Quebec now – one that respects our shared history and recognizes that keeping our country together requires a special relationship between that province and Ottawa. We must accept that Quebec will require expanded powers to sustain this new relationship, one that differs from those of the other provinces and territories with the federal government.

The federal NDP is the party that should spearhead the move to start these negotiations. The New Democrats should lead the way in supporting the Supreme Court's decision. By shifting the debate to this negotiation, the party will ensure that Quebec considers no further referendum necessary.

Parliamentary tradition allows leaders to make sweeping and radical changes to our constitutional structure. Even now, we spin our wheels discussing a new "social union" among the provinces, arguing about whose jurisdiction is whose and the danger of allowing Quebec more rights than other provinces. Where's the threat in that? We already recognize Quebec's uniqueness in the area of language, law, pensions, manpower training, and immigration. Some people oppose this devolution of powers, but it's had little or no negative impact on the country.

We're wrong if we think we can solve the Quebec equation by holding *vox populi* referendums. The search for unanimity or wide public consensus on such an emotional issue is bound to be futile. We end up arguing about whether a majority is fifty-plus-one, or 70 percent, or what. Our nation is too valuable to have its fate left to the randomness of competing or overlapping referendums. Referendums have more to do with lack of communication than communication. Often, a referendum represents a chance for polar opposites to register their stubbornness, reinforce their refusal to listen. I think we'd be better off if we left the issue to a serious dialogue between strong political leaders, got the deal done, then let the country argue its way to acceptance.

JUST AS THE NDP will never become a party of national significance without a presence in Quebec, so it will never make significant progress without the enthusiastic support of its allies in the labour movement. To gain that support, the NDP can't forget that improving the lot of working people must be the priority. To those NDP officials who believe, like Tony Blair in Britain, that you no longer need labour to govern, I'd suggest that you alienate labour at your peril. I don't believe the NDP can survive as a viable political alternative in the long run without labour on its side.

Some party strategists believe the NDP should "modernize," shift policy more towards the right, and marginalize – even expel – the more assertive and determined members of the labour movement and the left. This is dangerous thinking, and ultimately a death wish. We'll never educate the middle class to vote for a "middle-of-the-road NDP" (which is, or should be, an oxymoron). Mature voters do not switch political allegiances based on how good they feel. They switch out of a sense of grievance. The NDP will continue to lose credibility with every shift it makes to the right. Each time an NDP leader mouths platitudes about dealing with deficits and debts before talking about lower interest rates and job creation, the party loses labour support. I myself want what the NDP has always wanted: to take part in a realistic effort to save my country's citizens from further economic harm, to help the less fortunate to their feet, to assist workers and their families to gain back years of lost real wages and benefits. Yet I'm told my methods are extreme and my ideology is outdated!

Notwithstanding the two provincial NDP governments and the recent electoral success in Atlantic Canada, the "modern" NDP is in trouble right across the country. In the 1997 federal election, the NDP got 1.3 million votes, or 11 percent of the popular vote. That translated into twenty-one seats in the House of Commons. But voter turnout was at its lowest level (67 percent) since 1925. The vote for the Reform Party in English Canada was higher than the vote for the NDP. In once traditional "union ridings," Reform captured 20 percent of all voters. It replaced the NDP as the traditional alternative party in Ontario, Saskatchewan, and British Columbia. Clearly, in the 1997 election, the NDP lost the populist status it once held.

Federally, the party was at its peak in 1988. In the 1993 election it had a disastrous showing (a mere 939,000 votes, or 7 percent), and in 1997 it regained only one-third of the votes it had lost after 1988. In fact, the vote for the NDP in 1997 – which many in the party hailed as a great victory – was the second lowest since the party's formation in 1961. Given that the NDP is on the defensive, it needs to establish itself as an effective opposition. But the party, particularly in Ontario, does not seem capable of generating that kind of purpose. You can't be an effective opposition by preaching the politics of the middle.

As the labour movement has searched for an effective response to the corporate aggressiveness of the 1980s and 1990s, I believe that the real political leadership on the left has shifted away from the NDP. It was the unions, along with our social partners outside the NDP, that understood the significance of Free Trade, and led the fight against it. It was workers and unions, not the NDP, that began actively challenging the corporate agenda in the early 1980s when it became clear that the Mulroney government was essentially the legislative arm of business interests. It was working people, their unions, and community groups that conceived and carried out the Days of Action protests in Ontario, and that mobilized public anger in Atlantic Canada. And it was not the NDP but the labour movement, with help from the party and from organizations like the Council of Canadians and the Canadian Centre for Policy Alternatives, that led the fight against the Multilateral Agreement on Investment.

Through its increasingly conservative nature, or its simple lack of political will, the NDP has allowed a vacuum to develop on the left. The Ontario NDP, in particular, does not seem to know how to work in the best interests of its constituents. The Harris government's Bill 7 was, as mentioned, a piece of anti-union legislation that repealed the NDP's Bill 40 and, in some areas of labour legislation, sent Ontario back to the 1950s. On numerous occasions since, the CAW has asked the leader of the Ontario NDP, Howard Hampton, to make an unequivocal public statement that if the NDP were returned to power, it would repeal Bill 7. We're still waiting for that statement.

We expect a social democratic party to join with us in the fight to advance the interests of working people rather than the economic elite, to defend the interests of the underprivileged rather than those of Bay Street. The NDP seems to have lost sight of how to do that. The party does not have the money, resources, or top-down power of the corporate community. What it does have is the organizing potential of the labour movement. Labour can play a key role in mobilizing support between elections. It can help build a political structure that would make the NDP a real alternative for Canadians. But if the NDP is to tap that resource, it must respect the differences of opinion within the labour movement, not use those differences to divide it or dismiss it or reduce its influence.

The Ontario NDP might ask why a large percentage of the labour movement refuses to support the party. It might also ask whether we have the right leadership for the times. Debating leadership benefits the party. If the leadership is strong, debate can only strengthen it. If it's weak, debate will reflect that and allow the party to compensate for it. Debate also sparks public interest in the party and the movement. It exposes misconceptions, corrects fallacies, and challenges sometimes stereotyped depictions in the media. In doing so, it attracts new members with fresh ideas and points of view.

Unless the NDP gets its act together and goes on the offensive – provincially and federally – it will be relegated to third- or fourth-party status in the short term, and no status at all in the long term. Provincial debates as well as a nationwide debate, or series of debates, should be organized as quickly as possible. We can't afford to wait for the next convention. The party needs debate on where the left in Canada is going. There must be a clear purpose to labour's involvement with the NDP, or our political activists will either turn to more satisfying work with coalitions or else withdraw completely from political organizing. Labour represents three million voters. To appeal to that huge block, the NDP must put in place structures at the local, provincial, and national levels that allow for meaningful debate over policy and labour's role in developing it.

Too many people in the NDP today – fresh, bright people, full of new ideas, but limited in their understanding of history – refuse to recognize how the party got from there to here. Some have never been in a real debate in their lives. They think debate makes the NDP look messy, noisy, and confused. They see it as a sign of weakness, not a strengthening device. But that view is shallow and shortsighted. If they knew political history, they'd know that the NDP has been at its best when we were locked in impassioned debate about where the party was heading.

The NDP once had leaders that gloried in debate – Tommy Douglas, David Lewis, Stephen Lewis, Dave Barrett, Alan Blakeney, Grant Notley, Ed Broadbent, Howard Pawley, to name a few. These people brought differing views of social democracy and vigorously aired their differences. They debated in committee meetings and in public forums, at the federal council and at conventions. Despite hurt feelings, even bitterness, the party always came out stronger. Such debate forces us to think, to consider fresh ideas. It gives the public a look at a vibrant political entity with principles that people are not afraid to defend. And it reveals a collective conscience geared toward making a better society for all.

If my frustration with the NDP is evident, I'm certainly not alone. Many activists on the left in the CAW, and in other progressive unions, are similarly frustrated. Many in Ontario are still furious over the Rae government's Social Contract, and they're becoming increasingly impatient with the present leaders of the Ontario NDP. It's a party too timid by half, and one that's playing potentially destructive political games – games that erode any sense of commitment from the left.

Howard Hampton is a decent man, yet he argued in *Our Times* magazine against the street activism aimed at the Harris government, even though public demonstrations have been the best way of generating support and exposing the Harris agenda. I'm not clear what Hampton's reluctance stems from, but reticence is poor policy for a party deep in third place in the Ontario legislature, its support declining in almost every poll. The Ontario NDP could use a shot of courage.

During the Toronto Day of Action, I watched Hampton and Alexa McDonough join our organizing coalition on the speakers' stage. We were pleased to have them there. They both stood in front of the microphone when introduced. They smiled and waved. That was it. They stood there, smiling and waving at 200,000 people. When I asked why they didn't speak, they said they were reluctant to offend the non-political groups in the protest coalition. They did not want to politicize the event!

I was not on the speakers' list that day, but I grabbed the microphone and urged the crowd to stage more of this sort of street protest. It was a great show of solidarity and I congratulated the marchers for taking part. We all had one thing in common: we wanted to get a message to the Harris government. That day we did. I hoped my words would reassure them that we were doing the right thing. And while I appreciate that Hampton and McDonough had political reasons for not hogging the platform, their reluctance made no sense to me. If I'm close to a microphone at what is clearly a political event, I'll grab the opportunity to make political hay. So what if one or two coalition partners complain afterwards? My response would be: "the next time you spend thousands of dollars and a lot of your members' time, as the CAW did, to get 200,000 people at a street rally, then maybe I'll be quiet."

The question now for the left in Ontario is: How can the NDP attract the many voters who are turning away from the Harris government? The CAW is doing its part, creating forums for high-profile public debate through workplace closures, rallies, and demonstrations. We're trying to draw attention to the serious problems caused by the policies of the Chrétien government in Ottawa and the Harris government in Ontario. What's the NDP doing?

In early 1998 I suggested to Hampton that the Ontario NDP must provide voters with a reason to support it again. I suggested he set up a meeting of top labour and party leaders to discuss how we might best do this, and follow it up with focus groups in union halls across the province. His answer, as I understood it, was that the NDP was too busy preparing for a provincial election it assumed would take place in the fall of 1998 – highly unlikely, we in the CAW thought, given how committed the Harris government is to completing the implementation of its ideological agenda.

The Days of Action drew public attention to the reality that hundreds of thousands of Ontarians are angry and frustrated over the way the Harris government has conducted itself. We knew the Days of Action could invigorate angry citizens. Any time people feel an injustice has been perpetrated, the most effective way of drawing attention to it is to march in the streets. When you hit the streets, people know there is an opposition they can join. They know who their allies are, and what they stand for. The Ontario teachers proved that in their courageous stand against Bill 160. Because they went public, people witnessed the debate, listened to alternative points of view, and became involved and committed.

There's little dialogue these days between the CAW and the Ontario NDP. The CAW is perceived as militant and impertinent. In fact, it's fascinating to see how far the Ontario party will go to downplay the CAW's influence. I realize many party members do not like Buzz Hargrove personally, but their efforts to neutralize our union's aggressive leadership and progressive agenda sometimes border on the farcical. The NDP's house organ, *The Ontario New Democrat*, published an article on the Windsor Day of Action that made no mention of the CAW – in spite of the fact that our union had helped shut down more than eighty workplaces and taken 30,000 of our members off the job to join in the protest. We were by far the largest labour contingent at the rally. There probably would not have been a Day of Action without the organizing initiative of the CAW. There was no mention of my attendance, and the editors cropped their cover photograph – showing Bob White, Earl Manners of the Ontario Secondary School Teachers' Federation, Ken Brown of the Service Employees International Union, and Howard Hampton – to exclude me. The same photograph appeared in several community newspapers with me in the group, and the *Windsor Star* ran a similar photo that included me. If you picked up the Ontario NDP's own publication, Buzz Hargrove and the CAW did not exist.

Organizers of the Days of Action were aware of the substantial amounts of money and resources the CAW put into these events. Our members and political activists have not been impressed, to say the least, by the NDP's tactics in minimizing our contributions. Indeed, many of our members demanded that the CAW leadership look seriously at whether our union ought to be affiliated with the NDP.

In February 1998 the CAW's national executive board held a think-tank session at Port Elgin. My assistants and the CAW area directors took part in a debate about our relationship with the Ontario NDP. After two full days of heated discussion, it was decided – by a slim margin – that we should continue our affiliation. The decision took into account that, notwithstanding current difficulties, our union had enjoyed a long relationship with the NDP. The decision also recognized that severing formal ties with the Ontario NDP could set back our election prospects in Nova Scotia and, later, in British Columbia. It might also reflect poorly on Alexa McDonough, who's been working hard to rebuild the federal wing of the party.

A number of our members also made the case that cutting formal ties in Ontario might handicap our progress towards meeting our social goals. The best way, they said, to represent our traditional constituencies would be to fight harder within the party for more socially responsible thinking. The CAW had to remain in the party to make sure there was a strong, progressive voice representing working Canadians. But the decision to stick with the NDP was very close, and many of our leaders are still wary.

IF QUESTIONS ABOUT THE NDP'S DIRECTION are driving a wedge between the CAW and the party in Ontario, these same issues are also dividing the provincial labour movement. Many of the province's larger unions have bought into the argument that political change cannot be forced through street politics. How they can hold to this view in the face of one of the most anti-worker, anti-labour provincial governments Ontario has ever seen is beyond me.

A major split has surfaced within the Ontario Federation of Labour. It might be described as a split between the more conservative unions in the OFL, and the CAW joined by the Canadian Union of Public Employees (Ontario), the Service Employees International Union (SEIU), and some sections of other unions. The CAW is a major source of funding for the OFL, Ontario's federated body of labour unions. But our union has little influence on the OFL because it has no seat on the executive committee, despite being the largest private sector union in Ontario. The OFL's orthodox philosophical tone has been set by individual unions in the federation that are conservative and non-militant. This has also led to a significant division in thinking between the CAW and most of the OFL executive.

At a time when labour is under attack by business, government, and the media, we should be entertaining new ideas and staging major debates about how we might do things differently in a world that's rapidly changing around us. Instead, we've grown more rigid, cautious, and conservative. If the Canadian labour movement is to survive as a healthy, aggressive entity fighting to protect workers' rights, it needs open dialogue about how we can best do that, and how we can grow.

One of the reasons the CAW seems outspoken, standing alone on many public policy issues, is that many parts of the movement, such as the Ontario Federation of Labour, no longer play a meaningful role. The

OFL leadership does not share our passion for social equality, reform, and preservation of workers' rights. It does not share our interest in generating debate about where the movement should be going. As a provincial umbrella organization, it's largely irrelevant to working people.

Even within labour's major umbrella organization – the Canadian Labour Congress – there's a reluctance to debate the most archaic practices. In an age of extreme worker dissatisfaction – with unions as well as employers – the CLC does not allow members of one union to leave and join another. A union member is like an indentured servant. It makes no sense in an age when we talk about worker democracy.

The CAW is probably the only union that allows its members to decide if they want to stay with us or move to another union. We learned from experience that by giving members the option of choosing which union they're most comfortable with, we become stronger and more effective. Having the right to change unions allows our members to pressure the leaders to work more closely with them and to ensure that they're satisfied with our performance on their behalf.

The prevailing mood among affiliates in the CLC is just the opposite. Most unions want to make it more difficult for members to switch unions, not less, in the interest of maintaining a suitable number of dues-paying members. Among the majority of union leaders, the issue is not even considered worthy of debate. Yet it lies at the very heart of what the labour movement is all about. If we're going to be relevant to our members and strong enough to ensure that employers and government can't further dismantle the legislated rights we fought for decades to achieve, the labour movement has to be more open. It has to be the modern, progressive force it once was, not the static, conservative group it's become.

Our experience has been that when the labour movement is divided, as it is now in Ontario, the NDP, rather than helping to mend the rifts, exacerbates them. It is perhaps only natural, given that the NDP and the OFL share that conservative, middle-of-the-road thinking. A divided labour movement also allows the NDP not to have to respond as readily to demands for debate on policy and party direction.

These divisions are especially damaging at a time when we should be united in our effort to design a strategy to defeat the Harris government in the next election. They also make "solidarity" little more than a slogan on a T-shirt. Yet the Ontario NDP fails to see that, for a party trying to re-energize itself, it is astoundingly shortsighted in alienating a major portion of its constituency.

IS THE NDP – and especially the Ontario NDP – heading down a path toward irrelevance? At this writing in mid-1998 the Ontario party is foundering with a shaky 13 percent of voter support. More troubling to me personally is the idea that the NDP should no longer concern itself with the underprivileged in our society. After three decades as a dues-paying NDP member, I never thought I'd hear party leaders say that such people no longer matter – that regaining political power is the only issue. This group argues that the less fortunate are simply not part of the NDP's return-to-power equation: "when you think about it," they say, "people on welfare don't vote. It's admirable to defend them, but come election time there's nothing to be gained by fighting for them."

I've been told I seem angry much of the time. I've been asked why I demand more debate, not less, on NDP policies and platforms. To my mind, there's no reason for the NDP to exist if it's intent on walking away from the less fortunate, away from the traditions that brought us together as a party. What would Tommy Douglas say to that? Stanley Knowles? J.S. Woodsworth? David Lewis? These men knew that the NDP, and before it the CCF, was nothing unless it was caring and humane. The only reason we came together was to fight for a more equitable society for every citizen. Someone has to give voice to those without power and privilege. The NDP can't be just another political party in pursuit of votes. Its task is to show Canadians that there is no conflict between striving for a compassionate society while also working for a successful economy that provides us all with hope and opportunity. If the NDP completes its transformation into a party whose goal is merely to grasp power, the political left in Canada will be finished.

Who are these people trying to centralize the party? What brought them into the NDP? What other bizarre notions about democratic socialism do they have? They argue for the "rational approach" – it makes sense to concentrate exclusively on getting into power and then, once there, to act on your promises and introduce progressive legislation. Tell that to the former Rae government, the one that made it to Queen's Park and then forgot about the promises.

Many NDP advisers embrace the same sort of policies that Tony Blair does – the leader of a "labour" party so right wing that even Margaret Thatcher admires his work. These NDPers imagine they can gain power, as the Labour Party did in Britain, if they move to the right and throttle the influence of "labour." They're excited over what Blair has "accomplished." Tony Blair is a political accident of time and space. The Thatcher revolution had run out of steam. John Major was foundering. The Liberals were in disarray and the labour movement had atrophied. The "labour" of the British Labour Party had long ago lost its political clout and was no longer even a "movement." Given the state of worker disaffection, Blair did not need labour to win in 1997.

What is it that lights up the eyes of NDP operatives when Blair is mentioned? His version of social democracy is seen as a balance between "enterprise" and "fairness," a "sustainable socialism" aimed at balanced budgets, business-government "partnerships," and a "helping hand" to get the able-bodied "from welfare to workforce." Some call it Thatcherism with a bit of heart.

For the record, Blair pledged to reform the National Health Service; the waiting lists for hospital beds actually rose. Interest rates were to go down; they went up. Blair promised not to raise income taxes; gasoline taxes went up and new taxes were added on pension funds – a subtle way of raising income taxes. Blair brought in a new punishment regimen for young offenders, overhauled the welfare state to include a "no rights without responsibilities" slogan that tightened eligibility, introduced a working family's tax credit to encourage the unemployed to find work, and reduced corporate tax rates to what will soon be the lowest in Europe – all of which sounds as if it's right out of the Mike Harris policy book. And we're told by some NDPers that this should be the "modern face" of democratic socialism in Canada!

Unless the NDP makes major changes in policy direction and swings back towards democratic socialist principles, the leadership of the CAW will have a hard time getting our activists to work for Howard Hampton and the Ontario NDP in the next election. Staunch NDPer though I myself may be, I'll be damned if I'll risk my union's solidarity, and my credibility with our members, by working for a party that refuses even to listen to our concerns. The power brokers in the NDP do not seem capable of understanding the simplest rule of politics: you protect and please and listen to your friends, even though this will antagonize your adversaries. The only reason for the CAW to remain aligned with the NDP is to ensure that we make gains for working people and further our goals for social justice. If we can't do that with the New Democrats, we'll find a way to do it without them.

9

THE CORPORATE JUNTA

Every society needs some shared values to hold it together.
— *George Soros*

There is no such thing as society.
— *Margaret Thatcher*

What's happened in Ontario under the Rae government and now, much more viciously, under the Harris government, is in some ways a microcosm of what's happening in our nation and, more broadly, in the world at large. We're living under a system of government in which politicians get their votes from you and me, but take their marching orders from business. We have to go back to the late 1920s to find another time when the corporate agenda ruled as effectively and thoroughly as it does in the late 1990s.

It no longer really matters who gets elected to Parliament – Liberal, Reform, Conservative, even, in some cases, New Democratic Party or Parti Québécois – because their policy directions are essentially the same. In one way or another, most believe in the inevitability of free trade, global competition, price stability, elimination of deficits, debt repayment, reduced spending on social services, tax relief (especially for corporations and the upper class), deregulation of markets, and privatization of public sector institutions. All these issues were urged on our politicians by the corporations and have become governing liturgy, no matter who holds the most seats in Parliament. The common prayer of invocation in this right-wing crusade is so familiar by now that it carries its own religious certitude: governments must cut spending; corporations must downsize to be globally competitive; an economy in which wages fall and profits climb is "good," and an economy in which the number of jobs multiplies and wages go up is "poor." The Chrétien government has evidently decided that a good economy for Canada is one in which a million and a half people are unemployed. If this were South America, it would be no exaggeration to say that our democratically elected government had been overthrown by a corporate junta.

How did this happen? How did we lose control of the political agenda in our own country? How did working people yield the only democratic power available to them – the right to cast their ballots and expect that life for their families would, as a consequence, get better, not worse? I don't propose to answer these questions in a paragraph or a chapter, but I urge that they be aired and widely discussed because we, as a society, seem to have decided that the unemployed – along with the poor, the sick, the disabled, and the elderly – deserve less caring, not more. We seem to have accepted that the compassionate Canada of the past is destined to give way to the dog-eat-dog Canada that's replaced it. As we watch the rift widen between the haves and the have-nots, we're encouraged to believe that we're helpless to do anything about it – that our governments have no alternative but to yield to the supposed imperatives of a global economy.

Now that this corporate agenda has largely been implemented, where will it take us? Back to 1929 and the days of the Great Depression? The Depression represented the complete collapse of capitalism and left an entire generation destitute. When the markets crashed, the free enterprise system was exposed for what it was – a package of unproven theories. The corporate sector had no remedies for the Depression because economic collapse was simply not part of its dogma.

Everything people had been told about capitalism – its economic conventions and the social benefits thought to accompany it – turned out to be fraudulent, the damage deep and long-lasting. The only thing that saved us was a second global war and the recognition that government intervention – in the form of progressive new social and industrial policies – was needed to repair what capitalism had wrought. These new policies and structures formed part of the so-called welfare state. This humanely based approach helped bring us out of the darkest destitution North America had seen in generations.

Ironically, it has been the corporate-led dismantling of that welfare state that's now creating the conditions for a new global economic crisis.

In the name of free markets and globalization, the corporate elite appears to be doing to working people exactly what it did to an earlier generation. Over these past two decades, the corporations have been highly effective in turning back our economic and social clocks to the days of the late 1920s.

How were they able to rise from the ashes of their failure and eventually gain control of both the economy and our parliamentary system? In Western countries, the patriotism and sacrifice of the Second World War increased the demand for improvements in living standards, security, and equity. The postwar focus was on never returning to the days of devastation following the 1929 crash. A strong, growing labour movement articulated those demands, winning concessions from corporations and governments. Those concessions gave form and substance to a set of new public institutions and government-driven programs that guaranteed citizens a rising standard of security and equality.

This was also a period that saw the introduction of a form of "class compromise" – a social contract that legitimized and stabilized capitalism through the creative use of government regulation and investment. Only the intervention of activist governments helped capitalism get back on its feet. The welfare state in some ways bailed out the corporate sector, giving it new prestige at a time when we enjoyed general prosperity in the postwar period. An important lesson had been learned between 1939 and 1945: if we could win the greatest war in history, thanks to the guidance and leadership of government, why couldn't we maintain a generous peace using the same devices?

True, there were periods of social conflict after the war, strikes and work stoppages. Yet there was a fairly general acceptance that, even with corporations again running the economy, people would have jobs, feel protected through periods of economic change, and share in the benefits achieved under the shield of progressive legislation. Whatever hardships working-class families had to bear, they held to a fundamental assumption that social progress, from that point on, would be uninterrupted. Sons and daughters would inevitably end up better off than their parents had been. In the quarter century after the war, Canadian workers saw unemployment fall to relatively low levels and working-class families achieve steady increases in their standard of living. A progressive coalition lobbied for new social programs such as medicare and the Canada Pension Plan.

By the late 1960s, this consensus was showing its first signs of unravelling. Two developments changed the landscape. First, Europe and Japan had reconstructed their economies after the war and become serious trade competitors with North American business. Second, buoyed by secure times and social programs that provided entitlements independent of the marketplace, the working class became more confident and less responsive to corporate and market discipline.

With intense competition from Europe and Japan, North American corporations began fighting back to protect their postwar profits. Initially they transferred the shrinking of profits on to workers, but workers felt secure enough to resist being squeezed for concessions. The corporate sector turned to price increases as a means of maintaining profits, but higher prices led directly to demands for higher wages. The results included uncompetitive prices and escalating inflation.

Canadian banks, always a powerful arm of the country's political and corporate elite, viewed inflation with alarm. Because inflation reduced the value of their assets, the banks lobbied for government policies that would reduce it. Under these sorts of pressures, the corporate sector began moving towards a dramatic and radical conclusion, one that would eventually dominate our politics: that expansion of corporate profits was no longer compatible with the gains workers had made over previous decades. Corporations began searching for ways to undermine the welfare state, based on their assumption that it was no longer affordable or acceptable.

The corporations saw worker expectations as limiting their ability to perform satisfactorily in the marketplace. If a choice had to be made between profits and workers' expectations, the corporations would simply dismantle our expectations. One prong of the assault centred on the confidence and power of workers and their unions. It took the form of employer attacks on past standards of pay, benefits, and working conditions. Another prong was aimed at the policy intentions of elected representatives in the House of Commons and in provincial legislatures.

These assaults sought to undermine the political thinking behind labour laws that favoured workers and the social safety net constructed to protect citizens from a repeat of the Depression.

Unemployment levels began to rise in the late 1950s and early 1960s. The levels rose higher with the economic crisis of the mid-1970s. By the end of that decade, the Liberal government in Canada finally succumbed to the lobbying and made a major, but ultimately costly, alteration in our society. The Liberals switched the focus of economic policy from job creation to fighting inflation. The reasoning was straightforward, if heartless. Low inflation protects wealth. Since the main concern of the Canadian economic elite was inflation, unemployment would be allowed to grow as a means of fending it off.

Surprisingly, this shift in economic priorities was not followed by an outcry from Canadian workers. Except for the fight-back policies of a few large unions, rising unemployment did not trigger a sweeping new round of confrontations between labour and employers – or labour and government – as it had in the 1930s. Having enjoyed the affluence brought by steady jobs in the postwar period, working people feared nothing more than unemployment. They had tasted the benefits of progressive economic and social legislation, and they expected their children to go on to more prosperous lives. None of this would happen if they lost their jobs or had trouble finding new ones. By the time we entered the 1980s, that widespread fear of job losses was one of the things that had allowed our corporations to take control of the country's political agenda.

The corporations mobilized around a message that combined fear, resignation, and a promise that the good life would return down the road. If you do not buy into our economic interpretation, went the message, you'll lose, at an even faster rate, what prosperity you enjoy. There's no alternative to what we prescribe, in other words, and the present economic pain is the price if we're all to benefit in the longer term. This ideological offensive picked up the name "neoconservatism" and centred on three key elements: competitiveness, government deficit-cutting, and corporate cost-cutting. These elements were sold as the conditions necessary for future economic success. Competitiveness was the hammer used to keep workers' collective bargaining expectations in check. Deficit-cutting was the tool for keeping elected governments, which might be susceptible to popular pressure, from expanding or maintaining social safety net programs. Corporate cost-cutting was a brutal rider attached to these policies, and sold as "efficiency" – even though it meant job losses.

These solutions in some ways only aggravated the problems they allegedly addressed. They forced us into "stagflation" – a perpetually underperforming economy accompanied by high inflation. Governments found themselves with less tax revenue because more workers were without jobs. Nevertheless, governments cut spending on social programs, which many workers, now unemployed, needed more than ever.

Amid fear and uncertainty, workers were told that unemployment was the unfortunate cost of getting inflation under control. Ending inflation would make us competitive, keep the dollar strong, set the stage for steady progress. Free trade would close the productivity gap with the United States, bring more and better jobs, and secure our social programs. Deregulation would bring cheaper prices, a boon to consumers. Privatization of public assets would be a blessing to taxpayers. Getting the deficit in shape would protect future generations of Canadians. Or so we were told.

Canada has now had roughly twenty-five years of this neoconservative revolution, though its extent and devastating social consequences have only become evident in the past decade. Key pieces of the neoconservative agenda have been deeply entrenched. For working people, that agenda has brought falling real wages, a reduced standard of living, structural unemployment, massive downsizing, rollbacks of collective agreements, frozen wages in the public sector, two free trade agreements that have cost hundreds of thousands of jobs, closer integration into the American economy and culture, and a widening gulf between rich and poor. This right-wing revolution has also meant lower corporate taxes (while taxes for individuals increased), the erosion of the rights of workers to unionize, privatization of valuable public assets, and, of course, massive cutbacks in health, education, and social programs.

Over the past decade, in other words, Canadians have lived through one of the biggest lies ever perpetrated by government and the corporate sector, a lie aided and abetted by media whose owners have grown increasingly concentrated, business-oriented, and right wing. Before this assault on working people began, many of us assumed that Canada's social programs were untouchable. At one time the argument was over the best way to expand them to support an even higher standard of living for all. Few of us would have believed that steady double-digit unemployment rates could be sustained without riots in the street. We were terribly naive.

BETWEEN 1946 AND 1971, real per capita income in Canada more than doubled. In the twenty-five years since – and in spite of the acceleration of technology, corporate restructuring, longer work hours – real per capita income has edged up only a fraction of a percent each year. Between 1986 and 1996, the real median family income for Canadians actually fell.

In the first twenty-five years after the Second World War, with government taking on a strong leadership role in the economy, economic growth in Canada averaged about 5 percent per year, an amazing figure. In the second twenty-five years – under the corporate agenda – economic growth fell to less than 2.5 percent. In that first period, the unemployment rate in Canada averaged about 4.5 percent a year. In the second, under the corporate agenda, it doubled to more than 9 percent. The worst unemployment rate in the first period was 7.2 percent. The *best* unemployment rate, under the corporate agenda in the second period, was 7.5 percent. These days, we would kill to see 7.5 percent unemployment again.

When Paul Martin brought down his "golden age" budget in February 1998, he speculated that, if we were lucky, we might see unemployment in Canada fall to 8.5 percent over the next year. If we were lucky! A few months later, when the *Globe and Mail*'s Bruce Little and the Royal Bank of Canada's chief economist John McCallum were raving about Canada's economy being on a roll, it was reported that unemployment had dipped slightly (one-tenth of 1 percent) to 8.4 percent (in real terms, it was closer to 11 percent). By comparison, the U.S.

unemployment rate, at 4.3 percent, had dropped to roughly half Canada's official rate. While Little and McCallum were gleeful over Canada's "roll," Japan declared itself an "economic disaster" – partly because unemployment there had reached an unacceptably high 3.9 percent.

At about the same time, the National Council of Welfare pointed out that poverty rates in Canada had grown dramatically since 1991, to 17.6 percent of the population. That meant five million Canadians were living below the poverty line. Child poverty had leaped to 20.9 percent, meaning 1.4 million children are affected; the situation is worse today than when the federal government began its sanctimonious "War on Child Poverty" in the late 1980s. In Toronto, so long a model for other North American cities, one in three children lives in poverty. The poverty rate for seniors had also gone up to 18.9 percent by 1996. Nine out of ten single mothers under the age of twenty-five – an astounding 91.3 percent of them – were living in poverty. And a couple of well-heeled, middle-class pundits in Toronto were telling us our economy was "on a roll."

During the 1990s, Canada's poor have gotten poorer and its rich richer. Average earnings have fallen for all ages and levels of education, but the youth have been hardest hit. The drop in wages for those aged fifteen to twenty-four was a frightening 20 percent. And we wonder why so many Canadian kids are begging on the street and offering to squeegee our windshields?

The roots of our national malady go deep into the venality and incompetence of successive Liberal and Conservative governments. It was these politicians – Mulroney, Michael Wilson, Chrétien, Paul Martin – who ate up the notions supplied to them by neoconservative business organizations and right-wing think-tanks whose unproven theories about economics and society, and whose fetish for holding inflation in check, threw our economy into reverse and passed the burden on to the backs of working-class Canadians. The government's decision around 1980 to shift its economic focus from job creation to fighting inflation deliberately slowed the pace of economic activity. It undermined the bargaining position of working people and shifted the distribution of income strongly in favour of the owners of wealth. The average Canadian is worse off now, economically and materially, than she or he was in

1980 – or even 1972. The change in weekly earnings of the average Canadian between 1950 and 1980 was a 2.4 percent annual increase. Since 1980, the average annual wage has declined, in real terms, 0.8 percent a year.

Over the last two decades, our workforce has grown by almost four million jobs. The number of manufacturing jobs has actually declined, while jobs in the service sector – usually much lower paid jobs – have increased by 50 percent. One-third of all jobs "created" under the corporate agenda since 1970 have been part-time jobs. One-third of the people working in those part-time jobs want full-time jobs and cannot find them. Poll after poll indicates that unemployment is far and away the top concern of Canadians, ranking ahead of the deficit, inflation, even national unity. An estimated 750,000 workers have given up hope of finding employment. One in two Canadian families is now directly affected by unemployment. Meanwhile, income inequality is increasing. Between 1993 and 1996 the top 20 percent of our society saw their incomes increase by some $4,600 per year on average, while the bottom 20 percent – who average a little more than $17,000 in annual income – saw their incomes decrease.

Where is the evidence that high corporate profits are needed for new investment to produce more jobs? Between 1991 and 1996, after-tax profits for Canadian corporations rose by 116 percent, yet investment spending by business grew only a minuscule 6.6 percent. For each dollar in additional profits, corporations spent just 21 cents on new investment. When depreciation is deducted, new fixed investment by Canadian business in 1996 reached a post-1945 low. The last twenty years have shown us what's self-evident: corporations are not in the business of creating jobs. They seek instead to create profit, and one way of doing that is by eliminating jobs.

An effective argument corporate Canada makes is that this chronic state of recession is attributable to government deficits and the size of the public debt. Deficits and the debt, so we were told, had to be brought under control before we could begin to think that job creation and increased spending on social programs was remotely possible. But recessions create deficits. They cut into tax revenues because people earn less and spend less. They increase the cost of social programs because more people are forced to rely on them. The root cause of our deficits and debt has not been spending by governments on social programs; it has been the recessionary effect of the government's policy of maintaining artificially high interest rates.

From 1950 to 1980 the average short-term real interest rate, after inflation, was just over 1 percent. Since 1981 the short-term real interest rate, on average, has exceeded 6 percent. Similarly, the average real rate of interest paid by the government of Canada on the public debt from 1950 to 1980 was 3.9 percent. For bondholders, that was a decent rate of return; their investment, backed by the government of Canada, was virtually risk free. Since 1981 – the point at which the government swallowed the high interest rate argument – the rate of return virtually doubled to 7.7 percent on average.

Capitalists argued that high interest rates were needed to control inflation and maintain "faith" in the value of the Canadian dollar. In fact, these rates protected the value of their investments while guaranteeing that a large portion of the Canadian public would be forced out of their jobs. The Bank of Canada's high interest rate policy was, and still is, a duplicitous form of corporate and investor "welfare." It ensures that the assets of the rich continue to grow, while working people lose their jobs and any sense of long-term security they had.

A dramatic and permanent rise in real interest rates slows, or destroys, economic growth. Companies can't compete, so they close down. People are thrown out of work. Government deficits begin to accumulate, not because of inefficiency or overpaid public servants, or even because social program spending has to be expanded. Even with cutbacks in service and programs, governments cannot cut fast enough to keep pace with economic slowdown. Because the government must also pay its own interest at high rates, an initial deficit balloons into a full-blown debt crisis. We pay interest on interest as the debt expands. Any time the rate of interest exceeds the rate of economic growth, the debt will grow exponentially. The only way to stop it is to have huge government surpluses each year – a virtual impossibility when the economy is in permanent recession.

We need lower real interest rates to revitalize the economy. Low interest rates spur investment and create jobs. Jobs mean that people pay more taxes instead of collecting unemployment insurance. More tax revenue means governments wipe out deficits, without slashing into social programs. Tax revenue also allows governments to pay down the debt.

Rates today may seem low, especially to anyone who once took out a mortgage at 18 or 20 percent. But real rates are higher in Canada than in the United States, and they're higher because high rates suit the agenda of the corporate elite. In the years leading up to 1998, inflation dropped to low levels. Once that happened, we were told, the new-born sense of economic stability in the country would stimulate investment and produce new jobs. That has not happened. Why? Because our policy-makers keep unemployment in Canada at, or above, 8.5 percent. At this level of perpetual unemployment, they know Canadian workers will feel sufficiently insecure that real wages will stagnate and workplace "discipline" will remain high. We'll be too afraid of losing our jobs to fight back.

In the spring of 1998 the head of the Bank of Canada, Gordon Thiessen, said that Canada now had all its economic fundamentals right for a massive growth surge in the economy and a stronger Canadian dollar. The Canadian dollar is pummelled daily by international speculators – indicating they have no real confidence in what the Bank of Canada is doing. By August the dollar had fallen below US 66 cents. And growth projections into the millennium are modest indeed – less than 3 percent – for a nation that has presumably beaten the twin devils of inflation and the deficit.

The continuation of high real interest rate policies, in the absence of inflation, shows there is another agenda at work here. That sudden and – for Canadian workers – deadly policy of high interest rates put into place in 1981 had nothing to do with the normal flow of "free" financial markets. The long-term interests of investors and international financiers are best served by this state of semi-recession. A "jobless recovery" is a bonus for them. That's one of the reasons the stock market tends to rise on bad economic news. As recent headlines in the *Financial Post* have read:

Good economic news puts stocks in tailspin
Stock market can't get enough of that bad news
Markets shudder under new growth figures

Try to follow the logic. To lower unemployment, we have to make stockholders and shareholders happy so they'll invest in industries that produce more jobs. But if there's any hint that growth is returning and more jobs are actually on the way, Wall Street and Bay Street push for higher rates to slow down economic growth. Good news becomes bad news and bad news becomes good news. The Red Queen in *Alice in Wonderland* would understand perfectly: news is anything you want it to be.

I MET THE PRIME MINISTER in the lobby of Toronto's Delta Chelsea Inn for our drive to Chrysler's Bramalea assembly plant. It was May 1, 1998 – May Day, labour's traditional day of celebration – and the Prime Minister's Office had agreed that we would ride together in his Buick, along with his two RCMP bodyguards, to discuss the CAW's concerns. I'd have Jean Chrétien as a captive audience for forty-five minutes.

In April I'd asked Herb Gray, the deputy prime minister, if he could arrange a meeting with the prime minister to allow me to present him with petitions we had collected in support of Auto Pact tariffs. Ever since the Liberals were elected in 1993, the CAW, and organized labour in general, had been largely stonewalled by the Liberals. After a couple of phone conversations with Eddie Goldenberg, the Prime Minister's Office called and said the best they could offer was the ride. I leaped at the opportunity.

We were heading to Bramalea to take part in a ceremony marking the launch of two new Chrysler sedans – the LHS and the 300M series – and, more important, the third shift on the assembly line, something the CAW had been lobbying Chrysler to implement for a year. That third shift meant 1,000 new jobs. It was a huge morale booster for our members and for the community of Brampton.

The main issue I wanted to raise with Chrétien was the attack by Japanese auto manufacturers on Canada's 6.7 percent tariff on vehicles imported from outside North America. The Japanese were lobbying fiercely to have the tariff removed. They were investing heavily in auto manufacturing in Canada, they argued, and deserved the same access to the Canadian market as the Big Three. Removing the tariffs would open Canada to a flood of cheap vehicles from Japanese and South Korean plants, killing thousands of jobs in Canada.

The Japanese pointed to their existing investment in Ontario – Honda's assembly plant in Alliston and Toyota's plant in Cambridge – as proof of their commitment to generate new jobs in Canada. But the Japanese investment was peanuts compared to what General Motors, Ford, and Chrysler had invested. With its three shifts, Chrysler's Bramalea plant alone would employ nearly as many workers – roughly 5,000 – as there were at Honda and Toyota together. Chrysler employed more than 16,000 workers in Ontario – and it was the smallest of the Big Three in terms of investment in Canada. The Japanese lobbyists were having a tremendous influence on the federal industry minister, John Manley. I wanted to try to offset that pressure by going directly to the prime minister.

Politics is about grasping the moment, and I sure wasn't going to let this one get away. As we drove along, I emphasized that the launch of the new Chrysler lines, and the third shift, would not have happened if the Japanese had had open access to our market. This issue was about politics as much as it was about trade, and Chrétien is, if nothing else, a consummate politician. He knew the reality and understood the symbolism of the ceremony we were headed to.

The CAW had worked hard to catch the Liberals' attention on the tariff issue. We organized a support-the-tariff postcard campaign that resulted in 150,000 cards being forwarded to Ottawa. We held media events in every community in Ontario with a tie-in to the auto industry. We canvassed for public support in shopping malls and community halls. We were getting good media coverage, and the Prime Minister's Office had evidently noticed.

Our conversation touched on many things. I pointed out that the government had an obligation to put a long-term program in place to support workers in the east-coast fishery, devastated by the loss of the cod. I also emphasized the importance of federal aid for fishery workers on the west coast. I also told Chrétien I thought it was scandalous the way the Employment Insurance fund was being operated. Why was the government holding billions in surplus funds while making it harder for unemployed workers to qualify?

For every argument I had, of course, Chrétien had a smooth rebuttal. His facts were off in some cases (he understated the losses to east- and west-coast fisheries by a few hundred million dollars), but he was not shy about engaging in dialogue. On the tariff, he made the usual global- ization argument: How do you justify a set of rules for the Japanese that is different from that for the Americans? How do we avoid being chal- lenged for unfair trading practices by the World Trade Organization?

"The Japanese have a weak case," I said. "Their share of the Cana- dian market represents the largest market share they hold in any country in the world. Canada is sure not being unfair to them. For every job the Japanese create in Canada's auto parts industry, American companies create thirty. There's just no comparison. But thousands of Canadian jobs are at stake if you eliminate that tariff. Why would you even consider it now that the industry is doing well and is helping boost the economy?"

"Competition is supposed to be good," he shot back. "You can always argue that protected industries just get fat and lazy and less pro- ductive without competition."

"That's definitely not true of the Canadian auto industry," I said. "We've used that tariff protection to build one of the most productive, cost-efficient, and high-quality industries in the world. Everyone talks about how wonderful the Japanese are, investing in these two plants. They wouldn't even be there if it hadn't been for your old cabinet col- league in the Trudeau government, Ed Lumley, when he was running Industry."

Chrétien nodded. He'd been part of the cabinet decision in the 1970s to support Lumley's strong stand against the Japanese. If the Japanese were not willing to invest in production in Canada and help create new jobs, they would not have been allowed to sell their vehicles in this country.

"You Liberals have a long history of helping the industry expand and get stronger," I said, admittedly doing a little stroking. "The Auto

Pact, the introduction of tariff protection, shutting off the border to the Japanese. You've always supported the North American auto industry because it's so important to our economy."

When Chrétien spoke during the ceremony at the Bramalea plant, he said, "I picked up Buzz at the hotel this morning, and we had a good conversation – about the auto industry, about the fishing industry, about world problems. But let me rephrase that: Buzz Hargrove talked; I listened. I had just come back from Cuba, where I had to listen a lot to Fidel Castro. For a while in the car there, I thought I was back in Cuba with Castro!"

A funny line that got a few laughs, but a clever tack as well – equating me with the communist leader was also a way of dismissing me and suggesting that the CAW's concerns were over the top. When my turn came to speak, I got a heck of a greeting from the workers, and I didn't hold back. The tariff issue was critical to our members' livelihood and I was not about to play diplomat with so many key players on stage with me.

"I'm talking especially to you, Mr. Manley," I said, gesturing toward the industry minister. An ardent free enterpriser, Manley was philosophically in tune with the Japanese manufacturers and their campaign to erase the tariff. He's the sort of ideologue who would let the market determine every aspect of our lives.

"When that third shift kicks off in July," I said, "there'll be more people working in this one plant alone than the Japanese have in Canada. Let me put it in perspective: the sales of Japanese cars in Canada are about the same as Chrysler's. Figure that one out. Anyone saying the Japanese deserve the same rules as Chrysler doesn't understand the issue. This plant is one of the most efficient, productive, high-quality, low-cost operations in the industry. We could lose all that if the government doesn't establish a proper framework to protect plants like these and the jobs of workers in them."

I got a rousing cheer from our members, and noticed that even Chrysler management was applauding. I poked a finger at Mike Harris, the premier, who was waiting for his turn to speak, and compared his government to Chrysler management in the old days. Management then, I said, like the Harris government today, believed it had all the brains and know-how and could simply force its ideas on the union and its members. That style of management, I pointed out, had led to Chrysler's near bankruptcy, not once but twice. Only when management opened up the process and started listening to the union and its workers did Chrysler became one of the most successful auto companies in the world.

"There's an important lesson here for you and your government, Mr. Premier. Inclusiveness builds as surely as exclusiveness destroys."

I ended my speech by telling Harris and Chrétien, "I'm going to buy one of these new Chryslers. They're beautiful vehicles. I bought one when they first started building them here and today I'm ordering another. I invite the premier and the prime minister to make the same commitment." There were more than a thousand people in the audience and the place went wild.

Harris got up and began with some nonsense about how prepared he was to consult with Buzz Hargrove and the CAW. He added shrewdly: "When I announce our budget next week, our tax cuts will mean that everybody in Ontario will be able to afford one of these fine Chrysler products." It was a good line from a crafty politician, but there was little response. Not many of these people were buying the provincial government's line that tax cuts would make their lives better. They'd had three years of Harris, and they'd seen what had happened to their province.

A couple of weeks later, the Chrétien government announced that the 6.7 percent tariff on imported vehicles would remain in place. It was a major victory for the CAW and, indirectly, all Canadians. Was the harsh Liberal wind beginning to shift? Was the government starting to listen to working Canadians? I felt we were making real progress in our efforts to get a serious dialogue going with the Chrétien administration. Where once we could not get our calls returned, we'd recently been able to organize a dinner at the Château Laurier Hotel in Ottawa and get twenty-eight members of the Liberal caucus to attend to discuss the auto industry.

Shortly after my ride with Chrétien, I also got a call from Eddie Goldenberg. He said he wanted to discuss the CAW's views on the fisheries problem on both coasts, in particular the support program. He wanted our input. The CAW represents most of the affected fishers and processing workers, and our leaders helped put together a concrete proposal that we faxed off to Goldenberg. We followed this up with further discussions about how it might be implemented. (I couldn't resist saying to Goldenberg – an adversary since the fight over wage concessions at Canadian Airlines in 1996 – that if we'd been having these conversations years ago, perhaps we could have avoided a lot of pain and frustration among fishery workers on both coasts.)

Soon afterwards, Finance Minister Paul Martin invited a small number of private-sector labour leaders to meet to discuss job creation. We talked about Employment Insurance, pension clawbacks from working people, and the effect government policies were having on collective bargaining. We also raised the question of what impact the proposed bank mergers might have on workers.

I'm betting Martin will approve the mergers between the Royal Bank and the Bank of Montreal, and the Canadian Imperial Bank of Commerce and the Toronto Dominion Bank. There's too much at stake for the government to do otherwise. The big banks are just too influential in political terms, quite apart from the money they pour directly into Liberal Party coffers.

Martin will have two major problems if the mergers go ahead: branch closures in areas where services are duplicated, and layoffs. As many as 20,000 bank employees are expected to be set adrift. Martin will take some flak from backbench Liberal MPs representing small communities, but he'll survive that. The massive number of terminations are another matter. He can't legislate that there be no job losses. The government needs an innovative plan to reduce the impact of branch closings, one that provides workers with special layoff considerations as a trade-off for okaying the mergers.

I'm sure the Liberals will come up with one. Money talks, and if the banks run into public relations problems with these deals you can bet that money will simply raise its voice. Citing "global competitiveness" and the need for "greater efficiency," the banks will get their way again. Shareholders will reap the benefits, and workers will pay the price.

10

AS GOOD AS IT GETS

We are learning very fast that the belief that
a free market is all it takes to have a functioning society
– or even a functioning economy – is pure delusion.
— *Peter Drucker, 1996*

I suspect that when historians look back on this period, they will find it incomprehensible that Canadians sat by and allowed their elected governments to help engineer the largest transfer of wealth from the poor to the rich in our nation's history. How, they will ask, did it happen? What people, corporations, and organizations on the right pulled it off?

They could start with the C.D. Howe Institute. Formed in 1973, it's named after Canada's wartime and postwar government czar, one of the most powerful and controversial men ever to perform in public service. The institute is a privately funded organization that represents an eastern business elite seeking to control the direction of federal government policy. Its board is made up of members of Canada's largest corporations, such as Sun Life Assurance, Noranda, and Alcan. Linda McQuaig, author of *Shooting the Hippo: Death by Deficit and Other Canadian Myths*, believes the institute played a major role in building the hysteria over the deficit in Canada by insisting that the problem is government spending rather than high interest rates. The papers published by the C.D. Howe Institute are inevitably referred to in the newspapers as "independent" studies. The C.D. Howe Institute is about as "independent," in the non-partisan sense, as the CAW.

There's a whole herd of right-wing organizations now posing as independent think-tanks. Their pro-business, anti-government message is remarkably similar. The most effective is the Business Council on National Issues, which is made up of officers from about 160 of this country's most powerful corporations. The BCNI was once characterized as "tireless proponents of the American way of life," although this lobby group likes to see itself in a more benign light; it calls itself an organization "dedicated to the development of public policy in the national interest." Among its diverse policy interests, the BCNI championed free trade, NAFTA, the Charlottetown accord, reduction of federal deficits, and the lowering of the national debt through cuts to social services. There is no denying the BCNI's power and influence on Parliament Hill. It has frequently been asked to draft policy documents for consideration by the Chrétien government.

In March 1998 the BCNI sent a letter to Chrétien demanding a freeze on new government spending and an immediate, aggressive debt-reduction program. The letter was signed by Tom d'Aquino of the BCNI and Al Flood of the Canadian Imperial Bank of Commerce. If he had to boost spending on health care, Chrétien was told, the money should come from other, less important programs. "Don't get too cocky," these business leaders reportedly instructed our prime minister.

In mid-June, Finance Minister Paul Martin met with officers from the BCNI. The country's top executives advised him not to start spending any fiscal dividend the Liberals may currently hold, given the unknown future effect the collapse of Asian economies might have on Canada. Canadians can almost count on the Liberals announcing, perhaps even before this book appears, that they have placed constraints on any new government spending.

The BCNI opposes the Kyoto agreement on climate change – because environmental safeguards against global warming affect "competitiveness." Canadians can expect to hear less about any Liberal government initiatives on this issue. The BCNI has also been one of the strongest proponents of the signing of the Multilateral Agreement on Investment. Had the MAI been implemented on schedule in 1998, it would have further consolidated economic and political power in Canada in the hands of international investors and financiers. For the moment, MAI talks have been suspended, thanks to strong intervention by the Council of Canadians (led by Maude Barlow), the Canadian Labour Congress, and a coalition of anti-MAI forces that included large elements of the labour movement.

One of the more unusual neoconservative lobby groups is the B.C.-based Fraser Institute. It was formed in 1974 when "a slightly disgruntled federal civil servant" (as the *Globe and Mail* once put it) named Michael Walker left his job and convinced the forestry and lumber giant, MacMillan Bloedel, along with other well-heeled companies, to put up the $200,000 needed to start an institute dedicated to the study of capitalism and the workings of markets.

The Fraser Institute is modelled on the conservative U.S. Heritage Foundation, a right-wing organization formed in the early 1970s to help put Republicans back in power in Washington, and, in particular, to help put Ronald Reagan in the White House. The Fraser gets many of its economic ideas from economist Milton Friedman, whose conjectural, supply-side theories were once facetiously described as "a plan to help the poor by cutting the taxes of the rich."

Friedman's ideas run in tandem with the massive economic failure represented by two terms of Reagan's presidency and the one term of George Bush. Under these two supply-side presidents – both of whom were opposed to "big government" and public debt – America racked up the highest debt numbers in its history. These were also the years that saw the greatest increase in wealth for the top 1 percent of the U.S. population since 1929. Of all the new wealth created in that period, 60 percent went to that 1 percent of Americans. At the same time, middle-class Americans saw their wages fall in real terms by 10 percent.

The Fraser Institute has been effective in getting the debt and deficit issues near the top of governments' agendas. A large part of that effectiveness is due to a less-than-critical media. The Fraser Institute was once referred to regularly as a "right-wing" policy organization. Today, most newspaper and television reports fail to attach that subtle but important ideological marker. The Fraser is now commonly referred to as "a West Coast think-tank," a description that masks its political intentions. The "think-tank" label also camouflages a reality that many economists, political scientists, and students of public policy laugh about. At the Fraser Institute, accuracy and balance have never been prerequisites for commenting on public policy. Although the institute publishes a multitude of "papers," "findings," and articles for newspapers – and

refers to its contributors as "senior analysts" or "adjunct scholars" –
much of the material is simply right-wing rhetoric.

Newspapers seem to publish virtually everything the Fraser Institute
sends out. In the December 2, 1995, issue of the *Globe and Mail* ("A
bluffer's guide to think tanks"), the Fraser received more coverage of its
work, by far, than any other policy organization. Up to that date, the
Fraser Institute had been mentioned in the paper 139 times, while the
next highest figure was 39 mentions for the C.D. Howe Institute.

In his book *Bad Work*, lawyer Jeff Rose, the former head of the
Canadian Union of Public Employees, analyzed papers from a Fraser
Institute conference on right-to-work laws and concluded: "Scholarly
punctiliousness isn't job one" for this organization. "Proselytization is
job one." The Fraser can exhibit "a breathtaking ignorance of laws,
economics and labour relations in Canada," he said. The research can
be "superficial," and the papers "confused and confusing anti-union
polemic." In short, "the Fraser material is blighted by unsubstantiated
claims, dubious methodology and highly selective evidence."

One of the Fraser's principal crusades is right-to-work laws. The
institute views unions as a disturbing impediment to the success of free
enterprise, a cost to society rather than a benefit. According to the Fraser,
unions prevent the creation of jobs rather than help produce them. The
right-wing doctrine of the Fraser is so important to its members that it's
used to contradict reality.

To the Fraser, government is inherently bad for business. It argues
that social service spending in Canada – on medicare, education, insurance against unemployment, and public pensions for the elderly –
should be curtailed or eliminated. Payroll "taxes" on business (the
employers' share of contributions for the Canada Pension Plan, Workers'
Compensation, and Employment Insurance, for instance) should be
vastly reduced in the interest of creating new jobs, even though these
modest contributions from employers are already lower in Canada than
they are in most industrialized countries. Taxes on business in Canada –
among the lowest among the Group of Seven nations – should, according to the Fraser, be driven down, presumably in the interest of freeing
up capital to create more jobs.

The Fraser Institute is one of the most politicized lobby groups in Canada today. It's certainly the most extreme in its political goals. It is also no exaggeration to call the Fraser one of the most effective propaganda arms of the country's corporate community. In truly Canadian irony, taxpayers foot most of the bill for the Fraser. Revenue Canada has declared it a not-for-profit research and educational group – which makes it tax exempt under the broad category of "charitable" organizations.

IF THE ADVENT OF RIGHT-WING LOBBY GROUPS was the first ideological wave from the neoconservatives, the second wave arrived in the mid- to late 1980s, when successive federal governments began deregulating the energy, banking, and finance sectors, followed by the airline, telecommunications, and trucking industries. Deregulation freed these industries to make their own decisions about how they would serve us and what those services would cost. The net effect for consumers was higher prices, less choice (as companies merged to gain competitive advantage), poorer service, and fewer jobs (as corporations laid off workers to become "more competitive").

By the late 1980s the right-wing lobby got the Conservative government of Brian Mulroney to cut federal corporate tax rates from 36 to 28 percent. It also convinced the Tories to cut income tax rates for high-income earners from 35 to 29 percent. This largesse for corporations and wealthy Canadians was followed in the mid-1990s by more of the same, when a number of provinces cut their income taxes for high-income earners.

In 1988 the Conservatives ran an election campaign *against* free trade. The Mulroney government then went back on its promise and signed the Free Trade Agreement with the States. Hundreds of thousands of Canadian jobs disappeared. In 1994 Canada joined with the United States and Mexico – again, despite massive public outcry against the treaty – and signed the North American Free Trade Agreement. A majority of Canadians did not want NAFTA. Jean Chrétien rode to electoral victory on the promise to scrap it, then, like Mulroney, reversed himself.

Were these trade deals good for Canadian workers? Free trade has worsened the economies of both Canada and Mexico, and reduced manufacturing jobs in all three countries. Canada was the hardest hit by free trade, with manufacturing employment falling 12 percent between 1988 and 1996, more than three times the U.S. decline of 3.8 percent. Senior executive salaries in all three countries, meanwhile, have risen dramatically under free trade.

In the early 1990s a number of our respected public institutions – including Air Canada, Petro-Canada, and Canadian National Railways – were sold off to the private sector. The upshot was that the Canadian public lost valuable assets. The cost of the services these companies provided to consumers went up. The number of people they employed dropped by tens of thousands. Yet we're told that "privatization" of public enterprises has been a glowing success and has helped strengthen our economy.

The pressure from corporations and right-wing lobby groups to cut government spending on social services has succeeded unbelievably. By the mid-1990s, program spending by the Canadian government had fallen from 40 to 35 percent of Gross Domestic Product. This might have been well and good for the corporate elite, but it was not so good for working people and the underprivileged. Fall-back relief for the unemployed was taken away by successive federal governments through cutbacks to Employment Insurance benefits. By the end of 1997, less than 40 percent of Canada's unemployed qualified for unemployment assistance, down from 85 percent a few years previously.

Ontario, of course, eliminated anti-scab laws and weakened union organizing and certification procedures. Pushed by the Fraser Institute, the right-wing governments of Alberta and Ontario are contemplating right-to-work laws. These laws could seriously affect the status, pay, and benefits of all workers in both provinces. Various provinces, after cutting their social safety nets, weakened or eliminated pay equity and employment equity schemes, further penalizing half the workforce simply because it was female.

This widespread dismantling of what was once a compassionate system is peaking at a time when Canadians should be looking to the twenty-first century with confidence. Instead, the majority approach the future with an overwhelming sense of uncertainty and trepidation. Talk all you want about the Chrétien government's ability to rid us of the deficit; it's been done not through a fairer taxing of wealth, either personal or corporate, but rather on the backs of the poor, the elderly, the young, the less fortunate, even members of the middle class – who seem confused about who to blame, judging by the way they shift their votes from Liberal to Conservative to Reform and back again.

We have lived through the worst social and economic crisis since the Great Depression. At a time when we should be implementing a nation-wide job creation program, the Chrétien government claims we do not need one. Governments cannot create jobs, we are told; that's up to the private sector. But the private sector is not producing the number or quality of jobs it said it would. At a time when we should be expanding social programs to include affordable child care and an end to poverty (especially child poverty), offering more support for the ever-increasing number of elderly in our society, improving our public education system, and increasing support for the arts and our cultural communities, we're fighting to hang on to what's left of a once prosperous and decent society.

Neoconservative governments in the United States, Britain, and Canada have tried to deal with the insecurity of the times by promising a return to "traditional values." These values include denigrating the importance of government and bad-mouthing public servants. Neocon-servatives indulge in what John Ralston Saul calls a "vocabulary of con-tempt for the political process." Government is routinely depicted as "inefficient," "costly," and "bureaucratized." Public servants are "lazy" and "overpaid." Politicians are "corrupt," do deals "behind closed doors," pay themselves "fat salaries."

It suits neoconservatives to talk in sound-bite accusations because they require no documentation or proof. These accusations can be coun-tered with their own unproven theories based on the belief that the private sector is inherently better equipped to provide leadership than the public sector. The corporate sector, of course, is described by rote as "efficient," "competitive," and better able to bring "value" to shareholders.

In truth, the success of our public service is one of the reasons the United Nations declared Canada a world leader in social development. Our once-admired sense of public responsibility – building programs that cared for the elderly, looked after children and mothers, provided us with one of the world's best medical care systems – distinguished us as a nation as rich in human values and social conscience as it was in natural resources and skilled workers.

Three of Canada's major cities were recently ranked by UNESCO among the world's top ten – due largely to our public services. It's no accident that we have clean and reasonably safe cities, with high-quality public spaces and public attractions. Does anyone think the so-called free market produces cities like that? If you want to see a free-market city, go to New York, even the new, improved version achieved by Mayor Rudolph Giuliani. Stray a few blocks from the core of free enterprise – Wall Street – and watch the cars drive over garbage and slalom around potholes. Look at the crumbling public transit system.

Or go to Washington and see what life in America is like a few blocks from the White House. The United States has one of the highest infant mortality rates among industrialized countries. Some thirteen million children live in poverty. Fewer than one in five workers has union representation. The tragedy is that the States can well afford to supply its people with the kind of public services that would eradicate squalor. To a Canadian social democrat, America is an astonishing contradiction. To a neoconservative, America, with it huge division between rich and poor, is a virtual heaven on earth.

Visit the home of free enterprise and count the number of people you see who can't afford health care or better education; who can't afford to live in safe, well-policed, well-served communities. Forty-two million Americans do not have health care coverage. Twenty-nine million others (roughly the population of Canada) are seriously underinsured. The American private health care system is so expensive and exclusive that Dr. Benjamin Spock, the man who wrote the bible on child care – had to beg for cash handouts at the age of ninety-four to help him pay his medical bills. The bills he incurred after he suffered a heart attack and a stroke were so high that, by February 1998, he was penniless. His wife had to ask friends for the cash to keep going.

This is the "health care system" that the Reform Party, and neoconservative writers like the *Globe and Mail*'s Terence Corcoran and the *Financial Post*'s David Frum, claim is superior to the one Canada enjoys. It's a system even some Liberal cabinet members would like to see Canadians adopt. Industry Minister John Manley, for one, is known to favour privatizing the Canadian medicare system and replacing it with the American model.

IN JANUARY 1977 a confidential draft document entitled "Multilateral Agreement on Investment: Consolidated Texts and Commentary" was circulated among government and corporate officials in the Organization for Economic Cooperation and Development. Meetings over the MAI had been going on for a couple of years. Discussions among the OECD representatives were held in secret. In fact, for the first few years the entire MAI discussion process was carried out in secret. The issue only came to light when MAI critics obtained a leaked copy of the draft agreement and made it available on the Internet.

If this draft document had been adopted by OECD countries, including Canada, the foundation would have been laid for a new global economic constitution, the likes of which only science fiction writers used to dream up. The MAI began as a U.S.-driven objective to obtain what the Americans termed "a high standard multilateral investment agreement that will protect U.S. investors abroad." The proposed MAI was designed to establish a new set of global investment rules that would allow international speculators and investors the right to buy, sell, and move their money whenever and wherever they wanted, without interruption or hindrance from national governments.

The MAI would have meant open season on nation-states. Its purpose was to reduce or eliminate the capacity of governments to limit foreign investment in their own countries. It would have ruled out any government's attempt to impose national standards of behaviour on foreign investors. Consequently, the MAI would have restricted the ability of governments around the globe to shape their own policies to promote economic growth, or to meet social, cultural, or environmental goals. As columnist Richard Gwyn wrote in the *Toronto Star*, the MAI would amount to "a constitution for absentee landlords."

The MAI was essentially a global "charter of rights" for international capital. It was a declaration of global corporate rule. Under the MAI, Canada could not even have designed and implemented a serious job creation strategy if it restricted the free movement of capital. The MAI would have outlawed regulations that limit access of foreign capital to government contracts and privatization programs. Transnational companies operating in Canada would not have been obliged to hire Canadian workers or to invest any portion of profits in Canada. The MAI could have superseded earlier trade agreements such as the FTA and NAFTA and would have eliminated any exemptions negotiated by Canada in those agreements. Governments would not have been able to amend the MAI in their national legislatures. That power would have remained in the hands of international capitalists.

The MAI would have allowed transnational companies to qualify for government grants and subsidies currently offered only to Canadian industries. If the federal or a provincial government decided to privatize one of its public corporations, such as B.C. Hydro or TVOntario, transnational signatories to the MAI would have been given equal rights as Canadian companies to bid. If a transnational company had bought TVOntario, there would have been no requirement that it maintain Canadian or Ontario-based program content. Under MAI, regulations that protect Canadian content for musicians, broadcasters, and film-makers would likely have been illegal. Transnational companies could have received the rights to Canadian natural resources without obligation to renew or replenish them, or use them for the benefit of Canadians. As Bob White of the CLC put it, "If there had been an MAI in place earlier, Canada could never have developed as a nation the way it did. Canadians would never have enjoyed the benefits of our health care system, our public services, our education programs, our public hydro-electric utilities development, not our broadcasting system, our provincial automobile insurance plans, or even our industrial base."

Thanks to the CLC, the Council of Canadians, and more than forty organizations in the MAI Working Group, this little-known, secretive document was revealed for what it was – a massive threat to Canadian sovereignty. That revelation resulted in a large number of Canadians expressing their horror to the Chrétien government. The Liberals originally denied that such a draft document even existed. During the 1997 federal election, NDP leader Alexa McDonough was able to raise the profile of the MAI issue, forcing the Liberals to admit that MAI talks were indeed under way and to open the issue to parliamentary subcommittee hearings.

Public opposition to the MAI spread among the twenty-nine OECD countries. Opposition was loudest in France and Canada. As a result, talks over the MAI, which was supposed to have been signed in April 1998, were suspended for a minimum of six months. Some critics believe the MAI is all but dead. Given the huge stakes involved, however (U.S. companies alone invest more than $350 billion a year in OECD countries), and given the power of the corporate sector, it would be naive to think so.

There is already a move afoot by the more frustrated proponents of the MAI to move negotiations away from the OECD and put them in the hands of the World Trade Organization. The WTO has a larger membership and includes developing countries. Donald Johnston, the secretary general of the OECD (a principal proponent of the MAI), now has his $365,000-a-year, tax-free salary on the line.

Johnston is a former Liberal cabinet minister on whose behalf the Chrétien government lobbied long and hard to get him appointed as the OECD's first non-European secretary general. His European critics have been vocal in their displeasure over his inability to deliver the goods. Johnston will continue to press for the MAI, if for no other reason than to preserve his reputation, and the other powerful advocates of the MAI are already gearing up for the next round.

On May 5, 1998, the op-ed section of the *Globe and Mail* carried an article by Owen Lippert, director of the Law and Markets Project at (you guessed it) the Fraser Institute. The article was titled: "Where were the MAI's defenders? Global treaty supporters of the sidelined Multilateral Agreement on Investment were slow to defend it. What should they do next time?"

It was "inevitable" that the MAI would be reconsidered, Lippert proclaimed. He cast blame for its first-run defeat on the Chrétien government ("Work lies ahead in stiffening Liberal spines to defend their own policies"), the Council of Canadians' Maude Barlow ("It's irritating to see victory in this round of Canada's trade wars bestowed upon Ms. Barlow"), and the quality of its critics' attacks, which, according to Lippert, consisted of "wild claims based on forced extrapolations of opaque legal clauses." Observers of the MAI debate were left "bewildered," the Fraser Institute's spokesperson argued, because of the "quibbling" over Ms. Barlow's "bizarre legal reasoning."

Lippert claimed, erroneously, that the MAI does not give companies new "rights." There was a need, he said, to explain to a new generation "the fundamental insights of Adam Smith and David Ricardo" – two economic theorists whose ideas, when applied, have never served the interests of working people, though the mere mention of their names in right-wing circles elicits the same kind of reverence as mention of the Ayatollah Khomeini does for some Iranians.

Lippert insisted that "hoary myths" about the benefits of free trade must not go "unchallenged." Supporters of free trade in Canada "must be more aggressive." He ended his sweeping defence of the beauty and inherent decency of the MAI by stating: "The MAI will come back. Next time, we need to be better prepared."

For working Canadians, the interesting question to consider about the MAI, and the process that surrounded it, is this: If the treaty would have been such a good thing – for investors, corporations, and working people alike – why did the OECD and the Chrétien government seek to keep it a secret?

WORKING CANADIANS HAVE ENDURED a virtual state of siege under Brian Mulroney and now Jean Chrétien over the past fifteen years. The strategy of the corporate sector has been to seize control of public policy-making at both the provincial and the federal levels, and the strategy has succeeded brilliantly. There was no violent overthrow of our government, but the results were similar. In effect, the country's leading CEOs, assisted by right-wing institutes and lobbyists, mobilized what author Tony Clarke referred to in his book *Silent Coup* as "a powerful shadow cabinet in Ottawa to oversee and direct the basic reorientation of fiscal, economic, social and environmental policy-making in Canada."

What the corporations have achieved is nothing less than the systematic dismantling of the socio-economic system Canadians built over four decades. "We are now living in the midst of a coup d'état in slow motion" was the way John Ralston Saul put it in his 1995 Massey Lecture, published as the book *The Unconscious Civilization*. It's a revolution that, according to Saul, disfigured the ideal of the public good, "turning citizens into consumers, and weakening the fabric of democracy."

The corporate sector, led by the Business Council on National Issues, tells us that the democratic system we're familiar with is no longer an appropriate governing model. The BCNI calls for a return to "minimal government." Democracy, in other words, is incompatible with the interests of the corporate state. Capitalism requires control; it does not operate well under democratic forms of government, which are messy and inefficient. This attack on "excessive government" is really an attack on the democratic foundations of our society.

These past two decades, the state in Canada has been skilfully put to use by the corporate sector. CAW economist Jim Stanford reported that between 1988 and 1995, the federal government increased its loans from Canadian banks by more than 500 percent – from $15 billion to $80 billion. Ottawa now pays our banks close to $7 billion a year in interest on what are risk-free loans. The record-breaking profits the banks have been enjoying are partly due to a direct transfer of wealth from the average citizen to the banks' top executives and shareholders, in the form of interest on these government loans. The banks and other financial institutions have been feeding off our national deficits. The "debt" of Canadian taxpayers is an "asset" of Canada's banks. How could this happen without the complicity of our successive federal governments?

Banks, like other major corporations, no longer rely on domestic demand to sell their goods and services. They seek to broaden their horizons and take control of the international marketplace and governing structures, just as they did the domestic marketplace. Already, global competition has dramatically widened the gap between rich and poor. The ratio of the wealth of the top 20 percent of the world's population to the bottom 20 percent in 1965 was 30 to 1. Thirty-odd years later, the ratio is 60 to 1. I think of a line from "The Wizard of Id," the comic strip: "Remember the golden rule: them that has the gold, rule."

In the February 1997 issue of *The Atlantic Monthly*, the billionaire financier and investor George Soros wrote about the prospect of a global society, a world in which national hindrances to the free flow of capital have been removed and the disadvantaged have been left to fend entirely for themselves: "I now fear that the untrammelled intensification of laissez-faire capitalism and the spread of market values into all areas of life is endangering our open and democratic society," Soros writes. "The main enemy of the open society, I believe, is no longer communism but the capitalist threat."

Capitalism is undeniably effective at producing wealth for a minority of citizens. But when you see the inequality it generates, you have to ask: Is this as good as it gets? Is unfettered capitalism the best system to sustain – fairly and humanely – the human family? A well-regulated mixed economy of free markets influenced by the public sector can achieve impressive results, if the test is how many citizens, not how few, enjoy the benefits of wealth.

Capitalism is not working, despite what the *Financial Post* would have us believe. Two decades of declining standards of living and increases in poverty stand as clear evidence. The "Asian Tigers" were, as recently as a year ago, the epitome of free-market capitalism. The Asian economies were everyone's model for free enterprise. There was, we were told, no end to the benefits to be had by emulating their success. Since then, millions of Asian workers have lost their jobs, people are literally starving because of the absence of any social safety net, and the leaders of these suddenly destitute nations have no solution to their massive economic problems other than billions of bailout dollars from the International Monetary Fund. This is the best that capitalism can do? Most of its proponents – certainly in North America – are in denial: they refuse to believe there are real deficiencies and they don't accept that an alternative economic model might provide a fairer distribution of wealth.

Still, George Soros is not alone. Many leading thinkers around the world are sounding the alarm that capitalism might have become more of a geopolitical threat than an economic saviour. From management guru Peter Drucker to economist and author John Kenneth Galbraith to MIT economist Paul Krugman (who predicted the collapse of the Asian economies four years ago), many argue that leaving our fate entirely to free-market forces is undermining the values on which open and democratic societies depend. Their message: democracy is contracting as capitalism expands.

SO WHERE IS THIS CORPORATE AGENDA taking us? How much farther down the road must we go before we ask if we're heading in the right direction? Do we need some modern equivalent of the Great Depression to bring us to our economic senses? The ingredients seem to be there. As in 1929, the disparity in incomes has widened dramatically, consumer debt is at high levels, and there's excess capacity in a wide range of industries. The stock markets are overvalued and, as of midsummer, feeling the sort of tremors that sometimes signal a coming quake. There is great instability in international financial circles – not just in Mexico, South Korea, Indonesia, and Thailand, but now in Japan, the second largest economy on earth, and in Russia. The capitalist's solution is to solve our domestic economic problems by increasing exports of goods and services to other countries – while those countries try to do the same thing to us.

In Canada the corporate sector has changed the underlying assumptions and the direction of our nation. It has convinced our politicians that if we had only listened to the free-market liturgy, unemployment would be short term, low interest rates would make us competitive and strengthen the dollar, weakened unions would remove barriers to job creation, free trade would close the productivity gap with the United States and bring jobs, and our social programs would be secure. Deregulation would be a boon to consumers and privatization a blessing to taxpayers. We've done all that – and on every count the reverse has turned out to be true.

The members of Canada's corporate and political elite have either erred in their thinking about where free markets and open competition would take us, or misled us. Either way, it's the working citizen who loses. Even more alarming than the high price Canadians are paying for this folly is the thought that this is indeed as good as it gets. Chrétien's assertion notwithstanding, we're not entering any golden age. On the contrary, the economic growth we've experienced these past few years is peaking as I write. In July 1998, approximately 1.5 million Canadians were still unemployed. The unemployment rate remained stuck at 8.4 percent and there were indications it was beginning to rise again. During the best economic period in decades, our corporate leaders have been unable to produce more well-paid, full-time jobs. The number of full-time jobs in Canada actually stagnated during the 1990s, and there are more poor people living in Canada than there were ten years ago.

By mid-summer of 1998, the Liberal government was admitting its concern that Canada might now be catching the Asian flu. Russia was in chaos, the ruble plummeting. Economic growth estimates were hastily being adjusted downward. The so-called golden age was coming to a quick end. And who did the Chrétien government call for advice? Why, the Business Council on National Issues, of course. Under the banner of the BCNI, some of the country's top executives met with Paul Martin in June and greeted him with "a grim outlook on Asia and its impact on Canada," as the press reported. "We expressed some very, very serious concerns to Mr. Martin," the BCNI's head, Tom d'Aquino, said. "He is going to have to maintain his prudence, and, if anything, step up his prudence until we can determine how severe the crisis in Asia is going to become." There was no report indicating that Martin also held consultations with the Canadian Labour Congress, or even with members of Her Majesty's Loyal Opposition.

The corporate agenda that has reshaped Canada depends, ironically, on the loss of hope, and a growing sense of apathy, to sustain itself. The ideal world for corporations is one in which citizens feel insecure and powerless, their sense of democracy and equality undermined, their sense of community and society weakened. Margaret Thatcher, one of the chief heralds of neoconservative thinking, once said, "There is no such thing as society, anyway."

The reduction of society to little more than a platform on which to do business is typified by the MAI, which reflects the inherent logic capitalism uses to sustain itself: communities, and the rules and responsibilities by which we support them, are incompatible with capitalism. Milton Friedman, the ideological godfather of modern laissez-faire economics, said it best: "Business as a whole cannot be said to have responsibilities. The doctrine of social responsibilities is fundamentally a subversive doctrine." Friedman's thoughts are the sustaining theoretical diet for groups like the BCNI, the Fraser Institute, the C.D. Howe Institute, and the other right-wing organizations committed to the ascendency of business.

I understand that, under capitalism, the business of business is business. I've never believed we should expect corporations to act in a socially responsible manner. That is precisely why, in any society that sees itself as more than a giant factory, we need regulations to direct business in a way that incorporates, and meets, social and democratic needs. Business and society are closely interrelated. If we pretend they are not, and agree to leave business "alone," then the "business" of society is also reduced entirely to business. I don't believe most Canadians, given the choice, would want to live in a society with such a narrow, exclusive focus.

Governments once acted as a buffer between business and the people. They provided programs to offset the negative impact of business activity. They protected us. In carrying out that protection they became, ironically, straw men for the corporate agenda. Regulatory-minded governments became something to blame for the economic problems actually caused by the corporate agenda. Our parliamentarians could, on occasion, be turfed out of office for their sins, and voters were left with the mistaken belief that they could "correct" their economic situation simply by changing governments.

This turf-the-bastards scenario gives the corporate elite a major bonus. Even though their actions cause our economic headaches, they are able to join the throng of unhappy citizens and add their condemnation of "intrusive Big Government." They argue that unfettered free enterprise will, on the citizens' behalf, make things better. As business discredits government's role, government becomes less capable of acting as our protector and control of the economy shifts more fully to the corporate sector. As David Rockefeller put it in 1996, transnational companies "are now in the driver's seat of the global economic engine"; they're "setting government policies instead of watching from the sidelines."

Business may be "winning," but the failure of business to turn its victories into better lives for ordinary citizens is starting to raise widespread questions about the legitimacy of corporate domination. Where are the jobs? Where are the strengthened social programs the BCNI promised us in the run-up to the free trade debate? Where is the economic security Canadians were supposed to enjoy from global competition? If deficit and inflation control was meant to restore investor confidence, as the BCNI urged and the Bank of Canada orchestrated, why has the Canadian dollar fallen to record lows *after* the deficit dragon was slain? Since 1989, among all the Group of Seven countries, Canada's deficit has fallen fastest while our growth has ranked last.

If global competition is the way to go, why is the international economy out of control? How could the International Monetary Fund get it so wrong in Asia so soon after the economic collapse in Mexico? The IMF assured us in its 1997 World Economic Report that "there is no doubt that globalization is contributing enormously to global prosperity." In that report, the IMF cited Southeast Asia as a model of economic development – just months before it collapsed.

I talk to working people every day and I hear about their growing anger and frustration. Given that the media in Canada are largely controlled by such right-wing corporate interests as Thomson, Southam, Baton, and CanWest Global, it's not surprising that this anger is not given much media expression. But the message is starting to get out, nonetheless. Last December the *Washington Post*, analyzing the defeat of President Clinton's attempt to fast-track the extension of NAFTA into Latin America, commented, "no longer do Americans take it for granted that an open economy makes everyone better off." At about the same time, the *Los Angeles Times*, weighing the costs and benefits of financial bailouts, said, "The ordinary citizen, in both the United States and Japan, is starting to figure out the abusive political economics" behind them. As early as 1996, a New York *Times* poll revealed that a surprising number of Americans considered themselves "working class" and called on the government to do something about layoffs and high unemployment. The strikes in France in 1995 and 1996 were significant for the national support they enjoyed, in spite of the public inconvenience they caused. A French writer put it this way: "Gone was the optimism of the mid-80s, especially among young people, who now said they distrusted private employers. There was a loss of faith in business."

The tide could be turning in Canada as well. Such protests as the Days of Action and the Ontario teachers' strike revealed a level of unhappiness and resistance few could have anticipated. Our union's experiences at General Motors of Canada in 1996 and at PC World in 1997 helped reaffirm our belief that collective militant action still works. It will only become more widespread as more Canadians come to see the underlying mistruths and errors inherent in the corporate agenda. The July 1998 strike by the UAW against GM in the United States – involving more than 160,000 workers and lasting nearly two months – was another indication that workers are no longer prepared to watch quietly as management slashes jobs and lowers their standard of living in the name of increased profits. As a country and a society, we in Canada have to ask ourselves: Is a country's essence little more than a function of its corporations' profitability and market capitalization? This is our country, not Sony's and Coca-Cola's and Merrill Lynch's and Procter & Gamble's. What kind of country do we want?

The typical response from the business community – "There's no alternative" – has worked well for a couple of decades, but it's not sustainable. Why? Because it admits that capitalism has no solution to our problems, and effectively condemns the system rather than defending it.

Unfettered capitalism, we see, as we experience its shortcomings, is clearly not working. If you take into account the welfare of the entire nation, capitalism has been an abject failure. How do we fix it? How do we come up with viable alternatives? Where are the new thinkers? Where is the leadership on the left? We in the CAW are looking for broad public debate on this fundamental issue. Our challenge over the next few years is to build a forum to allow this debate to take place.

INDEX

The text of *Labour of Love* has been typeset
in Linotype Sabon, a face designed by
Jan Tschichold in the early 1960s and released
in 1964. Sabon was refined by Tschichold to meet
the mechanical and stylistic needs of the time.

The headings have been typeset in Clarendon,
and Gill Sans, both faces designed in the 1920s.

Designed by Public Good